BEYOND
THE
SECULAR MIND

BEYOND THE SECULAR MIND

A JUDAIC RESPONSE TO THE PROBLEMS OF MODERNITY

Paul Eidelberg

Contributions in Philosophy, Number 38

GREENWOOD PRESS

New York • Westport, Connecticut • London

Library of Congress Cataloging-in-Publication Data

Eidelberg, Paul.
  Beyond the secular mind.
  (Contributions in philosophy, ISSN 0084–926X ; no. 38)
  Bibliography: p.
  Includes index.
  1. Judaism—20th century. 2. Secularism. I. Title.
II. Series.
BM565.E38 1989   296.3'87   88–34732
ISBN 0–313–26663–8 (lib. bdg. : alk. paper)

British Library Cataloguing in Publication Data is available.

Library of Congress Catalog Card Number: 88–34732
ISBN: 0–313–26663–8
ISSN: 0084–926X

First published in 1989

Greenwood Press, Inc.
88 Post Road West, Westport, Connecticut 06881

Printed in the United States of America

The paper used in this book complies with the
Permanent Paper Standard issued by the National
Information Standards Organization (Z39.48–1984).

10 9 8 7 6 5 4 3 2 1

Copyright Acknowledgment

From *Democracy in America*, Volumes I and II, by Alexis de Tocqueville, translated by
Henry Reeve, revised by Francis Bowen, and edited by Phillips Bradley. Copyright ©
1945 and renewed 1973 by Alfred A. Knopf, Inc. Reprinted by permission of Alfred
A. Knopf, Inc.

For Sharen

Contents

Preface

The twentieth century, the century of triumphant secularism, is the bloodiest in human history. This palpable fact does not disturb the dogmatic slumbers of the most refined secularists. It is futile to remind them of Dostoevsky's admonition that without God everything is permissible; they could respond, rightly enough, that rivers of blood have been shed in the name of religion. Is religion the only alternative to secularism?

The twentieth century is also the century of triumphant democracy. As the century draws to a close, however, enlightened friends of democracy see signs of decay. Allan Bloom's compelling critique, *The Closing of the American Mind*, may readily be extended to the democratic mind: America is nothing if it is not democratic. Bloom, a distinguished professor of political philosophy, paints a dismal picture. Democracy, which enlarged freedom of expression, is witnessing an appalling decline of intellectual standards. Democracy, which elevated the principle of equality, is undergoing a leveling of all moral distinctions. Democracy, which championed human dignity, is now yielding to abject vulgarity. All this Bloom largely attributes to the university-bred doctrine of moral or value relativism.[1] It is this doctrine that has closed the American mind: closed it to the possibility that human reason can discover objective or universally valid standards of how man should live. It is this doctrine that renders all "life-styles" morally equal, for it denies any rational grounds for preferring the way of life of a Socrates to that of a Marquis de Sade. As a consequence, higher education undermines the quest for the Good, the True, and the Beautiful on the one hand, and fosters nihilism on the other.

Thus, in the very subtitle of his book, Bloom proclaims his accusatory thesis: *How Higher Education Has Failed Democracy and Impoverished Today's Students*. There is a confusion of causality here, perhaps deliberate. Bloom knows, as a translator of Plato's *Republic*, that no institution of learning can be entirely insulated from the influence of the political society of which it is a part. True, the relativism or moral egalitarianism propagated by higher education has impoverished the souls of countless students. But as Bloom surely learned from de Tocqueville (as well as from Plato), moral egalitarianism, or the leveling syndrome, is inherent in one of democracy's two cardinal principles, *equality*, or "equality of conditions." This all-pervasive principle shapes the minds of the educated as well as of the uneducated. It prompts them to extend equality to all domains, including morality or opinions as to how man should live. It thereby gives each individual a "moral" license to pursue his own "life-style." Equality thus reinforces, and is reinforced by, democracy's other cardinal principle, *freedom*—freedom understood as "living as you like." But this means that moral relativism is not only an academic doctrine competing with others in sequestered ivory towers. It is also the logical and psychological extension of democracy's constitutive principles. The thesis of Bloom's book, while correct in a most important respect, is nonetheless misleading.

Although Bloom's description of the contemporary American mind has cogency, it is essentially a rhetorical (or anecdotal) tour de force. While it makes reference to a score of philosophers, it lacks a truly theoretical formulation. It is devoid of any systematic discussion of human nature or of any theory of knowledge or mentality, let alone of history. Perhaps this is why it offers no cure for the mental malady in question. Also, Bloom views the American mind primarily from the perspective of political philosophy, with classical or Platonic-Aristotelian political philosophy as his paradigm. The political perspective, however, is too narrow for the study of mentality. Apart from the fact that Plato and Aristotle were not champions of democracy, nothing in their writings can solve the basic philosophical and political problems of the twentieth century. The American people will not escape the cave of moral relativism by reading Plato's *Republic* or his *Protagoras*, and they would find it rather cramped in Aristotle's polis. Indeed, I shall show in due course that the classical mind was closed to a reality now requiring elucidation if the "American" mind is to be opened. And so, even though it would be wrong and ungenerous to fault Bloom for failing to offer a remedy for the stultifying influence of moral relativism, he leaves us without light at the end of the tunnel.[2] A fresh and bolder approach is needed.

Bloom is an outstanding student of the late professor Leo Strauss, probably the most profound expositor of classical and modern political philosophy. He knows very well that moral relativism permeates every advanced democratic society. Nevertheless, to have entitled his book *The Closing of the Democratic Mind* might have been too provocative in our pluralistic age. But even this iconoclastic title would be theoretically inadequate. For the ascendancy of the democratic mind has gone hand in hand with the ascendancy of secularism. Involved here is not only the American or democratic mind, but the secular mentality of the modern age.

Nothing is more distinctive of modernity than science, more precisely, the mathematization of nature that originated with Galileo and Newton, the fathers of classical mechanics. The tremendous success of science has eclipsed every other intellectual discipline. While science has opened the mind to new vistas of the physical world, it has closed innumerable minds to the vistas of the nonphysical world. For this magnificent achievement of man, which revealed the mathematical hence logical order of nature, gave rise to an epistemology—a theory of what the mind can know and not know—that relegated all values to the domain of the subrational. Positivism ascended the stage of history and became the philosophical handmaid of science.

To grasp the significance of science *cum* positivism from a more theoretical perspective, let us briefly examine one of the most illuminating essays on physics and philosophy by the renowned Jewish philosopher and Talmudist, Rabbi Joseph B. Soloveitchik. The essay, which was written in 1944 but not published until 1986, bears the forbidding and somewhat misleading title, *The Halakhic Mind*.[3] Actually, it is primarily devoted to the scientific philosophical movements that have led to the closing of the contemporary mind.

Soloveitchik, whose mastery of science and philosophy is in the tradition of Maimonides, addresses a question that precious few have the capacity to answer: Is the scientist's interpretation of nature to remain the only cognitive and objective approach to reality? He points out that, until the twentieth century, philosophy accepted the dogma that the mind has access only to the scientifically chartered universe. Consistent therewith, philosophy distinguished between two world perspectives, the "postulated" and the "naive." While the postulated world perspective involved concepts such as time, space, and causality, the naive or "private" world interpretation consisted of qualitative sense data that were beyond the limits of cognition. This was as true of Platonic-Aristotelian philosophy as it was of modern philosophical criticism, be it Kantian, neo-Kantian, or positivism, except that the latter explicitly rejected ethical, metaphysical, and aesthetic values as objects of cognition or of true knowledge.

Now, as regards positivism, by limiting cognition to the quantitative domain, positivism closed the mind to the qualitative domain. Values descended, as it were, from the head to the heart and from there to the abdominal area, where they were explained in causal terms, be it volition, emotion, or biological drives. As a consequence, "good" and "bad," "right" and "wrong," were metamorphosed into likes and dislikes, or they were translated into the interests of this or that individual, group, or nation. Values thus became a purely personal matter, self-justifying or impervious to rational criticism, hence not to be taken too seriously.

And so the world comprising the sum total of our consciousness, the world of our senses and of our deepest convictions, was rejected by scientific positivism as relativistic, subjective, and ephemeral.

With the beginning of the twentieth century, however, the harmony between the philosopher and the scientist was shattered by the revolutionary concepts of relativity and quantum mechanics. Before elaborating on the purely theoretical aspects of the new mathematical sciences, Rabbi Soloveitchik remarks: "Mathematicians and physicists began expounding 'heresies' that undermined the accepted principles of classical mathematics and physics. . . . Whereas science accepted these revolutionary innovations and began to revise its systematic explanation of reality, philosophy found itself nonplused."[4] As a matter of fact, even though positivism (though not moral relativism) has been superseded in academic circles by analytical or linguistic philosophy, philosophy in general, and the so-called social sciences in particular, have yet to assimilate the new scientific constructs and have failed to keep pace with the accelerated progress of scientific research.[5] But this disjunction between mathematical physics on the one hand, and philosophy and the social sciences on the other, should be brought into sharper focus, the better to appreciate the emerging opportunity to open the so-called American mind.

When Galileo described matter as possessing this or that shape, in this or that place during this or that time, as in motion or at rest, he was virtually codifying the program of classical physics and laying the "scientific" foundation for positivism, the theory of knowledge that to this day dominates the secular mind (rendered no less secular by analytical philosophy). But when we enter the twentieth century and study Bohr's atom, which incorporates Planck's quantum of action, we learn that electrons "switch" from orbit to orbit without taking any actual journey from one to the other. Which means that, contrary to Galileo, atoms are not lumps of matter that can be represented in spatiotemporal or visible models. The classical concepts of time, space, causality, motion, and even quantity are inadequate for intepreting the vistas opened by the new mathematical sciences.

Moreover, in opposition to classical mechanics and its handmaid, positivism, quantum theory postulates an unavoidable interaction between the "observer" and the object of observation, the subatomic particles or microphysical events. The implications are far-reaching. For the intrusion of the observer or instrument of observation in quantum mechanics places in question the possibility of objective knowledge of ultimate physical reality—the contention of positivism. And to embarrass positivists even further, there is a de Broglie's discovery that matter as well as light has wave as well as particle properties. This means that both concepts are required to obtain a complete picture of reality, even though, as Soloveitchik points out, they are contradictory as regards precise mathematical formulation. Finally, both Einstein and Bohr, the fathers of twentieth-century physics, regarded their own mental constructs with skeptical reservations, much to the discomfiture of positivists, who want to believe in their final validity.[6]

Rabbi Soloveitchik thus shows that the claim of positivism that science alone has the exclusive right to cognitive or objective knowledge has been undermined by science itself. The dogma that metaphysical problems are pseudoproblems can no longer lean on the crutch of mathematical physics. During this entire century legions of academics, especially in the social sciences, have been genuflecting to an obsolete epistemology. There is no reason at all why college students should be bullied by any theory of knowledge that relegates the True, the Good, and the Beautiful to psychic, socioeconomic, or historical causes. Apart from political journalists and their mentors, the genetic fallacy is passé. Today "the task of the logician and philosopher is not to survey the cognitive act from a causal but from a normative and descriptive perspective."[7]

Having examined the (really partial) closing of the American or democratic or secular mind from an epistemological perspective, I shall now enlarge the picture even further by means of a theory of history (to be elaborated later).[8]

The closing of the secular mind was the price mankind had to pay for the conquest of nature. What made the conquest of nature possible was not only modern science (and technology), but the removal of all restraints on man's acquisitive instincts, and this required the ascendancy of capitalist democracy and its two constitutive principles, liberty and equality. Positivism and moral relativism have therefore served a world-historical function. By closing the mind to the nonphysical world, they facilitated the conquest of the physical world. At the present juncture of history, however, when the mathematical sciences have discarded the classical concepts of space, time, and causality, and are therefore blurring the distinction between the physical and nonphysical, the seeker of truth has been given the opportunity to go beyond the secular mind without falling into the lap of mysticism.

Now, as Bloom or the school of Leo Strauss knows, the conquest of nature is an idea utterly foreign and even hostile to classical political philosophy, and of course to any other worldly and ascetic religion. Hence his criticism of American higher education and especially of moral relativism, though valid, is one-sided. The Straussian school is a bit parochial and excessively antimodern. It lacks a philosophy of history that grades this or that philosophical doctrine, or this or that political system, in terms of its contribution to the fullest development of man's two-sided nature. Human nature exemplifies a complementarity principle analogous to the complementarity associated with particle-wave duality. Mankind tends toward two extremes: materialism and spiritualism, secularism and religionism. When the mind is open to one, it tends to be closed to the other. In the nuclear age, however, we have been given the opportunity—which we dare not decline—to be open to both worlds, and in a way unprecedented in human history.

Both the quantitative and qualitative domains can be objects of cognition, of veridical knowledge. This is the position explored by Rabbi Soloveitchik in *The Halakhic Mind*. The halakhic mind is fully rational and logical because it is fully open to both domains. It rejects the truncated rationalism of scientific positivism as well as the romantic and anti-intellectual reaction to that monotonous epistemology: the existentialism and phenomenological emotionalism that have so confused and corrupted the European mind. "It is no mere coincidence," writes Soloveitchik (who studied at the University of Berlin), "that the most celebrated philosophers of the Third Reich [above all, Heidegger] were outstanding disciples of Husserl. Husserl's intuitionism, which Husserl, a trained mathematician, strived to keep on the level of mathematical intuition, was transposed into emotional approaches to reality. When reason surrenders its supremacy to dark, equivocal emotions, no dam is able to stem the rising tide of the affective stream."[9] The halakhic mind does not eviscerate the emotions. Rather, it provides them with life-enhancing constraints.

The halakhic mind is not the religious mind, certainly not as the latter is portrayed by secularists and mystics.[10] Referring to the subjectivistic gods or mysticism that has reigned since the days of Schleiermacher and Kierkegaard, Soloveitchik warns that "this reduction of religion into some recondite, subjective current is absolutely perilous. It frees every dark passion and every animal impulse in man. Indeed, it is of greater urgency for religion to cultivate objectivity than perhaps for any other branch of human culture. If God is not the source of the most objectified norm, faith in Him is nothing but an empty phrase. . . . If cognitive approaches to reality exist apart from the scientific, then they must be based upon strictly logico-epistemological principles."[11]

As a man whose grasp of the history of philosophy *and* science is breathtaking (especially in view of the tremendous time, energy, and concentration of mind required to achieve his knowledge of the Talmud), Soloveitchik must be taken seriously when he says that "objectification reaches its highest expression in the Halakha." The Halakha converts the subjective experiences of human life into "enduring and tangible magnitudes." In fact, "Rabbinic legalism, so derided by theologians, is nothing but an exact method of objectification," of logically and rationally ordering "our response[s] to what supremely impresses us." The Halakha not only transcends the subjectivism associated with religiosity, but it frequently employs quantitative and therefore verifiable standards for analyzing and judging what is misleadingly called "religious experience."[12] Rabbi Soloveitchik does not succumb to chauvinism when he concludes: "Out of the sources of the Halakha, a new world view awaits formulation."[13]

To facilitate the formulation of a new worldview, it will be necessary to go beyond the secular-religious meaning horizon that dominates contemporary mentality, especially the democratic mind. The goal is not to denigrate democracy but rather to save its cardinal principles—again, freedom and equality—from the degradation of moral relativism and, in the process, to open and enrich the democratic mind. This can only be done by deriving these principles from a system of theoretical and practical knowledge having the following characteristics: (1) it must be neither secular nor religious on the one hand, and yet be supremely rational and ethical on the other; (2) it must be neither simply democratic nor antidemocratic, yet its principles of governance must synthesize popular consent and the rule of given law; (3) it must obviate the classical and modern dichotomy of law and justice (or of law and reason) so as to avoid the tension between civic duty (or moral obligation) and individual freedom; and (4) it must provide a rational and empirical foundation for human dignity that can preclude the tension between equality and excellence.

The only known system of knowledge that possesses these characteristics is that contained in Jewish jurisprudence, exactly what Soloveitchik means by the Halakha.

It is not commonly known (except among specialists) that Jewish law intersected and rendered more humane and rational the legal systems of the Egyptians, Persians, Greeks, and Romans. And while the salutary influence of Jewish jurists was felt throughout the Middle Ages, in no country has the impact of Jewish law been more evident than in eighteenth-century America. Indeed, the American Declaration of Independence, which was incorporated in many of the early state constitutions, is eloquent testimony to the fructifying influence of Jewish law in the progress of mankind.

Now, from this vast and oldest system of living law—to this day it guides and governs vibrant and highly sophisticated Jewish communities in various parts of the world—only those elements will be extracted that are pertinent to the task of enlarging the secular mind and of elevating democracy's formative principles. Such a task will obviously require something more than conventional modes of inquiry. It will be necessary not only to contrast Jewish law with political philosophy, but to transcend the latter's secular universe without compromising logical and empirical methodologies. The goal is to derive freedom and equality from a conception of man and society that goes beyond the usual political and social categories. Only then will it be possible to avoid a stultifying relativism without succumbing to a stultifying absolutism.

The concluding chapter of the book attempts to overcome, on theoretical grounds, the perennial problem of democracy: how to reconcile wisdom and consent. This it does in the process of sketching the basic institutions of a community wherein freedom dwells with virtue, equality with excellence, wealth with beauty, the here and now with love of the Eternal.

NOTES

1. See my critique of moral relativism and of higher education in *A Discourse on Statesmanship: The Design and Transformation of the American Polity* (Urbana: University of Illinois Press, 1974); *On the Silence of the Declaration of Independence* (Amherst: University of Massachusetts Press, 1976); and *Jerusalem vs. Athens: In Quest of a General Theory of Existence* (Lanham, Md.: University Press of America, 1983), cited hereafter as *Jerusalem vs. Athens*. My first published critique of moral relativism appeared in *The Congressional Record*, Senate, July 31, 1968, under the title "The Crisis of Our Times," and was subsequently published under the title "Intellectual and Moral Anarchy in American Society" in *The Review of Politics* 32:1 (Jan. 1970).

2. Bloom's understanding of the American regime, especially of its founding fathers, seems to have been influenced by the writings of the late professor Martin Diamond, whose democratic interpretation of the American Constitution is refuted in my *Discourse on Statesmanship* as well as in my *The Philosophy of the American Constitution: A Reinterpretation of the Intentions of the Founding Fathers* (New York: Free Press, 1968; rep. Lanham, Md.: University Press of America, 1986).

3. Joseph B. Soloveitchik, *The Halakhic Mind* (New York: Free Press, 1986). In the following analysis I shall interweave aspects of classical physics and quantum mechanics discussed in *Jerusalem vs. Athens*.

4. Ibid., p. 10.

5. Ibid. But see John C. Graves, *The Conceptual Foundations of General Relativity Theory* (Cambridge: MIT Press, 1971), who tries to develop a monistic philosophy based on contemporary physics.

6. Soloveitchik, *The Halakhic Mind*, pp. 24–27.

7. Ibid., p. 88.

8. See *Jerusalem vs. Athens*, ch. 4.

9. Soloveitchik, *The Halakhic Mind*, p. 53.

10. See Joseph B. Soloveitchik, *Halakhic Man* (Philadelphia: Jewish Publication Society, 1983), ch. 1.

11. Soloveitchik, *The Halakhic Mind*, p. 55.

12. Ibid., p. 85.

13. Ibid., p. 102.

I

THE WORLD OF
SECULARISM AND RELIGION

1

The Beginning and End of Secularism: From Socrates to Machiavelli

Mankind is tottering on an abyss. Violence punctuates daily existence in a world increasingly portrayed as meaningless. We are strangers, not only to each other but to ourselves. The "crisis of identity" has become a cliché. Familial and national ties have been eroded: we are homeless cosmopolitans.

Not knowing who or what we are, we lack the hauteur and confidence of cosmopolitans of the past. They believed in Universal Man, in man *sub specie aeternitatis*; we believe in nothing. Our humanism is hollow; we cannot even take our own humanity seriously. Nihilism and relativism have rendered the distinction between man and beast problematic in theory and hardly discernible in practice. What indeed is noble about man that anyone should boast of being a "humanist"?

When man becomes problematic, it is a sign of civilizational decay, but also of the possibility of renewal. Such was the case some twenty-four hundred years ago when Greek sophists like Protagoras exulted in teaching youth that "man is the measure of all things." This unheard of and skeptical doctrine—the dogma of today's universities—signifies that all ideas concerning the True, the Good, and the Beautiful are human creations, hence relative to time and place. Socrates saw that this secularism *cum* relativism, which was then spreading throughout the Mediterranean world, would eventually destroy the Olympian gods and was even then undermining public morality in Athens, the "open society" of the Hellenic Age. Various sophists, the Greek counterparts of today's "value-free" social scientists, were broadcasting the death of Zeus, the pagan god of justice. Without Zeus, what would hold society together?

Without the traditional understanding of right and wrong, men would devour each other like animals.

The task of Socrates, completed by Plato and Aristotle, was to substitute a restrained skepticism for the sophists' unrestrained skepticism, lest men revert to beasts. Their world-historical function was to construct a philosophy of man and the universe that would replace the no longer credible mythology of the Homeric world. Accordingly, and as dramatized in *The Republic* (when the god-fearing Cephalus leaves the dialogue), philosophy replaced religion, the philosopher replaced Zeus. No longer were the gods to rule mankind, but reason—unaided human reason—would henceforth determine how man should live.

Of course, neither Plato nor Aristotle was so naive as to expect the generality of mankind to defer to the rule of philosophers. Apart from other considerations, philosophers are not only as quarrelsome as the offspring of Zeus and Hera, but, unlike the Olympians, they are mortal: here today, gone tomorrow. Something impersonal as well as immutable and eternal was therefore needed to command the obedience of man. What else could this be but nature, nature divested of Homeric deities. Neither the gods nor man, but all-encompassing nature, was to be the measure of all things. And this nature, far from being arbitrary and mysterious, was fully accessible to the human mind.

The magnitude of Aristotle's program has not been surpassed in the history of philosophy. He merely set out to comprehend the totality of existence, to reduce heaven and earth and all between to an organized system of theoretical, practical, and productive sciences. To borrow the terminology of Rabbi J. B. Soloveitchik,[1] Aristotle would tolerate no randomness or particularity, no mystery to obscure the fleeting events of existence. Everything had to be fixed, clear, necessary, ordered. Nothing was beyond the grasp of the human mind because nature or the cosmos was an intelligent and therefore intelligible whole.

With Greek philosophy a new type of man appeared in the forefront of world history, Cognitive Man. Cognitive Man is a secularist who deifies the intellect. He is therefore to be distinguished from his secular rivals, Volitional Man and Sensual Man. Whereas Cognitive Man seeks to understand the world, Volitional Man wishes to change or conquer the world, while Sensual Man wants to enjoy it. It is only with the ascendancy of Volitional Man that secularism comes into its own as the regnant force of history.

Indeed, we are not used to thinking of Platonic-Aristotelian philosophy as secular. Not only do Plato and Aristotle refer to the divine and regard the intellect as divinelike, but the refinement of their writings conveys great piety. What gives the lie to this impression is that neither philosopher regarded piety as a virtue. We must also bear in mind their caution and civic-mindedness. Socrates, the master of irony, was given the hemlock for atheism. And what with the widespread corruption in Athens resulting from affluence, a disastrous war, and the unabashed atheism of so many intellectuals, it would have been reckless of these aristocrats of the mind to have joined the scoffers of a religion which, whatever its shortcomings, did provide some salutary restraints on the passions of men.

There are refined and vulgar forms of secularism. Plato's and Aristotle's is couched in pious language not only for political and pedagogical reasons, but because, in their species of humanism, the philosopher is virtually divine.[2] For these giants of the intellect, Cognitive Man is the passionate lover of wisdom, where wisdom is nothing less than knowledge of the organizing principles of the universe. But what is distinctive of Cognitive Man, be he philosopher or scientist, is his attempt to reduce the fleeting phenomena of existence to lawfulness. This is as true of Platonic-Aristotelian philosophy as it is of Galilean-Newtonian physics, despite their very different conceptions of lawfulness.[3] Both schools seek to discover the riddle of existence in some scientific order or pattern of the world. This is the aim of Cognitive Man.

However refined the quest of Cognitive Man, what unites him with his secular counterparts, Volitional and Sensual Man, is that, like them, he does not pursue the object of his desire at the behest of God or to glorify God. The reason is rather simple: for Cognitive Man such a God does not exist.[4] Otherwise, piety would be a virtue.

To be sure, the human psyche is not so easily compartmentalized. Cognitive Man may shade into Volitional Man. Thus Aristotle taught Alexander the Great political science, and politics, for that philosopher, was but the application of philosophy to action. Let us see how Aristotle accomplished this transition, the better to appreciate the greatest exponent of Volitional Man, Machiavelli, the central persona of this chapter.

When Aristotle inherited the concept of nature from his teacher Plato, it had already been demythologized and transformed into the impersonal and immutable standard of how man should live. Aristotle enriched and systematized the idea by developing an organic and teleological theory of nature.[5] Such was the success of this theory that it had no serious rivals in abodes of learning until the seventeenth century. Vestiges of organicism may be found even in Kepler, and it was not until Galileo and Newton, with the rise of the mechanistic conception of nature, that organicism was laid to rest. But I am getting ahead of the story.

What made the organic (and teleological) theory of nature so alluring and enduring is that it appealed to common sense. Observe the growth of a tree from its seed and it will seem that the processes of nature are inwardly directed toward an end, or telos. The end is that toward which a living thing strives in order to reach its completion. So it is with man.

Neither force imposed from without nor chance, so much as an immanent impulse, prompts man to form associations that can fulfill his potentialities. The most self-sufficient and comprehensive association is the political community, the polis, which alone can complete or perfect man's nature. Whatever contributes to that end is called "good." Nature is therefore the standard for judging what is good (or bad). There is no other.

Could there be a more impersonal yet intimate and benign substitute for the Olympian gods? Must we not marvel at Aristotle's genius? By creating a new foundation for morality, Aristotle became one of the greatest "legislators" of mankind. But there is more to his conception of nature.

Also to be seen in nature, and in nature as a whole, is a ruler-ruled relationship or hierarchy. It is natural for men to rule animals, for reason to rule the body, for parents to rule children, for the wise to rule the unwise. To be just, however, political rule must promote the common good; it must contribute to human perfection. The common good thus provides the criterion for distinguishing between just and unjust laws, hence between good and bad regimes.

At this point a brief review of Aristotle's sixfold classification of regimes will facilitate the subsequent analysis of his eventual antagonist, Machiavelli. Thus, the three good regimes, in descending order of excellence, are kingship, aristocracy, and republic (or polity). Their corresponding perversions, in diminishing degree of badness, are tyranny, oligarchy, and democracy. A republic, the best practical regime, combines elements of democracy and oligarchy. It is stabilized by a large agrarian middle class which holds the balance of power between the rich and the poor and whose way of life exhibits temperance or moderation. The best regime in theory, kingship, or aristocracy, requires men of exceptional moral and intellectual virtue, and such men are so few in number that their political ascendancy is very much a matter of chance. Nevertheless, the articulation of such a regime provides the model or standard for evaluating and, if possible, improving the laws, institutions, and policies of all existing regimes, good and bad.

The improbability of the best regime in theory or, conversely, the paucity of wise and virtuous men, clearly indicates that "nature" is the exception rather than the rule. Nature is a term of distinction—still intimated when someone is referred to admiringly as a "natural." Only if we understand what is distinctively human can we determine what is good and desirable in the conduct of life, private and public. Required, therefore, is a model of human excellence. Aristotle's *Nicomachean Ethics*, an inseparable part of his political philosophy, contains the paradigm of Secular, that is, Cognitive Man. It provides a meticulous treatment of the moral and intellectual virtues, those faculties or powers whose perfection is essential for private and public happiness. The better to appreciate Machiavelli, the four cardinal virtues should be borne in mind, namely, wisdom, justice, moderation, and courage. Their cultivation is the true purpose of politics. And to the extent that rulers pursue this end, the political order will approximate the natural order.

Notice how elegantly Aristotle translates a teleological conception of nature into a theory of politics with obvious implications for practice. But what needs to be emphasized here is that his theory of nature utterly eliminates the gods from human concern. Oracles, priests, prophets are rendered obsolete. Cognitive Man—the Philosopher—supplants the Olympian pantheon. Human reason, unaided and autonomous, replaces divine law. In this paradigm of classical political philosophy, which is one of the two sources of Western civilization, we behold an exquisitely modulated secularism, but one more congenial to the few than to the many.

Strange as it may seem, it required Christianity to bring secularism to the masses.[6] For to "render unto Caesar the things that are Caesar's and to God the things that are God's" is to confine spiritual concerns to the church and to leave a welter of political, social, and economic matters to the state, that is, to the more or less arbitrary will and contrivances of men. This is the price Christianity had to pay for discarding Jewish Law (the Oral Law eventually compiled in the Talmud), which the church had to do if Christianity were to survive and be accepted in the pagan world. Having no all-embracing revealed law of its own, the church had to adopt and, at the same time, desacralize the partially religious but pagan laws of a then decadent Rome.[7] To this day Christianity has been wedded to the mutable and contradictory laws of men and nations.

This mixed marriage of church and state, of religion and politics, was shattered by Machiavelli, the true father of modernity. Bearing in mind the centrality of volition in Machiavelli, the great Florentine will best be understood as the creator of Secular Man. By Secular Man I mean a logically coherent paradigm, not a vague appellation applied to casual and inconsistent nonbelievers. The secular tendency is as old as Adam. But it was Machiavelli who made secularism a universal ideology. Of course, the elaboration and dissemination of this ideology required philosophical collaborators or disciples, such as Hobbes, Locke, Spinoza, Rousseau, and Marx—to mention only a few of the disguised and undisguised atheists who constitute the legislators of the modern mind. These philosophers diluted Secular Man for the multitude, including a multitude of intellectuals. But to see this Promethean diluted, we must see him undiluted.

Machiavelli's deceptively simple book *The Prince*, so often trivialized, marks the Copernican revolution in politics.[8] In that sibylline work Machiavelli undertook the world-historical task of destroying nothing less than the two pillars of Western civilization, Christianity and classical Greek philosophy, both of which derogate from the complete autonomy of human will and desire.

The key to modernity will be found in Chapter 15 of *The Prince*. There Machiavelli lists ten pairs of qualities for which men, especially rulers, are praised or blamed.[9] Astonishingly, no mention is made of wisdom, justice, moderation, and courage—the four cardinal virtues of classical political philosophy! "Cunning" replaces wisdom, while "fierceness" replaces courage. (Today, in sophisticated democracies, wisdom and cunning have metamorphosed into "pragmatism," while courage and fierceness are often reduced to psychopathology.)

Moreover, religion (paired with skepticism) is placed last, inverting the Decalogue. Consistent therewith, the central and most significant pair of qualities is designated as "human" and "pride." One would have expected "pride" (the Christian vice) to be paired with "humility" (the Christian virtue, here silenced). But for the creator of Secular Man, humility is at once the virtue of the weak and the guise of the "proud"— the priests who denigrate pagan *virtu*, or manliness, while lording it over the people in the name of godliness, that is, of an impotent homotheism.[10] To complete the process of man's deification, the creator of Secular Man simply eliminates every semblance or pretense of godliness, rendering man entirely "human." He thereby advances Christianity's historic function, to destroy primitive idolatry on the one hand while facilitating the secularization of mankind on the other.

With justice omitted from the qualities for which rulers are praised, a radically new political science appeared on the stage of world history, one that sanctifies the commonplace, not to say vulgarity, in the name of "realism." (A smiling Machiavelli would remind us from the grave that when Mao Tze-tung and Chou En-lai died, Western statesmen and intellectuals praised these tyrants as "great men.")[11] In opposition to classical political philosophy, modern political science takes its bearing not from how man should live, but from how men do live—from the is, not from the ought. "There is such a distance between how one lives and how one should live that he who lets go that which is done for that which ought to be done learns his ruin rather than his preservation. . . . Hence it is necessary for a prince, if he wishes to maintain himself, to learn to be able to be not good, and to use it and not use it according to necessity." This separation of morality from politics is the historical or dialectical consequence of the Christian separation of church and state. Henceforth there are no moral limits as to what man may do. Man is at last fully autonomous. He stands, as Nietzsche was to say, "beyond good and evil."

Furthermore, in direct opposition to the biblical tradition, which exalts truth and truthfulness, the creator of Secular Man teaches would-be rulers to practice deceit and dissimulation constantly. "A prince ought to take great care . . . that he appears to be, *when one sees and hears him,* all pity, all faith, all integrity, all humanity, and all religion. . . . For men, universally, judge more by the eyes than by the hands. . . . Everyone sees what you seem to be, but few touch what you are."[12] We have here a politics keyed to the sense of touch, the most dynamic and erotic of the senses. For unlike sight and hearing—passive receptors of the written and spoken word—the sense of touch, especially in the hands, connects to the will, the will to power.

The greatest manifestation of the will to power is not the state but the founding of an entirely new "state." To establish such a state a founder must create "new modes and orders": he must make the "high" low and the "low" high.[13] To do this he must radically alter people's inherited beliefs as to what is deserving of praise and blame. This will require not only great force but monumental fraud or deception. Hence the founder must possess *virtu*, greatness of mind and body. Extraordinary cunning and fierceness—even terror—are essential in the founding of an entirely new state. In no other way can the founder perpetuate his "new modes and orders." Clearly, the "state"—Nietzsche will later say "philosophy"—is a construct of the mind and will of the "prince."[14]

Since all new states originate in force, say rather in revolutionary violence, their founders are, and by definition must be, "criminals." Only after they have established new "orders" do they become "legitimate" and respectable. What is decisive therefore in the study of politics is not laws or legal institutions but the dynamics of power, on which alone all laws are ultimately based. Indeed, laws are obligatory only insofar as they can be enforced; otherwise they are mere words having no "effectual truth"—like the best regimes in theory imagined by the philosophers of antiquity.[15] Hence there is no such thing as just or unjust laws or just and unjust regimes. (This is precisely the doctrine of legal realism or positivism that identifies the just with the legal, a doctrine that dominates law schools in the democratic world and makes it easier for democracies to recognize and have truck with tyrannies.) But to deny the distinction between just and unjust laws is to reject the concept of the common good, a concept that appears nowhere in *The Prince*.[16] Neither does the word "tyrant" (in a book that commends Hiero, Agathocles, Cesare Borgia, and others of their ilk as "princes").[17] This silent denial of the classical distinction between tyranny and kingship is one of the cornerstones of contemporary political science, which has spawned the journalistic relativism "one man's terrorist is another man's freedom fighter."

A political science that rejects the traditional distinction between kingship and tyranny can take no account of, in fact must deny, the distinction between the good man and the good citizen. The good citizen is of course the patriot who fights for his country and obeys its laws. His country, however, and therefore its laws, may be unjust—from the traditional point of view. But this means that the good citizen may be a bad man. From which it follows that contemporary political science denies the distinction between good men and bad men—which is why democratic journalists (and only democratic journalists) can publicly proclaim that "one man's terrorist is another man's freedom fighter." These relativists (and their academic mentors) are examples of Machiavellians tamed or democratized.

This leveling of moral distinctions is rooted in a leveling of the distinction between man and beast. The successful ruler will combine, in varying proportions (depending on circumstances), the cunning of the fox and the fierceness of a lion.[18] And just as it would be absurd to condemn a lion for devouring a lamb, so it would be absurd to condemn a "prince" (by calling him a "tyrant") for ravaging or subjugating a nation. "It is a thing truly very natural and ordinary to desire to acquire [note the deliberate redundancy]; and when men are able to do so do it, they are always praised or not blamed. . . . "[19] The ultimate criterion of praise and blame is not right and wrong, but success and failure.

We must now ask, What is the world-historical goal of Secular Man? The answer to this question will be found in Chapter 25 of *The Prince*. There Machiavelli subtly equates God with chance (*fortuna*). He then identifies chance with "woman" and playfully proclaims that man's task is to conquer her. What he means is this. "Woman" signifies nature, and man's ultimate goal is to conquer nature, which will require the overcoming of traditional views of human nature. This is why the word "soul" (*anima*) never appears either in *The Prince* or *The Discourses*. We are given to understand, therefore, that man's nature is plastic, is unbound by any moral laws or by conscience (another deliberately omitted word in *The Prince*).[20] And so, just as the Philosopher replaced the Olympian pantheon with a new conception of nature, so the "Prince" replaces nature and nature's God with a new conception of man. This requires elaboration.

The conquest of chance involves the overcoming of God and of all those who have traditionally diminished man by despising the merely "human." The enemy is the "proud": not only the priests, who denigrate the body, but the philosophers who exalt kingship and aristocracy. To conquer chance, therefore, is to lower the goals of human life. For the higher the goals of man, the more is he exposed to chance and accident. Turn now to Secular Man diluted, an inevitable by-product of the undiluted Promethean.

Lowering the goals of human life corresponds to leveling the distinction between man and beast on the one hand, and denying the existence of the soul on the other. Abolish the soul and human reason will have nothing to serve but the wants of the body or sensuality, and such external goods as wealth, power, and prestige. To deny the soul, therefore, is to deify, in effect, the "human, all-too-human"—what the priests referred to, pejoratively, as "human nature."

This deification of the merely human is the historical tendency if not the root meaning of human*ism*, the Machiavellian source of individualism and capitalism, of socialism and communism, of fascism and Nazism.

The prerequisites for the Machiavellian conquest of nature can now be more fully appreciated. The first thing needed is a new science of politics, a politics that liberates man's acquisitive desires in opposition to classical moderation and Christian asceticism. But the liberation of acquisitiveness on the massive scale required for the conquest of nature necessitates a rejection of priests, nobles, and kings in favor of the people. Commentators tend to minimize if not overlook Machiavelli's democratic bias. In *The Discourses* he challenges all previous political philosophy by claiming that "as regards prudence and stability, I say that the people are more prudent and stable, and have better judgment than a prince" (I, 58). And in *The Prince* (which is ironically dedicated to "The Magnificent Lorenzo Medici") he boldly declares: "The end of the people is more honest than that of the great."[21] Notice how the "people" versus "the great" corresponds to the qualities "human" versus "pride."

Viewed in this light, *The Prince* is a conspiratorial work. (Incidentally, its longest chapter, like that of *The Discourses*, is on conspiracy.) Yet it is far more than a tract for the times. This masterpiece of cunning may more accurately be regarded as philosophically armed propaganda addressed to thinkers who might be tempted to make common cause with the "people" and create a new dispensation for mankind. Needed were "co-conspirators," philosophers who would come after Machiavelli and bring to completion his world-historical project and ambition. And they were forthcoming.

Mention should first be made of that naughty plebeian Thomas Hobbes and his wily successor John Locke. Whereas Hobbes interspersed references to God by saying, as well as by insinuating, that everything is matter in motion, Locke paid homage to the deity by proclaiming that human labor is the source of all value—the seminal principle of Karl Marx. Following Locke's exaltation of commerce, Adam Smith proceeded to elaborate the essentially Lockeian principles of capitalism, and with the expectation that war could be replaced by economic competition (a prejudice that even two world wars has yet to dispel).

Advancing the Machiavellian program and drawing upon Hobbes, the lucid skeptic David Hume articulated a morality based on the passions, which alone were said to be "natural." "Nature" and the "natural" replaced God. So did the general will of Jean-Jacques Rousseau. Although he deplored the reign of commerce, Rousseau was the leading champion of democracy.

Building on Machiavelli, these (and other) philosophers made more explicit and enticing the ideological foundations required for the ascendancy of democracy and capitalism. To an unprecedented degree they liberated the acquisitive instincts of mankind, whose loftiest goal was now the conquest of nature.[22]

To achieve this earthly ambition, mankind required not only a new politics but a new science. Enter Machiavelli's countryman Galileo, who united physics and astronomy by the mathematization of nature, thus bringing heaven down to earth. But mention should also be made of a sympathetic reader of Machiavelli, Francis Bacon, who linked science to technology. The purpose of the new science? To alleviate the human condition. For the first time in history science, divorced from philosophy (the preserve of the few, i.e., the "proud"), was to serve the many.

Reason was thereby reduced to an instrument of the will or of the passions. This reduction of reason reinforced Machiavelli's soulless science of politics, the unheralded origin of today's social sciences. But let us read from Machiavelli's disciple Hobbes for a glimpse into the dark sources of the behavioral sciences: "For the thoughts are to the desires, as scouts, and spies, to range abroad, and find the way to the things desired. . . ."[23] Love itself is nothing more than desire, by which equation Hobbes makes explicit what Machiavelli insinuates in his political and literary works, thereby preparing the ground for Freud and today's sexual revolution.[24]

CONCLUSION

With Machiavelli, Cognitive Man became thoroughly secularized and shorn of sapiential wisdom. The functions of the intellect have been limited to the operations of pragmatic reason placed at the service of a welter of desires. The once ordered soul is now the disordered "self." All the emotions of the self, love included, are self-regarding. The only "natural" good is the private good.

And yet, despite his lowering the goals of humanity, there is something grand, not to say noble, in Machiavelli's world-historical ambition of which modernity is the sweet and bitter fruit. For his "new modes and orders" created a new dispensation for mankind, a democratic dispensation of which he remains the mocking prince.

One of the basic concepts of this dispensation is that of the sovereign state. True, this concept has its counterpart in the polis of classical antiquity. But the modern idea is unabashedly secular, based on the autonomy of the human will. If Louis XIV said "L'étât c'est moi," he was only echoing Machiavelli's reference to Louis XII as "France" (in Chapter 3 of *The Prince*). But with respect to the autonomy of the human will, there is no difference between proclaiming "L'état c'est moi" and saying "Vox populi vox Dei." In both cases law is a matter dependent solely on the will of the sovereign, be it the One, the Few, or the Many. The jurisprudent Isaac Breuer draws the only sensible conclusion: As long as states insist on their sovereignty and recognize no higher authority than their own laws, there can be no social or international peace. "The anarchy of mankind shows itself in continuously recurring historical catastrophes, foretold with tremendous insistence by all the Prophets, to which only the law of God can put an end." Forty and more years of the misnamed United Nations—itself a frequent instigator of conflict—lend weight to this conclusion.

Approaching its end with ICBMs and AIDS—soon salubrious clergymen may call for a sexual rather than a nuclear freeze—our century of triumphant secularism is not only the most violent but perhaps the most shameless in human history. It is a century in which timorous democracies, steeped in material abundance and sensuality, betray the liberty and human dignity of which they boast by appeasing monstrous and even petty tyrannies. It is a century in which, thanks to scientific technology and the media of mass communications, countless millions of people hear the bad called good and the good called bad. And so, as a consequence of the deification of man, humanity is being brutalized, driven to madness and death.

Disgusted with the moral decay of modernity, many people in the West are returning to traditional values, either to Christianity or to the "natural right" doctrine of classical Greek philosophy.[25] But as we have seen, modernity is itself the outgrowth of the secular ingredients of the Greco-Christian tradition. The contemporary phenomenon of Christian fundamentalism, to be applauded as a moral force, lacks the fecundity required for a renaissance of Western civilization. Looking at contemporary art, music, architecture, economics, literature, the professions, and entertainment, Christianity is conspicuous by its absence. Fundamentalism seems to be a historically limited reaction to the neopaganism now spreading throughout the West. (Similarly, the resurgence of Islamic fundamentalism is very much a result of Western retreat and decline. The words of once Westernized Moslems, most notably those of Harvard-educated Seyyed Hossein Nasr, reveal their disillusionment with the secularism and relativism of American and European intellectuals.) And then there is "liberation theology" to further secularize, fragment, and eviscerate the Christian religion, which was bound to become an increasingly private affair.

As for the classics, although Jonathan Swift was correct when he likened the ancients to the Brobdingnagians and the moderns to the

Lilliputians, the philosophic foundations of the classics are hopelessly obsolete. Newtonian mechanics (fully adequate for macro-objects moving below the speed of light) has relegated to the dust heap of history Aristotle's organic, teleological, and hierarchic conception of nature—exactly Machiavelli's own objective. But to refute Aristotle's conception of nature is to eliminate from serious consideration any return to his source of morality.

If this were not enough, the classics are also burdened by the Eastern cosmology of an eternal and cyclical (as opposed to a created and "linear") cosmology with all the consequences portrayed in Ecclesiastes.[26] This cosmology is exemplified in the Myth of Sisyphus alluded to at the end of Plato's *Apology*. Eternal repetition seems to be Plato's and, less explicitly, Aristotle's, assessment of human history. (In this most crucial respect there is no difference between Aristotle and Machiavelli, who also posited an eternal universe.)[27] Classical cosmology thus harbors a fundamental dichotomy: Whereas nature is purposive, history is purposeless.[28]

If history is purposeless or meaningless, if humanity is bound to eternal cyclicality, then Plato and Aristotle's political philosophy is nothing more than a "noble lie," a myth—as it may well have been so understood by one or both of these giants of philosophy. In that case, in the quarrel between ancients and moderns, the moderns have at least the advantage of candor, however deadly the consequences. But whatever the intentions of men, the road from Machiavelli's prince to Miller's Willy Loman may be traced back to the deicide of Plato's philosopher-king. Looking at this road as travelled today, it is strewn with innumerable casualties seeking meaning in drugs, sex, violence, cults—anything that may help the liberated self escape loneliness, anomie, angst, madness, and self-destruction. This torturous road is viewed, however, from the vantage of a Jewish theory of history that denies that history is purposeless or meaningless. This theory affords no grounds for pessimism, ICBMs and AIDS notwithstanding. For while man acts in freedom and pays the consequences, every act and consequence, good and bad, moves the system of history forward to an end ordained by a just and gracious God.

One example here must suffice to illustrate the theory of history that shall guide this study. The basic historical function of Greek philosophy was to destroy the Greek pantheon, that is, primitive idolatry.[29] The Olympian gods represented forces of nature. These forces had to be depersonalized if science were to develop. This was the task of the *physikoi*, the Greek natural philosophers. (Recall the great Democritus and his atomic theory, still current in the time of Galileo.) But in the process of demolishing the Olympian gods, these materialists of old also undermined the prevailing religion which, though far from having a refined morality, did place some salutary constraints on the conduct of men. What Aristotle did was to transform the *physikoi's* materialistic conception of nature into an organic one and to invest it with ethical significance far more elevated than the Olympian religion. Later, the decay of that religion threatened the Roman world with unmitigated barbarism. Such barbarism was avoided by the advent of Christianity.

Now, in the process of destroying paganism, Christianity also denigrated, in a most extreme manner, the sensuality of Roman naturalism. Thus, whereas Aristotelian philosophy presents nature humane and refined, Christian spirituality presents nature damned. In this way an otherworldly religion counteracted Aristotle's teleology of nature and its regressive anthropomorphism. It thereby helped to remove a barrier to the further development of science. Nevertheless, such was its understanding of man and nature that Christianity could never have given rise, any more than Greek political philosophy to modern science and to the subsequent conquest of nature enjoined by the biblical verse "Be fruitful, and multiply, and replenish the earth, and subdue it" (Gen. 1:28). Machiavelli's corrosive attack against Christian asceticism as well as against the aristocratic bias and agrarianism of classical political philosophy therefore provided a partial, albeit most dangerous, corrective to their respective conceptions of man and nature. By itself, nature provides neither a positive nor a negative standard of how man should live. Nature is something subordinate to human will and ingenuity. Paradoxical as it may seem, Machiavelli moved mankind a step toward a Jewish view of nature and, to that extent, toward a Jewish understanding of history.

EXCURSUS: MACHIAVELLI'S USE OF NUMEROLOGY

Machiavelli not only made use of numerology, but he seems to have been superficially acquainted with *Gematria*, the system by which the Hebrew alphabet is translated into numbers.[30] For example, as the late Professor Leo Strauss discerned, Machiavelli makes systematic use of the number 13 (and its multiples) both in *The Prince* and in *The Discourses*.[31]

Now, it so happens that 13 is the numerical value of the Hebrew word meaning "one." The "prince" is the "one" par excellence. The "prince," from the Latin *principi*, denotes the "first thing," the "beginning," something radically "new." "A New Prince Must Make Everything New" is the title of the twenty-sixth chapter of *The Discourses*, where Machiavelli subtly indicates that a new prince must imitate God. It can hardly be a coincidence that *The Prince* consists of twenty-six chapters: 26 is the numerical value of the four Hebrew letters comprising the Tetragrammaton, the Ineffable Name of God.

Turn, now, to the inconspicuous center of the book, Chapter 13, to the very last sentence. Referring to the great conquerors and how they "armed and ordered themselves," Machiavelli confides, "to which *orders*, I, in all things, *consign* myself" (italics added). Thus, in language borrowed from religion, Machiavelli confesses his faith: he bows to one god only, the god of power. (In the chapter's central episode, that of David and Goliath, the knife replaces God.)

But let us go back to the beginning. In Chapter 1 Machiavelli outlines, with remarkable brevity (a) the different kinds of "principates" and (b) the different modes by which they are acquired (where a + b = 13). He completes the treatment of the subject in Chapter 11. The central chapter of this group is of course 6. Accordingly, he there decides to "bring forward the greatest examples" of new principates founded by new princes, men who possessed extraordinary "virtue" (a term used thirteen times in this chapter). There he mentions Moses in the same breath, as it were, with three pagan lawgivers. One of the pagans is Romulus, the mythical founder of Rome, who murdered his twin brother Remus in order to be "alone," a first thing, a new beginning, a "prince" in the profoundest sense of the term.[32] We are also prompted to remember, moreover, that Romulus (together with his brother) was abandoned as an infant. This blurring of distinctions with Moses—the faithful brother of Aaron— this moral leveling, is diabolically methodical. But what is the significance of the number 6? The number represents the six directions (north, east, south, west, up, and down); six represents the physical world. Also, the world was created in six days. It is doubly revealing, therefore, that exactly in Chapter 6 of *The Prince* will be found the first reference to God.

It may now be asked: Why does Machiavelli invert the Decalogue in Chapter 15 and not elsewhere? The number 15 reduces to 6 (1 + 5). Man was created on the sixth day. Man, in the person of Machiavelli, becomes the creator in Chapter 15, for this is the only chapter of *The Prince* in which Machiavelli does not use historical examples to convey his radically new political science.[33]

To be sure, Chapter 24 also reduces to 6 (2 + 4). It ends with the statement: "And only those defenses are good, are certain, are durable, which depend on you yourself and on your virtue." God has no place in the world of men. This is an appropriate transition to Chapter 25 where, as we saw, Machiavelli equates God with chance. The number 25 reduces, of course, to 7 (2 + 5). To many, the number 7 signifies luck or chance.[34] To others it symbolizes completion or perfection, for it was on the seventh day that God rested from His creation.

Although Machiavelli can be adequately understood without numerology, his use of the latter is indicative of the great subtlety and painstaking care with which *The Prince* and *The Discourses* were composed.

But what is perhaps most significant about his use of numerology is this. By employing numbers and numerical sequences to modulate the communication of his revolutionary thoughts, less room was left to chance. Numerology added spice to his new science of politics and therefore made it more tempting to his unknown but knowing successors.

NOTES

1. Soloveitchik, *Halakhic Man*, p. 6.
2. By no means is the philosopher to be confused with the academic professor of philosophy. No one has portrayed the difference more powerfully than Friedrich Nietzsche in *Beyond Good and Evil*, Part Six, "We Scholars," trans. W. Kaufman (New York: Modern Library, 1968).
3. See Soloveitchik, *Halakhic Man*, p. 6.
4. Aristotle, like Spinoza, is a "pantheist." His Prime Mover is an extrapolation from the principle of motion (*Physics* 251b17–25, 266a5). As for Plato, his Demiurge is not a creator but an artificer that imposes order on a pre-existing chaos (*Timaeus* 30a, 52d—55, 69b). See my *Jerusalem vs. Athens*, pp. 112–120, for an elaboration of the subject. All this aside, however, one thing is clear: both philosophers rejected the idea of a personal God.
5. Aristotle's theory of nature and its relation to politics is discussed more fully in my *Jerusalem vs. Athens*, pp. 122–129.
6. It was Nietzsche who said that "Christianity is Platonism for 'the people'." See *Beyond Good and Evil*, Preface.
7. To be sure, and contrary to Pauline antinomianism (which was to be rejected by Protestantism), the Church perforce developed an extensive body of canon law that sought to govern man's relationship to society and to God, but primarily, or more directly, through laws governing the family.
8. All references to *The Prince* are from the brilliantly annotated and literal translation of Leo Paul de Alvarez, *The Prince* (Irving, Tex.: University of Dallas Press, 1980).
9. Actually, eleven vices are mentioned, for "miserliness' and "rapaciousness" are listed in opposition to "liberality." See Leo Strauss, *Thoughts on Machiavelli* (Glencoe, Ill.: Free Press, 1958), pp. 311 n. 63, 338 n. 139. This is by far the most profound work on Machiavelli, a work to which the following analysis is very much indebted.
10. See de Alvarez, pp. xi—xiv; Strauss, pp. 179, 207–208.
11. The author of *The Prince* writes in Chapter 18: "And with respect to all human actions, and especially those of princes where there is no judge to whom to appeal, one looks to the end. Let a prince then win and maintain the state—the means will always be judged honorable and will be praised by everyone; for the vulgar are always taken in by the appearance and the outcome of a thing, and in this world there is no one but the vulgar." Among the most notable adulators of Mao Tze-tung and Chou En-lai (the two must be held responsible for the slaughter of millions of Chinese) were an American president and his professorial secretary of state.

12. Ibid., ch. 18 (italics added). See de Alvarez, pp. vi–vii.

13. See Machiavelli, *The Discourses*, I, 26.

14. See de Alvarez, pp. ix–x. Founding an entirely new state must be the work of only one man. See note 32 below.

15. In Chapter 12 of *The Prince*, Machiavelli writes: "The principal foundations which all states have, whether new, old, or mixed, are good laws and good arms. And because there cannot be good laws where there are not good arms, and where there are good arms there needs must be good laws, I shall omit reasoning on laws and speak of arms." Arms are the counterpart of the "effectual truth" mentioned in Chapter 15.

16. See Strauss, pp. 26, 29. Although the concept of the common good appears in *The Discourses*, I, 2, Machiavelli asserts that the origin of justice is force. Incidentally, this chapter reveals what Machiavelli thought of Aristotle's classification of regimes. For a defense of the concept of the common good in opposition to behavorial political science, see my *A Discourse on Statesmanship* (Urbana: University of Illinois Press, 1983), pp. 9–14.

17. See Strauss, pp. 26, 29. Note that whereas *The Prince* is dedicated to a ruler, *The Discourses*, which does refer to Hiero as a "tyrant," is dedicated to two subjects. See de Alvarez, pp. xv–xix, and Harvey Mansfield, Jr., *Machiavelli's New Modes and Orders* (Ithaca, N.Y.: Cornell University Press, 1979), pp. 21–23. In Chapter 19 of *The Prince*, the just and gentle Marcus Aurelius and the unjust and ferocious Septimius Severus are both commended as virtuous by Machiavelli. Why? Because the ultimate criterion of "virtue," as of praise and blame, is success.

18. See *The Prince*, ch. 18. Contrast *The Ethics of the Fathers*: "Be the tail among lions rather than the head among foxes" (4:20) (cited thereafter in the text as *Ethics*). *The Ethics of the Fathers* may be found in almost any Jewish prayer book, or see, *Daily Prayer Book* trans. P. Birnbaum, (New York: Hebrew Publishing Co., 1949), p. 508.

19. *The Prince*, ch. 3. This generalization follows the account of Louis XII of France who "was brought into Italy by the ambition of the Venetians. . . . I do not want to blame the part taken by the King for wanting to begin gaining a foothold in Italy. . . . " In this chapter the founder of a "value-free" political science shows how to conquer his own country.

20. See Strauss, p. 26.

21. *The Prince*, ch. 9. Machiavelli explains in the sequel that whereas the great want to oppress, the people only want not to be oppressed. By no means does he regard the people as honest per se. "For one can say this generally of men: that they are ungrateful, fickle, hypocrites and dissemblers, evaders of dangers [and] lovers of gain. . . . " (ibid., ch. 17). Of course, only a "prince" can found a state; but thereafter Machiavelli takes the side of the people, as he must if he himself is to be a "founder," that is, of new modes and orders. Accordingly, his best regime is a commerical and imperialistic republic, reversing classical and medieval political philosophy. See *The Discourses*, I, 6, and Mansfield, pp. 152–155, 243.

22. It should be noted that Hobbes's *Leviathan* is based on the egalitarian principle of the social contract, which makes nonsense of his absolute monarch, an inconsistency corrected by Locke. Like these Englishmen, Rousseau's social

contract is based on the hypothetical construct of a "state of nature." Anticipated by Plato, "nature" takes the place of God as the source of morality. Finally, although Rousseau and Marx oppose capitalism, their secular teachings cannot but foster acquisitiveness, now rampant in social as well as in liberal democracies.

23. Thomas Hobbes, *Leviathan* (Oxford: Basil Blackwell, 1955), p. 46.

24. See *The Prince*, chs. 17 and 19 (beginning), and *Mandragola*.

25. A similar phenomenon is occurring in Islam. See Seyyed H. Nasr, *Islam and the Plight of Modern Man* (London: Longman, 1975), chs. 1, 2, 10.

26. See *Jerusalem vs. Athens*, pp. 311–312. The classical cosmology of an eternal universe may also be regarded as a consequence of the philosopher's deification of the intellect as capable of comprehending the principles organizing the totality of existence. Pride of intellect requires him to reject the idea of creation *ex nihilo*, an idea that offends logic or the spatial and temporal categories of the human mind. As we shall see later, this prejudice has been placed in question by quantum physics.

27. See Mansfield, pp. 202–203, commenting on *The Discourses*, II, 5.

28. Existentialists also regard history as devoid of purpose. Following the mode of thought inaugurated by Machiavelli, existentialism holds that man has no nature, no fixed or permanent nature. Hence there are no immutable standards by which to determine how man should live. Man, which is to say the individual, must choose his own ends or values and thereby endow life with meaning. But this leads to the nihilism deplored by Straussian traditionalists who find their (noble but questionable) standards of criticism in classical political philosophy.

29. See *Jerusalem vs. Athens*, ch. 4, for an elaboration.

30. See Nosson Scherman and Meir Zlotowitz, eds., *The Wisdom in the Hebrew Alphabet* (Brooklyn, N.Y.: Mesorah Publications, Ltd., 1983).

31. See Strauss, pp. 312 n. 22, 313 n. 24, 326 n. 183; Mansfield, pp. 32 n. 12, 67 n. 8, 73 n. 9.

32. Machiavelli defends Romulus's fratricide in *The Discourses*, I, 9, entitled "To Found a New Republic . . . Must Be the Work of One Man Only." The argument is largely symbolic. To be a creator of "new modes and orders" one must destroy or overcome what is nearest and dearest one's fraternal loyalties, one's subordination to ancestral beliefs and moral convictions. Nietzsche's creator of new values, the *übermensch*, is but the descendent of the "Prince."

Apropos of recent events, Machiavelli's statement "Where the act [Romulus's fratricide] accuses, the effect excuses" brings to mind the statement of two Christian clergymen who concluded, after a 1977 visit to Cuba, where political prisoners are tortured, that "there is a significant difference between situations where people are imprisoned for opposing regimes designed to perpetuate inequalities (as in Chile and Brazil, for example) and situations where people are imprisoned for opposing regimes designed to remove inequalities (as in Cuba)." As quoted in *Commentary*, Aug. 1986, p. 56.

33. See Strauss, p. 59.

34. Interestingly, Chapter 7 deals with Cesare Borgia who obtained power by chance and lost it by chance.

2

The Closing of the Secular Mind

Machiavelli's corrosive attack on the Greco-Christian tradition has left Western civilization with a tremendous but virtually unseen chasm into which mankind is blindly and blithely falling. By undermining the two sources of Western morality—belief in the benevolent purposiveness of nature and in the redeeming God of Christianity—Machiavelli left his successors with the awesome task of creating a new source of morality lest mankind relapse into barbarism. With a daring and subtlety worthy of the great Florentine they came to mankind's rescue by locating the ultimate source of morality in man himself (just as Protagoras had done upon the demise of Zeus).

But what is Man, deprived as he now was of the mind or wisdom portrayed by the Greek philosopher, deprived, too, of the heart or pious love of the Christian saint? Hence Machiavelli's successors had to reconstruct the mind and heart of man if they were to solve the perennial problem of political philosophy: How should man live? Their solutions were ingenious. Whereas certain philosophers decided to base political institutions on the passions, such as the fear of violent death or avarice, others selected the logical operations of reason as the foundation for a new moral order. Still others tried to solve the question of how man should live by constructing a philosophy of history in which either the passions or disembodied reason played the principal role of leading mankind to salvation.

Despite these great variations—I have been alluding to philosophers as diverse as Hobbes, Locke, Spinoza, Kant, Hegel, and Marx—all contributed to the rise of secularism and, directly or indirectly, to the ascendancy of the democratic state. All were optimists: all believed that unaided human reason could alleviate the human condition and solve the problem of political philosophy: What is the best regime for mankind?

Enter, now, the twentieth century. Here one finds a political science rooted in Machiavelli, but employing the facade of logical positivism, a doctrine that denies the possibility of political philosophy as just defined. There are no empirically verifiable standards of how man should live. Human reason is not dispassionate. The goals of men and nations are determined by subrational forces—psychological, social, and economic—and these are relative to time and place. The political scientist can describe the character, and perhaps predict the behavior, of different regimes, but he cannot know whether the goals and values of one nation are intrinsically preferable to those of another.

From this "humble" conclusion, so damaging to the pretensions of the "proud," it logically follows that a democracy is no more worthy of choice per se than any tryanny (a pretty encouragement to tyrants, to say nothing of their subjects). But note that this conclusion represents the most "progressive" thinking of the twentieth century, and not only of political scientists. "I know," wrote Albert Einstein in 1950 (five years after the Nazi Holocaust), "that it is a hopeless undertaking to debate about fundamental value judgments. For instance, if someone approves, as a goal, the extirpation of the human race from the earth, one cannot refute such a viewpoint on rational grounds."[1]

The philosopher of science, Hans Reichenbach, elaborates: "Ethical axioms are not necessary truths because they are not truths of any kind. Truth is a predicate of statements; but the linguistic expressions of ethics are not statements. They are directives [or imperatives]. A directive [e.g., "do not murder"] cannot be classified as true or false. . . . " Having decreed what constitutes a "statement," Reichenbach shifts from the grounds of logical positivism to those of historicism or historical determinism: "The attempts of philosophers to fashion ethics as a system of knowledge have broken down. The moral systems thus constructed were nothing but reproductions of the ethics of certain sociological groups; of Greek bourgeois society, of the Catholic Church, of the Middle Class of the preindustrial age, of the age of industry and the proletarian. We know why these systems had to fail: because knowledge cannot supply directives. . . . Science tells us what is, but not what should be."[2]

Although logical positivism and historicism may be refuted (or shown to be nothing more than partial truths), their refutation would not validate the claims of any political philosophy regarding how man should live. Now we can better understand why the Torah summarily prohibits, for example, murder. The fact that it does so without giving reasons (apart from the tacit reason that all men belong to their Creator) indicates that Cognitive Man—the most refined type of secularist—will never of himself eliminate murder (or even war) from the face of the earth. Philosophy itself now entails the conclusion that nothing in the history of philosophy will ever succeed in persuading a logical person that one ought not commit murder, even on a genocidal scale. On this life and death matter philosophy has at last made explicit what has always been known in the Torah world.

Before elaborating, it will be helpful to dissolve the critiques of logical positivists and historicists, whose superficial reading of the great philosophers must leave the Olympians laughing in their graves. For the truth is that the philosophic tradition, which has never refuted Glaucon's, that is, Plato's, defense of tyranny in *The Republic*, is a secret license to kill.[3] I say "secret" because great philosophers, like the moon, show only their bright side to the world.[4] Nietzsche was a reckless exception. He rightly defined philosophy as "the most spiritual will to power." The philosopher is not a discoverer so much as an inventor. To be sure, he presents his philosophy as the Truth; but it is nothing more than an "experiment," a "temptation" by which he lures intellectuals and becomes, through them, the "legislator" of mankind. In other words, philosophy is a "species of autobiography," a "tryannical drive to create the world in its own image."[5] Hence, not only Volitional Man but Cognitive Man—the philosopher as well as the prince—stands beyond good and evil.

If any one philosopher sounded the death knell of philosophy, it was Nietzsche. (This was the opinion of no less a person than Martin Heidegger.) Today we live in a postphilosophic era. No one can any longer say that philosophy provides a foundation for civilization and decency, or for what naive secularists call "humanism." This long-standing competitor of the Torah is dead. In fact, it is hardly an exaggeration to say that *philo-sophy*, the love of wisdom, has metamorphosed into *miso-sophy*, a hatred of wisdom. No more than a brief explanation is necessary.

In premodern philosophy, say before Descartes, the "thing" took precedence, as it were, over "thought." Only when thought conformed to the essence of the thing did one possess knowledge or science. In other words, it was presupposed that behind the appearance of things—the "phenomena"—there is a reality that exists independently of, but that is at the same time accessible to, the human intellect. With Descartes's *cogito ergo sum*, however, there was a shift from the primacy of things to the primacy of thought. This shift was fully systematized by Kant. With Kant philosophy became critical philosophy, that is, critical of the power of reason to apprehend nonphysical reality. Reacting to Newtonian mechanics or scientific determinism, Kant "found it necessary," as he says in his *Critique of Pure Reason*, "to deny *knowledge*, in order to make room for *faith*."[6] What Kant did was to confine knowledge, that is, science, to the domain of "phenomena," separating it from the domain of nonphysical reality, such as morality. (Therein is the source of logical positivism.) Kant tried to develop an autonomous and formalistic ethics based on universal categories of reason, an ethics independent not only of God and nature, but of experience. The attempt had no salutary influence on the conduct of mankind, to put it kindly. It soon came under the attack of historicism or the "sociology of knowledge." The point of the critique was this: Contrary to Kant (and Descartes), we do not think in our craniums. Rather, our thoughts are shaped by the prevailing ideas or material conditions of our society or of our historical epoch.

But the same could be said of the vehicle of thought—language. And so the critique of reason was transformed into a critique of language— an ironic if not paradoxical state of affairs that diminished the seriousness of philosophy. Certainly philosophy became more nebulous: from things (ontology), to thought (epistemology), to language (semantics and syntactics). In fact, the avant-garde school of "deconstructive criticism" makes nonsense of language. Language, we are given to believe, is nothing more than "random flights of signifiers" without anything signified. A book (with the possible exception of those written by deconstructive critics) cannot be said to convey the thoughts or intentions of its author, for the reader can do no more than read into it his own moods and predilections. (Substitute for authors and readers clients and their analysts, and ponder the implications.) Here language, written or spoken, is from the start fictive or illusory, which indicates that reality is elusive or mere phantasmagoria. "Truth doesn't slip away; it isn't there at the outset."[7] Viewed in this light, deconstructive criticism reduces all humanistic studies of man to "a tale . . . full of sound and fury, signifying nothing." This immolation of the intellect is foreshadowed in Scripture: "I am the Lord . . . that turns wise men backward and makes their knowledge foolish" (Isa. 44:24, 25).

But I have omitted what is perhaps the most important thing. The demise of philosophy and the current degradation of language are very much end products of modern science, of Galileo's discovery that mathematics is the proper language of nature. The precision and universality thereafter achieved in the study of the physical world contrasted starkly with the imprecision and lack of unanimity that still remained in the study of the moral and mental world. Philosophy, which had once pretended to knowledge of the whole, underwent a fundamental bifurcation. There were now two kinds of knowledge conveyed by two kinds of language, one quantitative, the other qualitative. But only the former yielded unanimity; only the former was "science." And so philosophy was left with the study of mind which, unlike matter, has no quantifiable units. The reign of quantity supplanted the reign of quality.

There are grave consequences. The reduction of "science" to quantitative analysis renders it incapable of telling us anything about the rich, qualitative world of sense perception and human values. Unlike classical and medieval science, modern science discards all considerations based on aesthetic and ethical principles. Distinctions between the beautiful and the obscene, the good and the bad, collapse into mere emotions or subrational forces. In other words, the discovery of mathematical laws of nature automatically implies the subjectivity and relativity of everything not susceptible to exact measurement. Given the reign of quantity, the language of ethics and aesthetics, two fields of philosophy, can hardly be taken seriously.

With the modern equation, knowledge equals quantified science, the cognitive powers of man's intellect were reduced to the direct and mechanical functions of reason (*ratio*). "Theory" was confined to logical and mathematical computations coordinated with the data of the senses on the one hand, and with the problem of relating means to ends on the other. What traditionally was regarded as direct or intuitive knowledge or wisdom was degraded to the subrational level of mentality.

While philosophy, the quondam queen of the sciences, retired to meta-metaland, such was the success of the new science of nature that all other disciplines began to "simulate" it. The classical fields of the humanities were converted into quantified social sciences that make even the institutions of great literature about the nature of man inaccessible to many students. The pseudohumanities being taught in many Western universities today are purveyed in an atmosphere of psychological inferiority vis-à-vis the sciences of nature and mathematics, a "humanities" that tries desperately to become "scientific" only to degenerate into a state of superficiality, not to say triviality. Indeed, there has never been as little knowledge of human nature—of the human in contradistinction to the subhuman—as one finds among contemporary behavioral social scientists, who like Hobbes, reduce man to *automata*. "For what is the *heart*, but a *spring*; and the *nerves*, but so many *strings*; and the *joints*, but so many *wheels*, given motion to the whole body. . . ."[8]

No less significant is this. Given the historical consciousness (or historicism) of the present era, an era, moreover, in which the doctrine of evolution modulates mentality, Western social scientists are trained almost entirely to study only change. Any change, no matter how trivial, is more often than not considered significant, while the immutable is almost unconsciously identified with the unimportant and the dead. Finally, because of the totalitarian but truncated rationalism of modern science (or of logical positivism), most social scientists have a very narrow and limited way of knowing things, namely through observation of their external aspects—their phenomena—such that man's intellect, reduced to ratiocination, is confined to this empirical contact with things.[9] Someone wisely said that stupidity and intelligence can live happily together at the level of rationality.

Once mathematics emerged as the proper language of nature, scientists began to refer to God as a "mathematician." As a consequence the language of Scripture began to appear as "more the slipshod invention of illiterate man than the gift of omniscient God."[10] How profoundly ironic. For today, some three centuries after Galileo, the computer, thanks to mathematics and solid-state physics, is beginning to reveal the linguistic precision and systematicity of the Torah at the very time when mathematical physics, commonly esteemed as the paradigm of knowledge, is itself in conceptual disarray, as I shall now explain.[11]

Whereas the field equations of general relativity presuppose that physical reality is continuous, quantum mechanics, constrained by Planck's infinitesimal quantum of action, must regard physical reality as discontinuous. And whereas the former posits an ultimate determinism in nature, the latter posits an ultimate indeterminism. Even the empirical dimension of physics has become problematic. The eminent historian of science, physicist Max Jammer, concludes, after an exhaustive study of the subject: "The immense diversity of opinions and the endless variety of theories concerning quantum measurements . . . are but a reflection of fundamental disagreements as to the interpretation of quantum mechanics as a whole."[12] To illustrate, Nobel laureate J. Robert Oppenheimer, reflecting upon the mysterious action of the electron in an atom, declares in all seriousness: "If we ask . . . whether the position of the electron remains the same, we must say 'No'; if we ask whether the electron's position changes in time, we must say 'No'; if we ask whether the electron is at rest, we must say 'No'; if we ask whether it is in motion, we must say 'No'."[13] Finally, to compound the confusion, Eugene Wigner, another Nobel laureate in physics, writes: "The laws of quantum mechanics cannot be formulated with all their implications, without reference to the concept of consciousness."[14] Thus physics is becoming "metaphysics."

Be this as it may, the intellectual rigor of the physical sciences is beyond the reach of the so-called social sciences. Indeed, no theoretical physicist would regard the social sciences as "science" in the strict sense of the term.[15] But this is not only a reflection on the pretentious character of the social sciences; it is also a commentary on the restrictive yet totalitarian character of modern science as the supposed paradigm of knowledge.

Because of its great empirical success and deserved prestige, modern science has endowed with an aura of scientific respectability various pseudosciences that have stultified academic and public discourse about man and mentality. In this century nothing has so titillated and distorted the popular view of man than the totalitarian emphasis which Freud gave to the id or the libido as the unconscious master of human thought. This scientifically unproven and unprovable hypothesis exempts the Freudian from his own theory: only his thought, and his thought alone, is free from the influence of the id or from his libido. All of which calls to mind the sign at the sideshow in Swift: THE LARGEST ELEPHANT IN THE WORLD EXCEPT HIMSELF TO BE SEEN HERE.[16]

Not only Freud, but modern psychology as a whole, denies the independence of human reason. The language of religion, for example, has been translated into sublimations of instinctual or biological drives. Man is portrayed as a repressed animal, bungled by morality.

Encouraged by the notion that the conscious state of man is not autonomous, radical behaviorists have simply jettisoned the "mind" altogether and reduced man to a stimulus-response mechanism, an object that can be readily manipulated and programmed. No wonder B. F. Skinner, the dean of American behaviorists, entitled one of his books *Beyond Freedom and Dignity*. The behavioral menagerie thus presents the curious phenomenon of human beings who glory in denying their own humanity.

To be sure, I have omitted a welter of nuances, but these only illustrate the phantasmagoria of the contemporary mind. Man is not only a complex animal. He is further complicated and even stupefied by the sophistication of his intellect, all too often the lackey of his imagination or desire for notoriety. The wag who said, "Harvard is a place you go to get your stupidity systematized," may have come from Yale. But only a product of "higher" education could broadcast the fatuity, "There is no truth . . . only news."[17]

In all too many universities the one-time quest for truth has given way to warring and decrepit ideologies, loveless sex, and grotesque music. The insipid "value-free" empiricism that now reigns in academia may be epitomized by William James's aphorism, "A Beethoven string-quartet is truly a scraping of horses' tails on cats' bowels."

The cultivation of human excellence was once the hallmark of the university. Today it is the breeding ground of egalitarian relativism, a doctrine that corrodes intellectual discernment, moral refinement, and aesthetic sensibility. But as noted in the Preface, relativism is also spawned by the egalitarianism of democracy. Notwithstanding its blessings, listen to what Alexis de Tocqueville says about the influence of democracy on the intellect and emotions of the Americans:

To evade the bondage of system and habit, of family maxims, class opinions, and, in some degree, of national prejudices; to accept tradition only as a means of information, and existing facts only as a lesson to be used in doing otherwise and doing better; *to seek the reason of things for oneself, and in oneself alone;* . . . such are the principal characteristics of [the American mind]. . . .

But if I go further and seek among these characteristics the principal one, which includes almost all the rest, I discover that in most of the operations of the mind *each American appeals only to the individual effort of his own understanding.*[18]

The phrases I have italicized clearly indicate that relativism is an intrinsic tendency of democracy. De Tocqueville almost makes this explicit when he says in the sequel that "in a country where the citizens, placed on an equal footing, are all closely seen by one another; and where, as no signs of incontestable greatness or superiority are perceived in any one of them, they are constantly brought back to their own reason as the most obvious and proximate source of truth." And later: "It is not only confidence in this or that man which is destroyed, but the disposition to trust the authority of any man whatsoever. Everyone shuts himself tightly within himself and insists upon judging the world from there." This leads the citizens of a democracy "to fixing the standard of their judgment in themselves alone. . . . Thus they fall to denying what they cannot comprehend; which leaves them but little faith for whatever is extraordinary and an almost insurmountable distaste for whatever is super-natural. . . . " But there is a terrible price to pay when everyone "makes it his boast to form his own opinions on all subjects. Men are no longer bound together by ideas, but by interests; and it would seem as if human opinions were reduced to a sort of intellectual dust, scattered on every side, unable to collect, unable to cohere." Therein is the reason why democracy generates individualistic loneliness and anomie.

But this is not all:

When the inhabitant of a democratic country compares himself individually with all those about him, he feels with pride that he is the equal of any one of them; but when he comes to survey the totality of his fellows and to place himself in contrast with so huge a body, he is instantly overwhelmed by the sense of his own insignificance. The same equality that renders him independent of each of his fellow citizens, taken severally, exposes him alone and unprotected to the influence of the greater number. The public, therefore, among a democratic people, has a singular power, which aristocratic nations cannot conceive; for it does not persuade others to its beliefs, but it imposes them and makes them permeate the thinking of everyone by a sort of enormous pressure of the mind. . . .

In the principle of equality I very clearly discern two tendencies; one leading the mind of everyone to untried thoughts, the other prohibiting him from thinking at all.

This prognostication, more than one hundred years before television and before anyone thought about the closing of the American mind, is truly astounding.[19]

To be sure, diverse ideas are tolerated in a democracy, but only because they are not taken seriously. This is to be expected in an era when the idea of equality extends to the intellect, such that all opinions regarding the good and the bad, the beautiful and the obscene, the noble and the base, are deemed equal. Here tolerance is nothing more than a facade for moral and intellectual indifference. It is the tolerance of closed, that is, dogmatic, minds.

CONCLUSION

This chapter commenced by reiterating Machiavelli's assault on the Greco-Christian tradition and its two sources of morality. We are witnessing the culmination of that assault in this century: The very notion of morality has been reduced to emotive utterances and relegated to academic dustbins. Meanwhile, positivism and historical relativism have led to the closing of the secular mind. This closing may be demonstrated by two observations.

First, given the false consciousness which positivists and historicists ascribe to mankind in the past, hence to the writers of the Psalms, Proverbs, and Job, television watchers are placed on a higher intellectual level than King David, Solomon, and Moses.

Second, secularists in the democratic world cannot draw any self-incriminatory conclusions from the palpable fact that the Soviet Union, the first regime in history to be based explicitly on atheism, has slaughtered tens of millions of its own people. (Much the same may be said of Communist China.) This slaughter was perpetuated not in the name of any god but in the name of Man, that is, of Soviet or Secular Man. Yet decent secularists—and they can be far more decent than many religionists—will not pause and reexamine the foundation of their decency in the light of the most advanced secular philosophy, which holds that there are no rational grounds for decency.

And so the decent secularist has nowhere to look. His mind is closed to religion, and rightly so, if only because countless people have been slaughtered in the name of some deity. If the decent secularist worships anything, it is science. Modern science is indeed testimony to the greatness of the human mind. But it is a dangerous error to think, as many half-educated people do, that this science, even when adorned by the humanities, can lead mankind to anything higher than commodious (but a still precarious) existence.

To prove this point I shall examine the case of Germany, which will bring to light the inadequacy not only of secularism but also of "religionism." In fact, the example of Germany will reveal why a cosmopolitan religion cannot overcome the evils of national chauvinism. Not that national chauvinism is exclusively a secular phenomenon (which humanists deplore, but without philosophical consistency). It is also a religious phenomenon, as will be seen when the case of Germany is supplemented by a survey of the creeds and conduct of various non-Western regimes. These brief studies will also serve the constructive purpose of warning democracies about their naive understanding of other nations, a naiveté rooted in democracy's own infirmities, the primary concern of the next chapter.

NOTES

1. Albert Einstein, *Out of My Later Years* (New York: Philosophical Library, 1950), p. 12. See my *Jerusalem vs. Athens*, p. 365 n. 4.

2. Hans Reichenbach, *The Rise of Scientific Philosophy* (Berkeley: University of California Press, 1959), pp. 280, 287. See David Hume, *A Treatise of Human Nature* (Oxford: Clarendon Press, 1955), p. 469. For a critique of logical positivism and historicism, see Leo Strauss, *Natural Right and History* (Chicago: University of Chicago Press, 1953) ch. 1, and *Jerusalem vs. Athens*, pp. 246–254.

3. It is not generally known, even among classical scholars, that in Book II of *The Republic*, Plato provides a justification for tyranny that has never been refuted in the philosophic tradition. There he has Glaucon challenge Socrates to refute the view that injustice is preferable to justice. This requires Socrates to prove that justice is the good of the soul, so that independently of reward and punishment, the just man will be happier than the unjust man.

Glaucon conjures the ring of Gyges, which enables its wearer to make himself invisible and thereby obtain, by murder and theft, tyrannical power, wealth, and every forbidden pleasure all the while appearing to be just. (The implication is that, by nature, men prefer injustice to justice, but that they desist from injustice only from fear of detection and retaliation.) He then portrays the opposite fortune of the just man, whose every act appears to be unjust, and who is punished accordingly.

Leaving aside the ludicrous impossibility of the two extremes, well understood by Plato, Socrates does not refute Glaucon's argument. To do so he would have to prove the existence of the soul and show how injustice renders it miserable. There is no definitive discourse on the soul in *The Republic*, nor in any other Platonic dialogue. Hence, even though the philosopher would not resort to murder or other heinous crimes, he can provide no logically compelling argument against injustice.

Indeed, the best city, the "just" city that Socrates constructs in speech in *The Republic*, is based on the greatest injustice, on force as well as on fraud! For its coming into existence requires that philosophers be compelled to rule and thus forsake the highest good, the contemplative life. (Besides, justice will eventually be defined as minding one's *own* business, i.e., doing one's *own* work well; and the proper work of the philosopher is not that of minding the business of the polis.)

Moreover, the best city is based on the famous "noble lie." Its citizens must be persuaded that they have all been born beneath the earth, of the same mother (for the unity of the city must resemble the unity of the family). But while the god put gold into the souls of the few, the "guardians" who are capable of ruling and who are most deserving of reverence, he put silver into the "auxiliaries" (or soldiers) and iron and copper into the farmers and artisans. In other words, the citizens must be made to believe that there is a natural hierarchy among men, and that the political order conforms to the natural order.

That there is a natural hierarchy among men is not a lie; the lie is in the pretended conformity of the political order to the natural order. The truth about the "noble lie" is that the best city will be based on hereditary classes with downward social mobility. For inasmuch as the farmers and artisans will not receive the education of the guardians, it will not be possible to know whether their offspring have natural talent. (See Chapter 6, on the hereditary ranks of Judaism.)

In any event, it will be obvious that only children would believe this tale of their origin. Hence, as Socrates makes explicit, the founders of the best city will have to "expel" all inhabitants over the age of ten—a "Cambodian" exodus—if the city is to be formed of uncorrupted or malleable material.

Although Plato surely knew that such an expulsion is a practical impossibility, such was his contempt for the unexamined life of the many that he would not have rejected the idea because of any moralism. Much the same may be said of his student Aristotle, who advocated hunting intelligent slaves for the proper use of a ruling class dedicated to the cultivation of intellectual and moral virtue. These "humanists" were not sentimentalists.

Viewed in the above light, the critiques of logical positivism and historicism are irrelevant, aimed at straw men, but still morally corrosive.

4. Political philosophy could hardly pose, in broad daylight, the question of how man should live unless it presupposed certain universal laws of morality proclaimed in the Torah. Even academic political science, with its specious "ethical neutrality," would be inconceivable were it not tacitly and commonly understood that it is wrong to deceive or cheat, to plagiarize or steal, to defame or murder. The moral relativists that dominate all levels of education in the West today take this minimum code of ethical conduct for granted, that is, they take decency for granted. The Torah does not, which is why it prescribes the minimum Noahide laws of morality (to be discussed later).

Incidentally, by recommending Romulus and Cesare as models for princes, Machiavelli does not deny that murder is evil. Rather, he is simply indicating that whatever is reputed to be good and evil must not be determinative of a ruler's conduct. To say "evil be thou my good" is to acknowledge that murder is evil, but that man's will transcends morality. The same may be said of the cheating which has become almost the norm among students, thanks largely to the moral relativism rampant among their mentors, who do not see that they themselves are the cheaters as well as the cheated.

5. Nietzsche, *Beyond Good and Evil*, Aphs. 9, 12, 42, 206, 211, 295.

6. Immanuel Kant, *Critique of Pure Reason* (London: Macmillan, 1956), p. 29.

7. Vincent B. Leitch, *Deconstructive Criticism* (New York: Columbia University Press, 1983), p. 51.

8. Hobbes, *Leviathan*, p. 5. Some indication of the contemporary degradation of man, especially among anthropologists, may be seen in Peter Shaw's critical essay, "The Demotion of Man," *Commentary*, Sept. 1986, pp. 30–36.

9. See Seyyed H. Nasr, *Islam and the Plight of Modern Man*, pp. 5–8.

10. Cited in S. H. Nasr, *Knowledge and the Sacred* (New York: Crossroad, 1981), p. 47.

11. See *Jerusalem vs. Athens*, pp. 1–3.

12. Max Jammer, *The Philosophy of Quantum Mechanics* (New York: John Wiley & Sons, 1974), p. 521.

13. J. Robert Oppenheimer, *Science and the Common Understanding* (London: Oxford University Press, 1954), pp. 42–43.

14. Eugene Wigner, *Symmetries and Reflections* (Bloomington: Indiana University Press, 1967), p. 202.

15. The basic elements of physical theory consist of (1) physical concepts (nonlogical terms like "particle," descriptive of physical reality); (2) mathematical formalism (translating physical concepts into exact empirical statements); and (3) experiment (i.e., empirical fact based on sense perception). See Jammer, pp. 10–13.

16. B. F. Skinner's mechanistic determinism is involved in an absurdity. It cannot account for the antecedent causes which produced his book *Science and Human Behavior*, for this would require a reflexive consciousness denied by Skinner. Lest his behavioral theory be nothing more than the (epiphenomenal) reflection of his personal history, and of his alone, Skinner must exempt himself from the deterministic mechanism to which all other men are supposedly subject. He must "either" deny his humanity "or" deify himself. The end of his book *Walden Two* reveals his "choice."

17. Peter Jennings, as quoted in Robert L. Loewenberg, "The Manipulative Powers of Journalism," *Scholastic* (Dec. 1982), p. 12.

18. This and the following passages are from Alexis de Tocqueville, *Democracy in America* 2 vols. (New York: Vintage Books, 1945), II, 3–12.

19. The relativism inherent in democracy refutes the attempts of morally sensitive scholars to redeem democracy within its own conceptual framework. For a Thomistic view of democracy, see Yves Simon, *The Philosophy of Democratic Government* (Chicago: University of Chicago Press, 1951), throughout. See also Claes G. Ryn, *Democracy and the Ethical Life* (Baton Rouge: Louisiana State University Press, 1978), ch. 1, for a summary of different democratic "theories."

3

The Failure of Secularism
cum Religionism

In this chapter I shall discuss the simultaneous failure of secular humanism and of Christianity in Nazi Germany. I shall then proceed to discuss the failure of Islam in Lebanon. This will expose me to the charge of denigrating two of the world's great religions. Whatever else may be said of these two religions, they have served a most important and salutary historical function, namely, to destroy primitive idolatry or paganism. True, in their crusades to spread the faith and save men's souls, Christians and Moslems have used the sword not only against pagans, but against each other as well as against innocent and refined nonbelievers. But it is also true that more people have been slaughtered in the name of Karl Marx than in the names of Jesus and Muhammed.

In any event, my purpose is not to denigrate any religion. Rather, it is to let the most shocking events of this century open the democratic mind to the failure of secularism on the one hand, and to the urgent need of transcending the ancient and destructive dichotomy of secularism and religion on the other. Hence the necessity of a two-sided critique. This critique will also place in question the dichotomy between religious doctrine and the actual conduct of religionists. It will be shown in this and in later chapters that the disparity between doctrine and practice is often the result not of hypocrisy or of human frailty, but of doctrinal deficiencies. But because religion is the minor theme of this book—it is primarily secularism that has closed the Western or democratic mind—the doctrinal deficiencies of Islam, a religion of the East, will be linked to those of Christianity and will appear more in endnotes than in the text.

To open the democratic mind, however, it will also be necessary to reveal the shortcomings of democracy, but not simply by using classical or Straussian criteria. For these are limited by a secular mode of thought which, however refined, is dichotomous and sterile.

Finally, inasmuch as I shall be accused of depreciating religion while showing that, despite its civilizing historical function, it is an inadequate alternative to secularism, I had better state here and now that, strictly speaking, Judaism is not a "religion." Only in the next chapter will I begin to reveal how the Torah transcends religion as well as secularism, whose failures will now be examined, beginning with Germany.

ON THE WARLIKE CHARACTER OF MANKIND

Not only was Germany the most advanced scientific country; it was the home of humanism, of refined culture: Goethe, Schiller, Lessing, Herder, Schelling, Leibniz, Kant, Hegel.[1] Philosophy meant German philosophy. Yet Heidegger, deemed by many as the greatest philosopher of this century, was a Nazi. The same Germany—the acme of civilization—precipitated the bloodiest war in human history and perpetrated, with the indifference of ostensibly humanistic democracies, history's most monstrous holocaust. The indifference was not only among secular humanists. Three of the six million Holocaust victims were murdered in Catholic Poland. Slaughter on such a scale could not have been carried out without the complicity of the Church.[2] But ponder the reflections of Elie Wiesel, a survivor of the death camps.

Wiesel notes how he had been "struck by a harsh truth: in Auschwitz all the Jews were victims, all the killers were Christians." He apologizes for embarrassing his Christian friends, but he is morally bound to tell the truth. He asks: "How is one to explain that neither Hitler nor Himmler was ever excommunicated by the Church? That Pius XII never thought it necessary, not to say indispensable, to condemn Auschwitz and Treblinka? That among the SS a large proportion were believers who remained faithful to their Christian ties to the end? That there were killers who went to confession between massacres? And that all came from Christian families and had received a Christian education?"[3] (Contrast this chilling remark of Rabbi J. B. Soloveitchik written in 1944, referring not to the Nazis but to men of the Middle Ages: "How many noblemen bowed down before the cross in a spirit of abject submission and self-denial, confessed their sins with scalding tears and bitter cries and in the very same breath, as soon as they left the dim precincts of the cathedral, ordered that innocent people be cruelly slain?")[4]

Returning to the Holocaust, Wiesel does not forget the few hundred brave Christians who came to the aid of the Jews. But he tacitly asks, without answering, why only a few hundred among hundreds of millions in all of Europe, the home of humanism?

In attempting to answer this tremendously complex and precarious question, I shall ignore the vast literature on "anti-Semitism," a mindless term if only because (1) Semitism is not a creed, (2) Jews do not constitute a distinct race, and (3) Arabs are also called "Semites." The phenomenon in question should be defined by its correct name: hatred of Judaism *and* of Jews. But rather than discuss this phenomenon, which some Christian theologians have recently traced to the New Testament,[5] it is far more pertinent to consider the older contention of orthodox Christianity, namely, that the destruction of Jews and of Jewish communities was a divinely ordained punishment for their refusal to recognize the divinity of Jesus.[5] I shall show that underlying this contention is a monumental yet virtually unknown error. This error must be brought to the surface the better to see why religion is an inadequate alternative to secularism.[7]

The Christian doctrine of divine reward and punishment is based on a fundamental and tragic misconception. Christian theology accepts Leviticus 19:2, "You shall be holy, for I the Lord your God am holy," as well as Deuteronomy 28:9, "And you shall walk in His ways" (imitatio Dei). But it fails to bring into correct juxtaposition Isaiah 55:8, namely, that "My ways are not your ways." That is, it confuses God's general ways, which men can know and imitate because they are prescribed in Scripture, and God's particular ways, which are not knowable. "The hidden matters belong to the Lord our God, but those things which are revealed belong to us and to our children for ever, that we may do all the words in this Torah" (Deut. 29:28). Why a righteous person is sometimes allowed to suffer, and why a wicked individual is sometimes allowed to prosper, involve particular laws known only to God. Of course, if the wicked were always punished here and now, and the righteous were always rewarded here and now, there would be neither wickedness nor righteousness, for man would be without free will. Human ignorance of God's particular laws of reward and punishment is a precondition of free will, hence of man's humanity.

God's ways often seem cruel from a human perspective—think of Job. And of this: when it rains, weeds also flourish, and with drought lilies also wilt.

Our knowledge is exceedingly limited, especially of what lies in store for us in the future. So far as conduct is concerned, we are given to know a finite set of positive and negative laws, infractions of which are dealt with in judicial courts. There judges apply the law to the questioned act or actions of specific individuals. They do not and cannot inquire into and evaluate the infinite train of causes and consequences of any human act. Only an Infinite Intelligence can do that. Put another way:

only the Supreme Judge of the world can weigh the exact harmfulness (or salutariness) of an individual's deed, can judge him not only in relation to all of his other deeds, good and bad, but in relation to all other individuals who may have been directly or indirectly responsible for his conduct. The particular laws or standards governing this infinite computation of reward and punishment, in which individuals and even nations are judged, are humanly unknowable. (Consider the song of Hannah, who understood that "the Lord is a God of Knowledge, and by Him actions are weighed" [I Sam. 2:3].)

Now, down through history Christianity (but also Islam) has committed the fatal mistake of presuming knowledge of the particular laws of divine reward and punishment. Without God's infinite knowledge, it has imitated God's particular ways which, from a human perspective, are often cruel, and it has applied these ways not only to individuals but to entire communities. It is in this light that we are to understand the negative side of "religion," so cruelly manifested in the Inquisition and the Crusades. And thus it is that, to save "errant" souls, Christians have oftentimes dispatched them to heaven.

All this is utterly foreign to Judaism. Its jurisprudence knows only of God's general ways, for these are set down in the Torah which is not in heaven but here on earth for all to see and learn (Deut. 30:12). Lacking omniscience, the Jewish judge leaves the saving as well as the damning of souls to the infinite judgment of God.

A less arcane reason for the failure of Christianity stems from its essence as an apolitical religion on the one hand, and its individualistic universalism on the other.[8] Christianity addresses itself directly and solely to the individual in complete disregard of nations and of their role as basic elements of history. To the suffering individual, the victim of injustice and oppression, Christianity promises reward or salvation in the life hereafter, or in the beyond of history when nations would (supposedly) cease to exist. It urges the pious Christian to turn the other cheek, not to resist evil, instead of seeking to steer his nation on the path of justice. Hence the Christian individual and his nation have drifted farther apart. Christian Europe has presented this interesting phenomenon: while individual citizenries of the nations abandoned paganism to become Christian, the nations comprising these very citizens remained pagan. The dogma "render unto Caesar the things that are Caesar's" armed the wicked, for the state was Caesar. It arrogated to itself absolute sovereignty and recognized no moral law but self-interest.

The idea of the sovereign state implies that the state is the source of justice, that every law is just. (This identification of the just and the legal, which in modern times may be traced to Machiavelli, was the defense used by the Nazis during the Nuremberg trials.) Given, however, the multiplicity of states and their different legal systems, a multiplicity of conflicting conceptions of "justice" will follow. Consequently, when the interests of these states come into conflict, force will be the arbiter. This is amply proven by the history of the last two thousand years. Europe, the predominantly Christian continent, has been drenched periodically in rivers of blood.

Although the above shortcomings of Christianity have often contributed to war and great bloodshed (and have therefore diminshed its contribution to civilization), there is a pacifist strand in Christianity—think of Tolstoy—which is evident in such apolitical precepts as "love your enemy" and "resist not evil." On the other hand, such unguarded precepts cannot but guarantee the victory of the wicked. Indeed, insofar as one can speak of Christian pacifism in the face of Christendom's bellicose history, this pacifism, duly secularized, is none other than the misguided and tragic policy of appeasement to which democracies are prone, the policy that precipitated the carnage of World War II.

Now, if only to warn democracies against the disarming optimism or naiveté of humanists vis-à-vis humanity as a whole, let us turn from the doctrinal and empirical defects of the one religion that has dominated the West to various creeds in the East. Surely the words "I have not come to bring peace, but a sword" (Matt. 10:34) could have been the battle cry of Muhammed. What a handful of scholars have known in the past has, in recent years, become familiar to millions, namely, the militancy of Islam. Who does not know that the *jihad* is a basic religious obligation for the myriads of Moslems who now populate the globe?[9] The Koran teaches them: "Believers, take neither Jews nor Christians for your friends." "Allah does not forbid you to be kind and equitable to those who have neither made war on your religion nor driven you from your homes. . . . But he forbids you to make friends with those who have fought against you . . . or abetted others who do so." From this passage comes the necessity on the part of Muslim Arabs to describe Jews—but not only Jews—as "aggressors." The Koran's imperative on dealing with aggressors? "Kill them wherever you find them."[10]

Doctrine aside, it is now notorious that war, including fratricidal war, has ever been the modus operandi of Islamic states, as is so horrifyingly evident throughout the Middle East and North Africa today.[11] Consider the case of Lebanon, where the moral infirmity of secular democracies is only exceeded by the barbarism of religious sects and autocracies. We need look no further than this commentary on a report appearing in the *London Observer* by one of Israel's leading writers, Eliyahu Amiqam:

"In the corners of the streets of Beirut, small children exhibit bottles which contain human ears dunked in acid, like pickles or artichokes in vinegar. Bodies are

laying in the streets immersed in their coagulated blood, some lacking their pro-
creative organs, which were cut off and put in acid for exhibition by children. . . ."

This report was printed not in June 1982, during Israel's Operation Peace for
Galilee. It was printed in January 1976, during the Civil War in Lebanon. We
read further: "The number of those killed and wounded, and worse than anything, the kidnapped whose fate was usually horrible and awesome, reached
about 40,000, with both sides [Muslim and Christian Arabs] competing between
themselves for the most ferocious actions. Complete villages were robbed, set
on fire, and all their populations eliminated. The Palestinian terrorists [the PLO]
were the most extreme and cruelly vicious of all. . . . "

What did the world say at that time to this frightening situation? Nothing.
What did Pope Paul VI say when nuns were raped in front of their parents and
brothers and afterwards had their elbows cut? His holiness did not say anything.
He was busy at the time protesting against the construction that was going on
in Jerusalem. . . . [12]

What did the world do at the time to stop the carnage and the horror in
Lebanon? Nothing. But six years later [during Operation Peace for Galilee], the
world saw various attempts to allow the [PLO] terrorists to remain in their
positions where they had succeeded in destroying Lebanon, slaughtering tens
of thousands of its population, while establishing a central base for exporting
murder on a worldwide scale [all this with the arms of the Soviet Union, the
money of Saudi Arabia, the military cooperation of Syria, and the diplomatic
patronage of Egypt].

Until then everything was just fine in Lebanon. The disaster started only after
the Jewish army entered Lebanon and began its "genocide" and its "final solution" to the Palestinian problem. Now [all of a sudden] the world showed on
TV screens the pictures of war, the killing and destruction, the mothers fleeing
with their children in their arms.[13]

The "world" in this context is the one influenced by the grotesquely
distorted and distorting media of the United States and Western Europe,
which denigrated Israel and portrayed the Jew as the villain, more monstrous and ugly than any other.

But if one looked into the hospitals of Israel during Operation Peace
for Galilee, he would have seen many Lebanese children who had been
wounded and mutilated by the PLO terrorists. Also, wherever Israel
had expelled the terrorists there was joy; there was peace of mind and
relaxation from years of oppression. But not for long. Fratricidal war
again rages in Lebanon, exacerbated by the same PLO terrorists who,
thanks to the intervention of the United States and other democracies,
were rescued from the clutches of Israel and have now been welcomed
back, and not only by certain Muslim factions, but even by various
Christians. Indeed, some of these PLO cutthroats were hired by the
United States to guard its embassy in Beirut![14]

Unfortunately, Islam, which contributed to the elimination of primitive idolatry as well as to the preservation of Greek philosophy, suffers from the same theological error ascribed above to Christianity. Moreover, Islam (like Christianity and also Manicheanism) is a religion whose founder forms an integral part of the faith. It is not sufficient to believe in the gospels of these messengers, but in the messengers themselves. This is another reason why Moslems have wielded the sword to spread the faith and to send "infidels" to eternal rest. The crusades are going on even today.

But Islam is not the only militant religion. The Hindus, another numerous people, worship Shiva, the god of destruction. Their sacred text, the *Bhagavad Gita*, exalts war. Rulers, who necessarily come from the warrior caste, are obliged to discipline their subjects to wage aggressive wars against neighboring states whenever feasible. As one writer observes: "peace emerges from India's literature and history either as stagnation, or as a time for plotting military action, or as a ruse of war meant to induce somnolence and moral disarmament in enemy ranks."[15] The horrors of Bangladesh may here be omitted.

Although Buddhism arose in protest against the Hindu caste system, it did not alter the prevailing orientation toward war and peace. In Japan, Zen Buddhism combined with Shintoism to establish the martial tradition (innocuously portrayed in the theatrical West). Throughout Southeast Asia warfare has been accepted as the natural expression of the religious or political order. Much the same may be said of all the regions of sub-Saharan Africa.[16]

But it is in China that the science of war achieved perfection. The martial classics of China exhort rulers to make their people "delight in war" and to expand the frontiers of the state. "It is a misfortune for a prosperous country not to be at war; for in peacetime it will breed ... the cultivation of goodness, filial piety and respect for elders, detraction of war and shame at taking part in it."[17] In his classic, *The Art of War*, Sun Tzu teaches that costly battles may be avoided and the enemy states taken over intact if generals remember that all warfare is based on deception. Hence it is the commander's task to confuse the enemy in peacetime as well as in war; to manipulate the enemy's basic values and perception of reality while dissimulating one's own intentions; to cover the enemy's country with networks of spies and agents, all engaged in sowing dissension and subverting morale. In short, the objective is to encircle the enemy's mind so that he will contribute to his own destruction.[18] Mao Tze-tung was a disciple of Sun Tzu as well as of Karl Marx.

But lest the Orient be cast in too dismal a light, let us return to the Occident; first, to that great Swiss historian of civilization, Jacob Burckhardt. Though more subdued than Nietzsche, his younger colleague at the University of Basel, the refined Burckhardt nonetheless extolled war, only adding the hope that it be "just and honorable." He writes: "Lasting peace not only leads to enervation; it permits the rise of a mass of precarious, fear-ridden, distressful lives which would not have survived without it and which clamor for their 'rights,' cling somehow to existence, bar the way to genuine ability, thicken the air and, as a whole, degrade the nation's blood. War restores real ability to a place of honor."[19] I shall pass over this last statement in silence. But clearly Burckhardt was not enamored of our democratic dispensation, to which I now turn.

THE FAILINGS OF DEMOCRACY

Leaving war and warlike creeds behind, let us reflect on the only kind of political regime where pacifism can flourish, where the enjoyment of freedom and equality renders war utterly disturbing and abhorrent. I am referring, of course, to democracy, today the haven of secular—some would add religious—humanism. Grateful as we must be to those who saved no small part of mankind from horrendous tyranny, the honest friend of democracy will not ignore its deficiencies. Indeed, the seeker of truth will even question the principles of which democracies are most proud, freedom and equality.

Partisans of democracy have reasons for such pride. Democratic freedom and equality have facilitated man's conquest of nature, have produced tremendous wealth and creature comforts, have eliminated slavery and unrelieved drudgery, have liberated talents hitherto suppressed by economic scarcity if not by tyranny. And yet, while men and women in democratic countries enjoy unprecedented freedom and equality and material abundance, a frightful number find their lives empty and meaningless. Broken homes, promiscuity, and drug addiction abound, along with boredom, stress, and violence. Democratic freedom and equality, together with widespread affluence, do not ensure private and public happiness. Political or external freedom does not yield inner freedom or harmony. Social equality does not ensure self-respect and abiding friendship. As for wealth, while it has the distinct advantage of enabling many men and women to choose their own form of misery, it has not endowed the life of democracy with grace and beauty. Let us go to the root of this malaise.

When Machiavelli placed the concept "human" in the center of *The Prince*'s decalogue, he was subtly proclaiming that Man is the center of all things. And when he placed "religion" last in that revolutionary canon, he was preparing the grounds for the ascendancy of Secular Man.

Secular Man, or secular humanism, dominates the political, educational, and economic institutions and daily activities of all liberal and social democracies. Having been spawned by Machiavelli, secular humanism is tainted by his corrosive attack not only against Christian asceticism, but against the distinctive virtue of classical political philosophy, temperance, better understood as modesty. Notwithstanding the refinement of some of its advocates, secular humanism cannot free itself from its intellectual origin, from that separation of morality and politics which removed all restraints on man's acquisitive instincts. This liberation of acquisitiveness transformed the soul of man into a veritable democracy of desires. Hobbes was only following Machiavelli when he baldly denied that covetousness is a vice. Thus was born the era not merely of capitalism, but of Democratic Man.

To be sure, Democratic Man did not spring full-blown from the pages of *The Prince* and the *Leviathan*, not even from the *Social Contract* and *Confessions* of Jean-Jacques Rousseau. In democracy's youth, statesmen could openly deplore and seek to mitigate its leveling and licentious tendencies. The blessing of political freedom, they thought, did not entail moral laxity or permissiveness. Nor did freedom of speech require toleration of obscenity. Speech, which elevates humanity above brute nature, and which is inseparable from reason, was linked to public inquiry and criticism, to man's quest for truth and justice. In contrast, obscenity, it was universally understood, reduces the distinctively human to the subhuman and fosters not the quest for truth but vulgarity, not concern for justice or the common good but self-indulgence.

Before democratic relativism gained ascendancy over men's intellects and leveled or dulled their moral and aesthetic sensibilities, legislators banned the obscene on grounds of its appeal to "prurient interest." Today such language is admittedly too vague. Hence one scholar recently proposed a more vivid and revealing definition of obscenity (or pornography), namely, that it consists in making a gross public display of physical intimacies, presenting graphically and in detail a degrading and reductive picture of human life, inviting the reader or viewer to wallow in it to the accompaniment of desire or loathing.[20] A noble effort, in vain. We are no longer in democracy's youth when judges understood that just as the laws must prohibit defamation of an individual, so must they prohibit the obscene degradation of man. The laws restrained not liberty but license.

Of course, such laws, designed to safeguard a person's honor and to uphold human dignity, originated in aristocratic ages, in ages of faith. With the complete ascendancy of the secular democratic state, however, virtually all restraints have been removed from freedom of expression. Today the media are more concerned to titillate and shock than to refine and enlighten. And so democratic man has become jaded. Every few years he may vote or exercise his political freedom and then relapse into moral servitude.

When democracy was in the flush of youth, freedom took precedence over equality; now, with the senescence of democracy, equality has taken precedence over freedom. No one has explored this phenomenon more minutely than Alexis de Tocqueville. In his 1838 classic, *Democracy in America*, this friendly critic of democracy writes: "I think that democratic communities have a natural taste for freedom; left to themselves, they will seek it, cherish it, and view any privation of it with regret. But for equality their passion is ardent, insatiable, incessant, invincible; they call for equality in freedom; and if they cannot obtain that, they still call for equality in slavery."[21]

With extraordinary prescience and perspicacity, de Tocqueville warned of the vices of democracy which, unless checked, would eventually overcome its virtues. He traced these vices to one architectonic principle, that of equality of conditions (which he by no means opposed if only because he deemed it providential). He saw that as men became more equal in their conditions, they became more intolerant of any vestiges of inequality.[22] In other words, democracy breeds egalitarian envy. Moreover, under conditions of equality, where no one is bound to the station of his birth, nothing is greater or more brilliant than commercial callings, in consequence of which the ultimate criterion of social status is money. *You are what you make.* And so the door was opened to universal competition, dominated by acquisitiveness or the ceaseless striving for physical comfort.

To be sure, democratic equality emancipates the individual; but thrust upon himself he becomes animated by self-interest (class affiliation having lost its compelling power in democracies). At the same time, however, his very freedom or independence renders him virtually powerless. Accordingly, he must combine with others, restrain his egoism, and learn the give-and-take of democratic life if he is to pursue his interests intelligently. Democracy thus cultivates what de Tocqueville calls, famously, "self-interest rightly understood." This utilitarian morality, he saw, would generate "virtuous materialism," the gratification of petty desires. Virtuous materialism, he predicted, would eventually "enervate the soul and noiselessly unbend its springs of action."[23] In short, de Tocqueville foresaw that modern democracy would sanctify and thereby spread human selfishness on the one hand, and diminish effective individual freedom on the other. While he prescribed ways of mitigating these tendencies, he very much feared that secular democracy would lead to the most benign and subtle form of despotism:

I seek to trace the novel features under which [this] despotism may appear in the world. The first thing that strikes the observation is an innumerable multitude of men, all equal and alike, incessantly endeavoring to procure the petty and paltry pleasures with which they glut their lives. Each of them, living apart, is as a stranger to the fate of all the rest; his children and his private friends constitute to him the whole of mankind. As for the rest of his fellow citizens, he is close to them, but he does not see them; he touches them, but he does not feel them; he exists only in himself and for himself alone; and if his kindred still remain to him, he may be said at any rate to have lost his country.[24]

Over this multitude of self-enclosed and politically apathetic individuals de Tocqueville saw the rise of a centralized and encroaching government, obliterating, by the uniformity of its mundane legislation, the moral and intellectual distinctions among mankind. For given the quantitative principle of equality, which does not discriminate between the words of the wise and the words of the unwise, the only politically acceptable (and effective) standard of democratic life is the lowest common denominator called "public opinion," whose only responsible instrument is, of course, the towering government of the secular state. Finally, inasmuch as democratic man is animated by the "taste for physical gratifications," the paramount purpose of that government will be to promote commodious living rather than moral and intellectual refinement. Here, then, is a new tyranny, that of benign and inescapable vulgarity.

CONCLUSION

Surveying the panorama of mankind's warlike creeds and conduct with the verse of Genesis, "God created man in His own image," one may draw the conclusion that the worshippers of Shiva have the only realistic religion. In no way, however, do the enormities and atrocities committed in the name of religion justify what is redundantly called "secular humanism." The victims of the Gulag Archipelago, many of them devout Christians, were slaughtered in the name of a secular creed that still threatens the world with the darkest of tyrannies (the reforms of a teflon tyrant notwithstanding).[25]

But while justly condemning tryanny, no one should wax complacent over democracy. Go to almost any university campus. There secular humanism has its priesthood. There a welter of liberated students discard national prejudices, titivate in the garb of pacifism, and peregrinate through eastern cults oblivious of their native violence. While their mentors casually identify with humanity, the bulk of humanity, riven by what can only be called pagan nationalism, murder and mutilate each other. This makes the ventilations of secular (as well as religious) humanism so much drivel.

Nevertheless, there is light at the end of the tunnel, if we but turn away from the shadows on the wall. From the above discussion alone it should be obvious that the evil of pagan nationalism cannot be lifted from history by Christianity nor by secular humanism or philosophy. Mankind is in dire need of concepts that can endow nations as well as individuals with intrinsic moral significance.[26] Neither the philosophic tradition nor Christianity can fulfill this function, if only because both are inescapably cosmopolitan. As Gustave Flaubert portrays esoterically in *Madame Bovary* and *Salammbo*, the Greco-Christian tradition, with its abstract universalism and ostensible humanitarianism, undermines familial and communal or national ties and thereby renders the individual at once autonomous and homeless.[27] In contrast, Torah Judaism teaches that nations, and not only individuals, are creatures of God. (See Deut. 33:3.) Hence the Torah precludes both national chauvinism and cosmopolitanism. No nation is an end in itself. All have distinct historical functions; indeed, their actions and interactions make history.[28]

Given their variety, however, conflict among nations can be avoided only if they abide by the Seven Noahide or Universal Laws of Morality.[29] These laws (of which, more later) are based on the principle of ethical monotheism, which is expressed positively by requiring the establishment of courts of justice and negatively by prohibiting idol worship, murder, stealing, immorality, blasphemy, and cruelty to animals.[30] Only if nations live in accordance with this minimal code of morality can they contribute, in their great diversity, to the overall perfection of mankind. Otherwise, no memorial will prevent the atrocities of World War II.

Forty and more years have elapsed since Europe's long black night. Yet there is not a single discipline in the universities of the democratic world that can argue against that unmitigated evil on logical grounds—as Einstein's and Reichenbach's above-quoted remarks suggest. Twenty-four hundred years of humanistic philosophy, modulated for so many centuries by an avowedly compassionate religion, have failed to provide an adequate answer to the question of how man should live. The time has come to transcend the dichotomy of secularism and religion.

NOTES

1. For an exemplar of humanism see Friedrich Schiller, *An Anthology for Our Time*, trans. F. Ungar (New York: Frederick Ungar Publishing Co., 1959), pp. 68–69, who writes:

Man should feel not only permitted but called upon to reconcile desire and duty; he should obey the dictates of his reason joyfully. A sensuous nature was wedded to his pure spiritual nature, not that he should cast it off as a burden or rid himself of it as of a course shell, but that he might accord it intimately with his higher being. When Nature made man a rational-sensual being, i.e., when she made him man, she implied for him a duty not to sever what she had combined, not to leave behind the sensual part of his being in the purest manifestations of his divine part, and not to build the triumph of the latter on the suppression of the first. When the morality of his thought emanates from his total humanity as the combined effect of both principles, when it has become natural for him to think thus, then only is his morality safely established, for as long as the moral principle in man applies coercion, so long the natural drives are bound to be possessed of force to oppose it. When the enemy has merely been drowned, he can rise again, but when he is reconciled, his enmity is truly vanquished.

Schiller's model is that of natural man perfected by universal culture. The "divine" part of natural man is reason and has nothing to do with God. (Schiller was a pantheist.) Contrast the Torah man in chapter 9 below.

2. In all fairness it must be stated that the lapses of the Church extend to its own flock. See Armando Valladares, *Against All Hope: The Prison Memoirs of Armando Valladares* (New York: Alfred Knopf, 1985), who claims that after 1961 "never again did the Catholic Church in Cuba raise its voice against the crimes and tortures or demand that the firing squads be abolished. During that time it was not only a silent Church, but something much worse, a Church in complicity." As quoted in *Commentary* (Aug. 1986), p. 58. As for the Vatican, not only did it issue passports to thousands of Nazis seeking asylum, but, more recently, Pope John Paul II granted an audience to the successor of the Nazis, PLO chief Yasir Arafat, whose villains murdered and raped Marionite Christians in Lebanon. But see note 12 below.

3. Elie Wiesel, *A Jew Today* (New York: Random House, 1978), p. 11.

4. Soloveitchik, *Halakhic Man*, p. 93.

5. See, e.g., Alan Davies, *AntiSemitism and the Foundations of the New Testament* (New York: Paulist Press, 1979).

6. See note 12 below.

7. I am indebted to the incomparable Torah philosopher, the Gaon Dr. Chaim Zimmerman, for the following explanation, but for whose present formulation I alone am responsible.

8. The remainder of this paragraph is adapted from Isaac Breuer, "Judaism and the World of Tomorrow," in Leo Jung, ed., *Israel and the World of Tomorrow*, 2nd ed. (New York: Herald Square Press, 1949), pp. 87–91.

9. Before one concludes that Anwar Sadat was a man of peace, see my *Sadat's Strategy* (Montreal: Dawn Publishing Co., 1979). One year after he signed the March 26, 1979, treaty with Israel, Sadat told his National Democratic Party: "Despite the present differences with the Arab 'rejectionist' rulers over the Egyptian peace initiative, the fact remains that these differences are only tactical not strategic, temporary not permanent." *The Egyptian Gazette* (Cairo) (April 16, 1980).

10. *The Koran*, trans. Dawood (New York: Penguin Books, 1974), pp. 393, 267, 352. On May 10, 1979, Cairo's ancient and prestigious al-Azhar University, which represents within Egypt the official Islamic position on all matters, sacred and profane, had this to say in the wake of the Egyptian-Israeli peace treaty: "Since the period of prophecy Islam has given clear examples concerning treaties signed between Moslems and their enemies. The Koran commanded us to make peace with the enemy when the *imam* sees there is some advantage for Moslems in it, as Allah says: 'If they are turning towards peace, then you likewise do so, and depend on Allah.' The Muslim authorities concluded that this verse complements the verses which talk about fighting the enemy and is not abrogated by them, because here fighting the enemy is an obligation...." (More fully quoted in Ronald Nettler, "Muslim Scholars on Peace with Israel," *Midstream* [Nov. 1980], p. 15.)

11. Islamic militancy is facilitated by the doctrine that the mere seizure of state power gives religious authority to its holder. The doctrine may be traced

to al-Ghazzali, reputed as Islam's greatest theologian. (But see Gen. 16:12 and Nachmanides' commentary thereon concerning the descendents of Ishmael.)

12. See Harold Fisch, *The Zionist Revolution* (New York: St. Martin's Press, 1978), pp. 133–134, who writes: "To the astonishment of Israel's [secular] leaders, the Vatican and the Churches did not seem to be overwhelmingly concerned at the onslaught made on the Christians in Lebanon by the extreme Muslim groups in 1975 and 1976. It seemed as though the Jewish occupation of Jerusalem was somehow more important than the fate of entire Christian communities threatened with destruction! And of course it was." It was, Professor Fisch might have added, bcause the re-establishment of the state of Israel in 1948 contradicts Catholic theology, specifically, that God abandoned the Jews to damnation for refusing to recognize the Christian messiah.

13. Eliyahu Amiqam, writing in the (Hebrew) daily press *Yediot Aharanot*, June 18, 1982, cited in, and adapted from, Chaim Zimmerman, *Torah and Existence* (Jerusalem: 1986), pp. 349–350.

14. See Edward A. Lynch, "International Terrorism: The Search for a Policy," in *Terrorism: An International Journal*, vol. 9, no. 1 (1987), p. 58.

15. See Adda B. Boseman, "The Nuclear Freeze Movement: Conflicting Moral and Political Perspectives on War and Its Relation to Peace," *Conflict* 5:4 (1985), p. 274.

16. Ibid., pp. 274–275, 280.

17. Ibid., p. 277.

18. Ibid., p. 278.

19. Jacob Burckhardt, *Force and Freedom* (New York: Meridian Books, 1955), pp. 232–233. Most significantly, the concept of the "hero," let alone of the military hero, will not be found in the Bible of Israel. Judaism celebrates no man, not even Moses, whose name, incidentally, will not even be found in the Passover Haggadah commemorating the exodus of the Jewish people from Egypt. Unlike humanism, Judaism exalts God, not man.

20. This defintion is based on, and elaborated by Harry Clor, *Obscenity and Public Morality* (Chicago: University of Chicago Press, 1969).

21. Alexis de Tocqueville, *Democracy in America*, II, 102.

22. Ibid., II, 147.

23. Ibid., II, 141. "The passion for physical comforts is essentially a passion of the middle classes; with these classes it grows and spreads, with them it is preponderant. From them it mounts into the higher orders of society and descends into the mass of the people" (II, 137).

24. Ibid., II, 336. In this passage will be found some of the reasons why democracy today is the home of cults, and not only of cosmopolitanism.

25. See Richard M. Nixon, "Dealing With Gorbachev," *The New York Times Magazine* (March 13, 1988), and David Satter, "Why Glasnost Can't Work," *The New Republic* (June 13, 1988), pp. 18–21. Neither *glasnost* nor *perestroika* will alter the world-historical function of Soviet communism, on which see *Jerusalem vs. Athens* pp. 152–153, 157.

26. Although Islam does not suffer from Christianity's apolitical separation of church and state, its militant character renders it an expansionist creed that does not recognize international boundaries. Hence it, too, cannot be said to understand the historical function of nations.

27. See Harry Neumann, "Philosophy and Moloch: An Interpretation of Flaubert's *Madam Bovary* and *Salammbo*," in *The Independent Journal of Philosophy*, vol. 3, 1979, pp. 79–85, for a brilliant exposition of Flaubert's insights into modernity's devastating effects on familial and communal ties.

28. See Zimmerman, *Torah and Existence*, ch. 1.

29. It should be noted that the Torah forbids Israel from waging war against any nation that keeps the Noahide Laws. Even so, no war can be declared against any nation before it is offered peace terms. Nevertheless, humanists are fond of condemning the Torah for sanctioning the decimation of the Canaanites. They may be answered as follows. Assume that these humanists are not moral relativists, for then they would have no rational grounds for condemning anything. But if these humanists acknowledge some standard of excellence that would distinguish the human from the subhuman, the animalistic practices of the Canaanites relegate these people to the subhuman level. (See Gen. 19:5; Lev. 18:3–27; Deut. 12:31, 20:17–18; Ps. 106:34–38.) Hence, without resorting to theological arguments (which humanists dogmatically ignore), one could employ his own standards to justify the incomplete eradication of the Canaanites, one of the most depraved and disgusting peoples of antiquity. (It is significant that allowing the Canaanites to dwell among them had a corrupting influence on, and brought disaster to, the people of Israel.)

30. Hugo Grotius, the renowned seventeenth-century legal scholar, often cited the Noahide laws as an early source of international law. But as Aaron Lichtenstein has shown in *The Seven Laws of Noah* (New York: Z. Berman Books, 1981), these laws are actually general categories which involve no less than 66 of the 613 basic laws of the Torah codified by Maimonides. Also, to convey the humane and progressive character of this most ancient body of laws, Lichtenstein quotes extensively from that remarkable work, *The Unknown Sanctuary*, in which the French author Aimé Pallière tells of how his knowledge of Hebrew led him to renounce Catholicism, how he sought to convert to Judaism, to which end he consulted the Italian rabbi, Elijah Benamozegh, who introduced him to Noahism as the "true catholicism."

II

JUDAISM AND DEMOCRACY

4

Why Judaism Is Not a Religion

When we see a stone fall, a gyroscope spin, the tides recede, a pendulum oscillate, a rocket blasting off into outer space, we do not see the single law that governs these diverse phenomena, the law of universal gravitation. The truth is that we cannot see any law of nature, any more than we can see the quality "justice" or "graciousness." What we can see are their spatio-temporal effects or manifestations. And yet, while we cannot see the laws of nature, we believe in their existence. If we ask, What is it that sustains these laws? the answer proffered by conventional scientists and philosophers is that they are self-sustaining. But this is no less mysterious than to say that the laws of nature are sustained by an invisible and omnipotent God. In fact, and as will be seen in the following chapter, twentieth-century mathematical physics unwittingly provides theoretical as well as evidential grounds that indicate that the laws of nature are not self-sustaining.

The purpose of these preliminary remarks is to inform the reader that the word "God" as used in this treatise is connected to a thoroughly logical, coherent, necessary, and applicable body of knowledge. Patience and an open mind will be required to appreciate the source of this knowledge.

Over 3,300 years ago the people of Israel accepted the laws of the Torah at Mount Sinai.[1] This same system of jurisprudence is alive and vibrant today. All the old religions of the nations have either been abandoned or have been so changed that their founders would not now be able to recognize them. The Torah, however, is not a religion, a reflection of man's thoughts about some deity and his relation to that deity. The laws of the Torah, like the laws of nature, do not spring from the breast of mortal and mutable man. This is why the Law that was received in a desert is the same Law that is practiced today in New York and Jerusalem, the same Law that has been practiced in Babylonia and Yemen, in Turkey and Morocco, in Spain and England, in Germany and Russia.[2] In other words, the same basic way of life has been practiced for more than thirty-three centuries by Jews living in the most varied cultural surroundings and under the most inhospitable human conditions. Wherever they have been scattered—whether they have worked as farmers, shepherds, woodcutters, shoemakers, tailors, shopkeepers, teachers, doctors, translators, printers, merchants, financiers, advisers to kings— Jews have carried with them their "portable homeland," the Torah, and have lived by its laws and wisdom. Is it not cause for wonder that, despite its antiquity, the system of law contained in the Torah is, in the words of a twentieth-century jurisprudent, "as comprehensive as any codification of the whole complex of private and public law of a living modern state can possibly be"?[3]

Strange as it may seem, Judaism was not regarded as a religion before the modern era, at least not by scientists and philosophers like Rabbi Moshe ben Maimon, that is, Maimonides. The author of the _Mishneh Torah_ saw Judaism, more precisely, the Torah itself, as the all-comprehensive system of knowledge about man and the universe. This outstanding logician would have deemed it fallacious and even pernicious to classify the Torah under the non-Jewish category of "religion."

Turning to our own century, Alfred North Whitehead defined religion as "the art and theory of the internal life of man, so far as it depends on himself and on what is permanent in the nature of things."[4] As we shall see more clearly in a moment, no one who has studied Judaism seriously could include it under Whitehead's definition, as he mistakenly does. But inasmuch as this might also be said of Christianity and Islam, let us draw some sharp contrasts between religion and its competitors.

Whereas religion is said to be based on revelation, philosophy is said to be based on reason. And whereas religion is rooted in the particularity and subjectivity of faith, science is based on the universality and objectivity of verifiable knowledge. Reason versus revelation, knowledge versus faith, seem to be irreconcilable dichotomies. If the Torah does not exemplify a religion, how does it avoid or overcome these dichotomies?

The Torah is often referred to as the Law. In the domain of nature, the term "law" is ascribed to repetitive and predictable phenomena, so that the laws of nature are characterized by invariance or permanence. In contrast, the Torah emphasizes the domain of history, and history accentuates change. The Torah suggests, moreover, that there are laws of history, but laws which are dependent on the free-willed action of men. Can it be that Judaism, as understood by that great rationalist, Maimonides, transcends the contradictions of mankind? To answer this question it will be necessary to define what is meant by the "Torah."

The Torah comprises the Written and Oral Law, that is, the Pentateuch and the explanatory laws and rules without which one cannot properly understand and fulfill the Written Law. The Oral Law, carefully preserved from generation to generation, was eventually compiled in the Mishnah and subsequently in the Talmud.[5] Intimately related to the Torah are of course the teachings of the Prophets, the Hagiographa, and the voluminous Midrashic commentaries which, like the Talmud, contain scientific, homiletic, and esoteric knowledge. This immense body of wisdom prompted an eminent biopsychologist to write: "One may say without hestitation that the Torah is the most complete science of man and above all the most coherent and unified that we possess."[6]

The Jewish Sages go further. The Midrash states: "God looked at the letters of the Torah and with them created the universe."[7] This means that the Torah contains, in code form, the blueprint for the totality of existence. Computer experts at the Israel Institute of Technology (the Technion), as well as in other academic institutions in Israel, have begun to take these words seriously. Various studies have discovered a profound linguistic systematicity in the Book of Genesis, indicating that it had only one author. (The documentary hypothesis of multiple authorship spanning different time periods has been refuted on mathematical grounds.) Moreover, at least one computer study has shown that the Written Torah contains hidden sequences of letters, that encoded in the text is evidence of names, concepts, and events occurring in the present era.[8] (This helps to explain why, for thousands of years, countless Jewish scholars, many of them mathematicians and scientists, have examined every letter of the Written Torah with meticulous care and reverence.)

The findings of these computer studies—and they have hardly scratched the surface—surprise no one who has mastered, or at least has worked with the few who have mastered, the logical controls and hermeneutical rules of the Talmud, without which the Written Torah, long trifled with by outsiders, remains a closed book. No mere philosopher, Spinoza included, has entered this exclusive domain.

If the Torah is viewed as the blueprint for the totality of existence, then, logically, it cannot be comprehended by any category extrinsic to itself. Religion is such a category, and the one most commonly applied to the Torah. But inasmuch as the Torah is *sui generis*, nothing is a greater obstacle to understanding its uniqueness than placing it under the category of religion. This is exactly the position of one of the most outstanding philologists and Torah philosophers of modern times, Rabbi Samson Raphael Hirsch (1808–1888), who writes:

Every European language speaks of religion. We, the People of Religion par excellence, have no expression for it. As soon as anything is used to designate some special relationship to our life as religious, it specializes just this, and implies that there are phases in life which have no relation to it. It makes it a separate realm. But where everything from birth to death belongs to religion, this conception cannot exist inasmuch as every phase of life is penetrated with it and nothing at all is left out. The word religion, if it comes from the Latin 'religare,' to bind, is even contrary to the Jewish point of view. Our relation to God makes us free. . . .[9]

Elsewhere the great commentator is still more specific.[10] Thus, unlike religion, by which is to be understood the conception that men have formed and are still forming of a deity and their relationship to this deity, the Torah is, or may be regarded as, the "codified thought" of God and His message to and about man. (Strictly speaking, therefore, Judaism has no theology.) Although aspects of what is sometimes understood as religion will be found in Judaism, the Torah is infinitely more comprehensive and different. In religions God has only temples, churches, priesthoods, congregations, and so forth, whereas in the Torah God establishes a nation having a world-historical function. (See Gen. 12:2–3, 17:4; Exod. 6:7.) And insofar as this nation was given a religion, it is a religion of (dynamic) reason embodied in axiomatic and immutable law reaching to the nation's everyday life.

Now it will be easier to understand why the Torah, in contrast to religion, is not based on faith.[11] The concept of faith, unlike the concept of reason, is not logically related to the idea of man's creation in the image of God. Besides, the Hebrew word _emunah_, misleadingly translated as "faith," signifies a state of mind one has not at the beginning, but at the end, of a process of observation and experience informed by rational contemplation, a process that results in clear-eyed and unwavering conviction and confidence. (See Exod. 14:31, 19:4–8.) Torah Judaism begins with either inquiry or practice, one proceeding toward the other. The aim is to understand the totality of existence and to live in accordance with the laws thereof. Hence the Torah, like scientific inquiry, must and can be tested by its internal logical consistency and by its power to elucidate history and nature.[12]

This last statement contradicts the dichotomy between reason and revelation. In his _Kuzari_, Rabbi Yehuda Halevi writes: "God forbid that there should be anything in the Torah that contradicts reason." Consistent therewith, principles based on logical reasoning have the validity of a biblical statement and therefore do not require biblical proof. (See _Ketuvot_ 22a.) If, by logical reasoning, one arrives at a biblical statement, the latter must have additional meanings that can be rendered explicit by various hermeneutical rules contained in the Talmud.

But the Torah itself warns us against the mind-stultifying dichotomy of reason and revelation that has led skeptics and believers alike to confuse the Torah with the fantasies of mysticism and with the otherworldiness of religion:

[The Torah] is not in heaven that you should say: "Who will go up for us to heaven and bring it down to us and make us understand it and keep it." (Deut. 30:12)[13]

What is decisive in revelation (or prophecy) and scientific thought alike is not the subjective process by which the mind gains knowledge or insight into some reality, but the linguistic product of that process, which alone can be communicated and tested by logical and empirical means. Mental processes are not in themselves communicable because, unlike language, they transcend space and time. Language is the tangible means by which thought links the nonfinite to the infinite. An analogy from quantum physics may make this clearer.

According to quantum physics, the macrophysical world—the world of sense perception—is a derived world. Though real, it is not, physically speaking, the ultimately real. To discover the latter we must grasp the microphysical world, the world of subatomic processes. But because the mind can only think in terms of space and time, we can only know about the microphysical world indirectly, that is, by its macrophysical or observable effects. The spatial and temporal concepts used to describe these effects are really metaphors or anthropomorphisms. They do not literally describe the microphysical world in itself—just as the anthropomorphisms in the Torah do not describe God in Himself, but only His tangible manifestations.

This is what is meant by calling the Torah the "codified thought" of God. Because the Torah, in its entirety, is here on earth and has been ever since the law-giving at Mount Sinai, it must, on principle, be wholly accessible to the human intellect and fully applicable to human concerns. We are even told that

[The Torah] is something very close to you. It is in your mouth and in your heart [i.e., it is something you can discuss and intimately understand], so that you can fulfill it. (Deut. 30:14)

Drawing upon Hirsch's commentary: What the Torah is primarily about is you yourself, here on earth. To understand its teachings you need only examine yourself and your circumstances. And what you require beyond the Written Torah, you have in the tradition that is to be taught and learned from mouth to mouth, that is, by living teachers and students engaged in rational investigation and dialogue. Neither prophetic inspiration nor any priesthood, but only erudition and publicly tested scholarship can lay claim to any validity regarding the teachings of the Torah.[14]

By "teachings," Hirsch obviously means, primarily, the all-embracing laws of the Torah called the Halakha. (The term comes from the Hebrew root verb meaning "to walk." To live by the Halakha is to walk in God's ways, but as a unique individual.) It is precisely knowledge of, and devotion to, the Halakha that distinguishes the Torah man from religious man. A most brilliant and contemporary elucidation of the subject will be found in Rabbi J. B. Soloveitchik's essay, *Halakhic Man*. The essay begins by distinguishing between "cognitive man" and *"homo religiosus."* As already noted, cognitive man is content to reveal what is fixed, clear, and lawful in existence, that is, to solve, through unaided human reason, the riddle buried deep in reality. *Homo religiosus* is very different:

When he confronts God's world, when he gazes at the myriads of events and phenomena occurring in the cosmos, he does not desire to transform the secrets embedded in creation into simple equations that a mere tyro is capable of grasping. On the contrary, *homo religiosus* is intrigued by the mystery of existence—the *mysterium tremendum*—and wants to emphasize that mystery. He gazes at that which is obscure without the intent of explaining it and inquires into that which is concealed without the intent of receiving the reward of clear understanding.[15]

This is not to say that religious man denies objective knowledge or the validity of the cognitive act. He does not necessarily adopt the position of Tertullian, "Credo quia absurdum est" (I believe because it is absurd). He may even be eager to cognize natural phenomena and understand empirical reality. But unlike cognitive man, he is profoundly dissatisfied and unhappy with such knowledge and seeks a more purified existence.[16] Sometimes he abandons the world to all its evils and sufferings. Other times he battles with carnal, this-worldly pleasures. Clearly, these different psychic states of *homo religiosus* make him "highly subjective," if not dangerous.[17] For unlike most religionists who have come to terms with this mundane world, *homo religiosus* is not halfhearted in his religiosity. Not to be overlooked are those examples of this type who, to this day, slaughter the innocent or force them to enter the "faith."

Contrast, now, Rabbi Soloveitchik's description of halakhic man, the master of Torah jurisprudence:

Halakhic man does not long for a transcendent world, for "supernal" levels of a pure, pristine existence. For was not the ideal world—halakhic man's deepest desire—created only for the purpose of being actualized in our real world? It is this world which constitutes the stage for the Halakha, the setting for halakhic man's life. It is here that the Halakha can be implemented to a greater or lesser degree. It is here that [the ideal laws of the Torah] can pass from potentiality to actuality. It is here, in this world, that the halakhic man acquires eternal life! "Better is one hour of Torah and *mitzvot* [good deeds] in this world than the whole life of the world to come. . . ." (*Ethics* 4:22), and this declaration is the watchword of the halakhist. Not only will the universal *homo religiosus* not understand this statement, but he will have only contempt for it, as if, heaven forbid, it intended to deny the pure and exalted life after death.[18]

Contrary to appearances, halakhic man is not a secular, cognitive type unconcerned with transcendence. But whereas *homo religiosus* starts out in this world and ends up in mystical realms, halakhic man takes up his position in this world and deals with it in a manner comparable to that of a mathematical physicist who, at the same time, is also a physician. Like the physicist he has "a priori, ideal constructs" (the laws of the Torah). If he were only a physicist, his sole aim would be to reveal the correspondence between the ideal world and concrete reality. But since he is also a physician living in an imperfect human world, he tries, on a case-by-case basis, to make part of that world approximate the "a priori, ideal constructs" of the Halakha.[19] Here halakhic man displays not only individuality and creativity, but a "distinct streak of aristocracy." Unlike *homo religiosus*, who yearns for *unio mystica*, or "who stands and waits for the revelation of truth and inspiration by the spirit," halakhic man does not require any transcendent assistance to understand the Torah or to achieve his own, individual perfection:

He approaches the world of Halakha with his mind and intellect, just as cognitive man approaches the natural realm. And since he relies on his intellect, he places his trust in it and does not suppress any of his psychic faculties in order to merge into some supernal existence. His own personal understanding can resolve the most difficult and complex problems. . . . He recognizes no authority other than the authority of the intellect (obviously, in accordance with the principles of tradition).[20]

Thus equipped, halakhic man explores every domain of existence—physical, biological, mental, social, political, cultural, the concerns of the family, of workers and businessmen, in short, of every kind of human relationship—and all in the minutest detail and with the documented experience of millennia.[21] This halakhic man can do because he is the recipient of a system of law unequalled in comprehensiveness and rationality. This system of law, moreover, is not the preserve of a distinct or privileged class, but the possession of the Jewish people as a whole.

In fact, there was a time when, thanks to their educators, Jews of the humblest callings were scholars. Aristotle's disciple, Theophrastus, described them as "a nation of philosophers."[22] But ponder the words of Nietzsche: "Wherever the Jews have attained to influence, they have taught to analyze more subtly, to argue more acutely, to write more clearly and purely: it has always been their problem to bring people 'to *raison.' "*[23]

Anyone with some knowledge of Judaism would know, however, that the rationality which Nietzsche here attributes to the Jews must be credited to their study of the Talmud, whose volumes of Jewish law involve the most rigorous and exhaustive training in logic, a logic linked to the entire gamut of human life.

What most distinguishes the Torah man, therefore, is his knowledge not of the Written Law but of the Oral Law. This requires some elucidation.

Dr. Chaim Zimmerman has pointed out that the Written Torah stands to the Oral Torah as short notes to a comprehensive, explicit system.[24] The notes are coded in exact logical characters. To decipher the code one must apply the hermeneutical rules that Moses received at Mount Sinai and conveyed to Joshua and the Elders, and that were subsequently transmitted to the Prophets and the Men of the Great Assembly. Only by mastery of these logical, linguistic, and numerical rules is it possible to translate, as it were, the Written Torah into the Oral Torah.

As previously noted, the Oral Torah is embodied in the Mishnah. Its contents were compiled by the Mishnaic Sages, the Tannaim, in continuity with the Men of the Great Assembly. The final compilation was executed by the court of Rabbi Judah HaNasi at the close of the second century of the present era. Moreover, the laws and legal opinions of the Mishnah were thoroughly discussed and analyzed by the post-Mishnaic halakhic scholars, the Amoriam, to determine their logical relationships and the functions of their application. The Jews have authentic records of these discussions, which are called Gemara (from the Aramaic word meaning "to study"). The Gemara were collected and, together with the Mishnah, were embodied in the Talmud (about 500 C.E.).

Despite its having been put into written form, the Oral Torah remains essentially oral, for only under the apprenticeship of a Torah master can one learn the various methods of expounding and applying the Halakha.

It is to Maimonides (1135–1204), one of the greatest minds the world has ever produced, that we owe the first complete and systematic presentation of Jewish law. His fourteen-volume magnum opus, the *Mishneh Torah* (Repetition of the Law) reveals, in the most logical and lucid manner, the unity of the Torah. From his monumental work there emerges a comprehensive view of Judaism as a guide to life, at once rational and humane. There is no dichotomy here between law and reason or between law and morality (a subject to be discussed in Chapter 11).

As a code of law, the *Mishneh Torah* deals only with what is explicit in the Gemara and not with what may be deduced from it by the dynamics of halakhic argument and refutation; in other words, it does not teach the student or the judge how to arrive at halakhic decisions. For this one must learn the dialectics of the Talmud, a most formidable discipline requiring many years of concentrated study under a halakhic master. Only a person who believes in the divine origin and totality of the Torah would undertake such a discipline.

Far from being static—the impression one may gain from a code of law—the Halakha is a dynamic and ever-expanding system of jurisprudence intrinsically capable of dealing with the ever-changing conditions of mankind—social, political, economic, and technological. Thus, building on Maimonides and other halakhic masters, Rabbi Joseph Karo (1488–1575) wrote the *Shulkhan Arukh,* to this day the authoritative Code of Jewish Law. It should be noted, however, that Halakhic decisions cannot be made from the Code alone; one must also understand the logic and methodologies of halakhic jurisprudence. Also, the Code is continually brought up to date by case law, that is, by the Responsa literature of which there now exist several thousand volumes. It is in the Responsa literature that one finds pristine halakhic thinking applied to day-to-day problems. Here the halakhic authorities have to decide how the immutable laws of the Torah are to be applied in concrete cases. There is thus an unbroken chain of Jewish tradition connecting the days of Moses with our own. Never in the whole course of Jewish law has any change been made that was not consistent with the logical structure of the Torah.[25] All new ordinances were only logical deductions and applications of the law to new conditions.[26]

Contrary to widespread prejudice, the Halakha is not merely a vast body of laws and rules having only practical significance.[27] For underlying these laws and rules is a logic conceptually comparable to that of mathematical physics. This means that the Halakha is a thoroughly axiomatic system of law that determines the logical status and comparative value of the concrete variables coming under its purview. In any case or controversy, the judge has to follow the halakhic rules in the same manner as the quantum physicist has to follow an algorithm, a set of rules telling him how to make calculations using observed data as a starting point but in conformity with the laws of nature. Moreover, just as the scientist in his laboratory has no interest in the "whys" or metaphysical explanations of the laws of nature, so the judge is not concerned with the reasons underlying the laws of Halakha. ("Why" questions, in both cases, would lead to an infinite regress. Such questions may be raised for heuristic purposes, but not for deciding the validity of any law.) The judge, *qua* judge, is only concerned with the clear and immutable rules of the Halakha, and their logical consequences and practical effects. There is no dichotomy here between theory and practice (a subject to be discussed in Chapter 10).

Interestingly, the Halakha may be said to contain an important democratic dimension. Thus, when a court or a judge issues a decree (*gezera*), it must not only be consistent with the immutable laws of the Torah, but it must be acceptable to the community. On the other hand, no custom (*minhag*) which may have evolved in a community has any binding power if it is contrary to the Halakha. But such is the breadth, sobriety, and vitality of the Halakha that it can accommodate divergent customs, as may be seen among Ashkenazi and Sephardi Jews. In fact, customs that do not contradict the Halakha may themselves attain the status of law. In short, whereas no court would issue a decree unless the community is able to conform to it, no court would feel bound by any custom that violated the Halakha. Here is a beautiful blending of theory and practice.

Although theoretical truths are the basis of action in Judaism, no Jewish philosophy is valid unless it is grounded on, and terminates in, the Halakha. There is, of course, an important difference between the realm of thought and the realm of action. In the realm of thought the mind must have freedom, there must be latitude. For it is not only difficult to define or circumscribe metaphysical ideas, but unlike the logic of the Halakha, such ideas inevitably undergo change in transmission from one mind to another. Hence it is impossible to establish a supreme authority regarding notions that involve the world beyond our senses. No exponent of Judaism is deprived the right to give his own interpretation to even universally accepted doctrines so long as his views do not contradict the Halakha.[28]

As regards action or conduct, conformity to the Law is essential. Whatever degree of flexibility may be inherent in the laws and rules of the Halakha, the theoretical principles that guide their application in specific cases are fixed and authoritative, as they must be in any axiomatic system. Jewish law is based on logic, not on personal predilection, convenience, or sentiment. It needs to be emphasized, however, that the Oral Law leaves the intellect free to speculate, to produce philosophy, science, and poetry. This is one reason why the Torah can provide conceptual constraints for democracy without stifling freedom, nay, can bring freedom to its highest perfection. A further step in this direction will be taken in the next chapter.

NOTES

1. See Eli J. Gottlieb, *The Inescapable Truth* (New York: Feldheim, 1971), ch. 6. On the rapid growth of the Israelite population in Egypt (which has aroused the skepticism of Bible critics), see Eliyahu A. Schatz, *Proof of the Accuracy of the Bible* (New York: Jonathan David Publishers, 1973), pp. 43–44.

2. See Avigdor Miller, *Behold a People* (New York: privately published, 1968), p. 128.

3. Isaac Breuer, *Concepts of Judaism* (Jerusalem: Israel Universities Press, 1974), p. 31.

4. Alfred North Whitehead, *Religion in the Making* (New York: Meridian Books, 1961), p. 16 (originally published in 1926). He goes on to say: "Religion is what the individual does with his own solitariness. It runs through three stages, if it evolves to its final satisfaction. It is the transition from God the void to God the enemy, and from God the enemy to God the companion." Clearly this is not the God of Abraham. I mention Whitehead not only because he is a philosopher-scientist of the first order whose reflections on religion are profound, but also because he held that "reason is the safeguard of the objectivity of religion" (ibid., p. 63), a position closer to Judaism. Contrast the aesthete Clive Bell, *Art* (New York: Capricorn Books, 1958), who writes: "Religion, like art, is concerned with the world of emotional reality, and with material things only insofar as they are emotionally significant" (62). Moreover, "Religion which is an affair of emotional conviction should have nothing to do with intellectual beliefs" (p. 183).

5. Unless otherwise indicated, all references in this work will be to the Babylonian Talmud (B. T.), as distinguished from the less comprehensive Jerusalem Talmud. References to individual tractates will appear between parentheses in the text. See the *Babylonian Talmud*, 18 vols. (London: Soncino Press, 1978).

6. Henri Baruk, *Tsedek* (Binghamton, N.Y.: Swan House Publishing Co., 1972), p. 80.

7. *Genesis Rabbah* 1:1.

8. See Daniel Michelson, "Codes in the Torah," *B'Or Ha'Torah*, no. 6 (in English) (Jerusalem: "Shamir," 1987), pp. 7–39. Dr. Michelson is currently a professor of mathematics at UCLA and at the Hebrew University. See also Yehuda T. Radday et al., "Genesis, Wellhausen and the Computer," in *Zeitschrift Fur Die Altetestamentliche Wissenschaft* (Berlin and New York: Walter de Gruyter, 1982), pp. 467–482, using statistical techniques such as cluster analysis to refute Wellhausen's hypothesis regarding multiple authorship of the Book of Genesis. For a nonmathematical but nonetheless devastating refutation of "higher" biblical criticism, see A. Cohen, "The Challenge of Biblical Criticism," in Leo Jung, ed., *Judaism in a Changing World* (New York: Oxford University Press, 1939), pp. 193–210.

9. Samson Raphael Hirsch, *The Pentateuch*, 2d ed., 6 vols., trans. Isaac Levy (Gateshead, England: Judaica Press, 1982), I, p. 214 (cited hereafter as *Hirsch Commentary*).

10. See Samson Raphael Hirsch, *Judaism Eternal*, 2 vols. (London: Soncino Press, 1956), I, 89–95; II, 67–69. See also *The Collected Writings of Rabbi Samson Raphael Hirsch*, 3 vols. t.d. (New York and Jerusalem: Feldheim, 1984), III, 89.

11. See Martin Buber, *Two Kinds of Faith*, trans. N. Goldhawk (New York: Harper Torchbooks, 1961). Buber suggests that the concept of "faith" in Christianity involves the believer in a fundamental tension because the concept connotes its opposite, the denial of God's existence, leaving to the individual the choice between belief and unbelief (p. 38). He exaggerates, however, when he says that "The supposition for a decision between faith or unbelief is lacking in the world of Israel. . . ." (p. 40). King David, who was certainly part of that world, declared: "The fool [alternatively, scoundrel] said in his heart: 'There is

no God' " (Ps. 14:1). Here, as elsewhere, Buber is an unreliable commentator on Judaism. Thus, it is misleading and I dare say tendentious on his part to aver: "In the Hebrew Bible Torah does not mean law, but direction, instruction, information. . . . It includes laws, and laws are indeed its most vigorous objectivizations, but the Torah itself is *essentially* not law" (p. 57, italics added).

Not only is this view belied by the law-giving at Mount Sinai, but it is contradicted by Judaism's greatest codifier, Maimonides, and the entire rabbinic tradition to which Buber was personally opposed. Torah does mean "direction" and "instruction," but it is the direction and instruction derived from the teaching of the laws, i.e., the Halakha. Buber rejected the Halakha (of which he had no substantial knowledge), having married out of the "faith" and having denied the Jewish people's exclusive title to the Land of Israel. But see Chapter 11 below, which contains a refutation of Buber based on actual cases in Jewish law.

12. Empirical evidence for this statement will be found in the Michelson study cited in note 8 above. For corroborative evidence, see Zimmerman, *Torah and Existence*, ch. 1, edited for the general public in my *Israel's Return and Restoration* (Jerusalem: privately published, 1987).

13. Should the voice of God Himself intervene in a judicial dispute, the Sages would reply: "The Torah is no longer in heaven; it has already been given us at Mount Sinai. We pay no attention to heavenly voices [in the matter of judicial decisions]! For Thou hast already written for us at Sinai (Exod. 23:2): 'Incline toward the majority' " (*Baba Metzia* 59a–b). But see below, p. 66, on the Judaic view of majority rule.

14. *Hirsch Commentary*, VI, 602–603.

15. Soloveitchik, *Halakhic Man*, pp. 6–7.

16. Ibid., pp. 11–12. Soloveitchik goes on to point out that "the echo of the longings of *homo religiosus* for a supernal existence succeeds, from time to time, in making itself heard in the world of knowledge and science" (p. 14). Plato's world of ideas as the paradigm of true being comes first to mind. Hence cognitive man and *homo religiosus* may in some instances overlap.

17. Ibid., pp. 66, 83.

18. Ibid., p. 30.

19. Ibid., pp. 18–20, 83.

20. Ibid., p. 79.

21. Ibid., pp. 22–23.

22. See Isaac Herzog, *Judaism: Law and Ethics* (London: Soncino Press, 1974), pp. 213–214.

23. Friedrich Nietzsche, *The Joyful Wisdom*, trans. T. Common (New York: Frederick Ungar Publishing Co., 1960), p. 289.

24. See Chaim Zimmerman, *Torah and Reason* (Jerusalem: HED Press, 1979), pp. 239–242. See also *Hirsch Commentary*, II, 288–289.

25. For an authoritative explanation of the divergences of legal opinion in the Talmud (as well as in various codes), see Maimonides, *Introduction to the Talmud*, trans. Z. Lampel (New York: Judaica Press, 1975), pp. 88–92.

26. Ibid., pp. 69–103. See also Abraham H. Rabinowitz, *The Jewish Mind* (Jerusalem: Hillel Press, 1978), chs. 5 and 8–10, who points out that the Oral Law, in all its details, including the Responsa, is contained in the text of the Written Law. All that is required to bring them forth are the hermeneutical rules. The

author is of course aware of those who reject the immutability of the Halakha. See, e.g., Haim H. Cohn, *Jewish Law in Ancient and Modern Israel* (New York: KTAV Publishing House, 1971), throughout. Cohn is a former justice of Israel's Supreme Court. His amateurish understanding and caustic approach to talmudic law should be compared to the more positive but nonetheless secular position of former Deputy President of Israel's Supreme Court, Moshe Silberg, *Talmudic Law and the Modern State*, trans. B. Bokser (New York: Burning Bush Press, 1973), to be discussed in Chapter 11. For a truly learned work on talmudic law, see Isaac Herzog, *The Main Institutions of Jewish Law*, 2 vols. (London: Soncino Press, 1936). Herzog (1888–1959) was a Chief Rabbi of Ireland and subsequently of the Holy Land.

27. See Zimmerman, *Torah and Reason*, pp. 176–178.

28. See Salis Daiches, "Dogma in Judaism," in Leo Jung, ed., *The Jewish Library*, second series (New York: Bloch Publishing Co., 1930), pp. 249–250.

5

Forward to Genesis

It was shown in Chapter 3 that the malaise of democracy is rooted in the extreme, not to say totalitarian, tendencies of its formative principles, again, freedom and equality. In the past, the founders of popular governments sought to curb the excesses of democracy by institutional means.[1] These have proven insufficient to prevent the moral and even intellectual decline now evident in contemporary democratic societies. Urgently needed are conceptual constraints on democracy's two cardinal principles, something no democracy has ever had. It is futile to call for "freedom with responsibility," or for "equality with competence," as moderate democrats are wont to do, for democratic freedom and equality remain preferential and paramount.

Inasmuch as freedom and equality, singly or together, cannot of themselves teach man how to live, the only way to prevent their degradation or save what is precious in these two principles is to derive them from a conception of human nature, or rather, from a body of knowledge, that transcends the dichotomy of secularism and religion. That body of knowledge will be found in Jewish law. But first a note of caution.

Intellectual integrity requires the truth seeker to avoid the facile efforts of certain Jewish apologists to equate the basic principles of democracy with those of the Torah. The entire tradition of political philosophy, which modulates contemporary mentality, embodies various dichotomies that are foreign to the Torah and Jewish law. Such dichotomies as the individual and society, freedom and authority, happiness and morality, justice and law, freedom and necessity, reason and revelation, religion and the state, punctuate the writings of philosophers as diverse as Plato and Rousseau, Hume and Kant, Hegel and Marx, J. S. Mill and

Nietzsche, John Dewey and Leo Strauss. These dichotomies are especially pronounced in democracy. Transposing the language of democracy into the domain of the Torah can therefore be most misleading. Here is a simple example.

The word "democracy" literally means the "rule of the people," or popular sovereignty. Clearly this notion clashes with the Torah which proclaims the sovereignty of God, the creator of heaven and earth. Moreover, popular sovereignty reduces to the rule of the majority. Although majority rule is an important Torah principle (see Exod. 23:2 and *Sanhedrin* 3b), not only is its operation constrained by higher principles, such as the Ten Commandments, but its meaning is rational rather than volitional.[2] In Torah jurisprudence the majority principle is a subset of the probability principle.[3] Not the will so much as the judgment of the majority has moral authority, for it is more likely to accord with truth on matters of law. And because truth is the aim and criterion, there are numerous cases in Jewish law when the opinion of an outstanding individual teacher was accepted against the rest of his colleagues.[4]

Notice, however, that liberal democracies impose constitutional limitations on majority rule. On what grounds? The answer involves the Western idea of "limited government," the roots of which will be found in Genesis.

HUMAN NATURE V. HUMAN DIGNITY

The insistence on limited government in the West may be derived from a less tangible idea, namely, the "dignity of the individual." From the discussion in Chapter 2 alone, however, it should be evident that this idea has no foundation in the social sciences: Man has no intrinsic dignity. Shocking as it may seem, this confirms the Torah view, unless the idea of human dignity is derived from its only possible rational source, the Genesis account of man's creation in the image of God. What does this mean?

To endow the idea of human dignity with rationality by deriving it from the Genesis account of man's creation, the meaning of the Hebrew word for God, *Elohim*, needs to be clarified. The great Torah commentator, Nachmanides (1194–1270), writes that the word *Elohim* is a composite of two words, *el* meaning "force," and *heim* literally meaning "they," but alluding to the multiplicity of forces in creation.[5] Consistent therewith, the name *Elohim* is used exclusively in the account of the first six days of creation. Not unitl the seventh day, the Sabbath, is the name *Elohim*, God, conjoined with the Great Name, the Tetragrammaton, *YHVH*, usually translated as "Lord." The difference between the two is this. *YHVH* is God in Himself, the ultimate source of all existence. But when He is referred to as the one who places limits, measures, and stable form on the forces of creation, He is called *Elohim*.[6] (See Deut. 4:39.) This is why *YHVH* relates to freedom and graciousness, while *Elohim* relates to the rigor of law or justice. (Contrast Abraham's remonstrance with God over Sodom.)

Now, as noted earlier, ever since Galileo and Newton, the laws of nature have been expressed by mathematical equations. This means that nature obeys laws that correspond to the logical operations of the human mind. A pre-established harmony therefore exists between the laws of nature and the laws of human reason. This pre-established harmony corresponds to the Torah's account of man's creation in the image of *Elohim*. Hence we see that man is, to begin with, a rational being capable of comprehending the laws of nature, that is, the laws governing repetitive or cyclical phenomena.

It may be noted in passing that countless behaviorists never get beyond this level of existence in the study of man. They regard man as a highly complex animal governed by the forces and determinism of nature. Political scientists, sociologists, economists, and psychologists alike construct theories based on the primacy of the passions. If it is not the Hobbesian fear of violent death or the desire for gain or glory, it is the Freudian libido or the Nietzschean will to power. They may agree that man is a rational being, but they very much limit rationality to the determination of means to ends. As Hobbes lucidly stated: "The thoughts are to the desires, as scouts, and spies, to range abroad, and find the way to the things desired."[7]

Returning to Genesis and man's creation in the image of God, a penetrating insight is offered by Rabbi Reuben Denenberg (in *Rosh L'Ravenu*).[8] His insight can best be presented by first recalling the incredibly lifelike human faces, say, in London's Wax Museum. Rabbi Denenberg points out that man is not what you see but what you do not see. You do not see man's soul; you know man only by his speech and actions. Bearing this in mind, consider the "second" account of man's creation:

The Lord God formed man of the dust of the ground and breathed into his nostrils the breath of life (*Nishmat Haim*): and man became a living being (*Nefesh Haya*). (Gen. 2:7)

The Malbim's commentary is most pertinent. The expression "breath of life" is never used for describing animals breathing; in fact, the expression appears nowhere else in the Torah. This godly "breath of life," which cannot be seen or measured, energizes man's physical and mental powers.[9] And because it is given to man alone, all the human structures and functions through which it operates differ fundamentally from those of animals. From this it follows that the higher functions of man are not reducible to his lower functions. Genesis 2:7 is therefore telling us that,

because of his *Nishmat Haim,* man's "being alive is different from that
of the animal; he [alone] can choose freely, this being the meaning of
"Let us make man in our image."[10]

Because choosing or choice involves cognition as well as volition, the
Nishmat Haim may be defined as the "cognitive-volitional" power of
man.[11] It is this power that enables man to say No to his appetites, that
is, to transcend the vegetative and sensual aspects of his soul. Put another way, because of the cognitive-volitional character of his soul, man
has the capacity for spontaneous and critical reflection, which liberates
him from the immediacy and servitude of sensuous, animal-like experience. Man transcends nature.

Of course, man is influenced by the laws of nature operative within
and outside his body. If he wills, he can use his intellect as a mere
instrument of his sensuous desires and thereby act contrary to his having
been created in the image of God; for such is God's graciousness that
He endowed man with the freedom to disobey Him, that is, to disregard
The laws of the Torah. Hence the Sages say, "All is in the hands of
Heaven except the fear of Heaven." Man's intellectual and moral perfection therefore depends on himself, but only in the sense that he is
graced with the freedom to accept or reject the Torah as the paradigm
of how man should live.

When the verse "God created man in His own image" is construed
to mean that man is endowed with intellect and free will, the premise
is that God is the Supreme Intellect and the ultimate source of freedom.
From this it follows that the laws of the Torah are the highest manifestation of reason, and that to live by these laws is to enjoy the highest
form of freedom. Accordingly, consider now what the God of reason
and freedom said to Adam:

Of every tree of the garden you may freely eat; but of the tree of knowledge of
good and bad, you must not eat of it; for in the day that you eat thereof you
shall surely die. (Gen. 2:16–17)

This prohibition—this No to man's desiring nature—presupposes that
Adam's faculties were mature, that he possessed free will and intellectual
discernment; otherwise the prohibition would have been pointless. Also,
this first no is indicative of a fundamental difference between man and
animals. Unlike man, an animal cannot say no to his appetites. An animal
eats whatever appeals to his senses or innate instincts. These are his
gods who tell him what is "good" and what is "bad." This corresponds
to Hobbes's conception of man (the obvious source of moral relativism):

But whatever is the object of any man's appetite or desire, that is it which he
for his part calleth *good*; and the object of his hate or aversion, *evil*; and of his

contempt, *vile* and *inconsiderable*. For these words of good, evil, and contemptible, are ever used with relation to the person that useth them: there being nothing simply and absolutely so; nor any common rule of good and evil, to be taken from the nature of the objects themselves; but from the person of the man, where there is no commonwealth . . . [12]

What is "good" and "evil" is relative to the likes and dislikes of each individual or of each nation of which he happens to be a member. This moral relativism among men and nations is analogous to the "moral relativism," as it were, among different species of animals. Just as one cannot rationally condemn a wolf for devouring a lamb, so one cannot, on rational (or at least relativistic) grounds, condemn one nation from devouring or annihilating another. Eating from the tree of knowledge of good and bad makes man at once godlike and beastlike.

Notice that Adam was permitted to eat from all the other trees, including trees of knowledge. In no other way could he fulfill the positive (and antiascetic) commandment to "replenish and subdue the earth," say to conquer nature. The only tree he was prohibited from eating was the most tempting of all, the one rooted in the nature of man, in the power of his intellect and will: the tree whose fruit yields a knowledge of good and bad which is only relative to the tastes of the person that eats of it. Eating from this tree leads to untimely death, for it provides only human as opposed to divine knowledge concerning how man should live. For the crystallization of this divine knowledge one must repair to the Torah, the Tree of Life (Prov. 3:18; *Berachot* 32b).

By eating of the tree of knowledge of good and bad, Adam was asserting, in effect, that man, and not his Creator, is the legislator of how man should live (or the measure of all things). But this is to deny the Torah, including man's creation in the image of God. The consequence is soon made clear. Cain will murder his brother, and he will deny that he is his brother's keeper. The egoism or individualism is obvious. Less obvious is this: To deny that man is created in the image of God is to deny the moral unity of human nature and to degrade man to the level of the beast. Machiavelli adds nothing essential to what we learn from Cain. If Cain (or Romulus) is not his brother's keeper, then, in any conflict between two individuals each will be the ultimate judge of his own interests, so that in the last analysis "might will make right" (whether the might is of the one, the few, or the many).

Returning to Genesis, by proclaiming that man is created in the image of God, the Torah provides the only solid foundation for the moral unity of human nature. Consistent therewith, and notwithstanding contrary inclinations, man is the only creature that is mentally capable of being concerned about his own species *qua* species, and even with the welfare of other species. This is evident from the following verses:

Six days you shall do your work, but on the seventh day you shall rest: that your ox and your donkey may have rest.... (Exod. 23:12)

You shall love your neighbor's well-being as your own (the correct rendering of Lev. 19:18).[12]

But we are also enjoined to be gracious and magnanimous to our enemies. Thus:

If your enemy is hungry, give him bread to eat, and if he is thirsty, give him also water to drink. (Prov. 25:21)

On the other hand, we are cautioned against maudlin sentiment:

Let favor be shown to the wicked, yet he will not learn righteousness. (Isa. 26:10)

I hate them, O Lord, that hate You...I hate them with utmost hatred. (Ps. 139:21, 22)

The sobriety of the Torah is famously epitomized by Rabbi Hillel:

If I am not for myself, who is for me? And if not now, when? But if I am only for myself, what am I? (*Ethics* 1:14)

To understand the Torah it is extremely important not to overmoralize it. Because each individual is a creature of God, he is obliged to take intelligent care of God's "property," be it himself or others. Just as murder is prohibited, so is suicide. Self-preference, however, is the law. Thus:

If two are travelling on a journey [far from civilization], and one has a canteen of water; if both drink they will both die, but if one only drinks, he can reach civilization. The son of Patura taught: It is better that both should drink and die, rather than one should behold his companion's death. Until Rabbi Akiba came and [correctly] taught: "that your brother may live *with* you" (Lev. 25:36): your life takes precedence over his life. (*Baba Metzia* 62a)

Only after you have first taken care of yourself are you obliged to take care of your brother—that he may live *with* you. Generally speaking, the Torah does not go against the grain of human nature. But when Rabbi Hillel says "If I am only for myself, what am I?" he means that a person who is only for himself is simply governed by his natural inclinations. In contrast, the Torah-educated person is concerned about the good of others, and without ulterior or self-interested motives. To this extent he acts contrary to nature. But how can one act contrary to nature? The concept of nature requires some clarification.

Until the twentieth century, both science and philosophy conceived of the universe as eternal and of nature as self-sustaining. This dogma has been (unwittingly) rendered questionable by quantum mechanics, which holds that the laws of nature are ultimately statistical. One need only ask: If the universe is eternal, what is it that sustains the stability of the mean associated with statistical law? For however remote the probability, the structure of the universe should have "collapsed" given its supposed eternity on the one hand, and its merely statistical foundations on the other.

Also, there is an insurmountable contradiction between eternally self-sustaining laws of nature and the second law of thermodynamics, that of energy decay or entropy. This law states that every system left to itself always tends to move from order to disorder, its energy tending to be transformed into lower levels of availability, finally reaching the state of complete randomness and unavailability for further work. When all the energy of the universe has been degraded to random motion of molecules of uniform low temperature, the universe will have died a "heat death." The fact that the universe is not yet dead is clear evidence that it is not infinitely old. And so, whereas the second law, that of energy decay, requires the universe to have a beginning, the first law, that of total energy conservation, precludes its having begun itself.

These difficulties are overcome in the Torah. Nature is not self-sustaining and cannot be in a created universe. The universe continues to exist only by virtue of the ceaseless will of the Creator, but Whose will manifests itself to man as "laws of nature." Stated another way, what the physicist postulates as a law of nature is in reality what the Talmud calls a *Shevua*, an oath or promise that God will not change some stable form or predictable regularity of existence. Man himself, however, is not a mere automaton. Because he possesses free will, his behavior is not simply a function of the laws of nature. Besides (and as will be shown at greater length later), the laws of nature are only statistical manifestations of qualitative laws of existence. For example, Rabbi Hillel's epigram refers to self-concern and concern for others. Both are qualitative laws. But their manifestation in human beings varies probabilistically, both in intensity and in frequency. Although self-concern takes precedence over concern for others and applies to all men, concern for others is distinctive of the Torah man and of those influenced by the Torah's teachings.

Self-concern and concern for others are logical extensions of man's creation in the image of God. Hence the Mishnah: "Let your friend's honor be as dear to you as your own" (*Ethics* 2:15). Note the words "your friend's honor," in contradistinction to the honor of someone who is not your friend, which means that the honor due a person depends on his status and on his relationship to you. You owe more honor to your teacher than to your father, to your father than to your mother (unless they are divorced, in which case the honor a son owes his mother is equal to that which he owes his father, and in the event of conflict, he may choose for himself who should take precedence). In Jewish law, therefore, a person's honor (which in Hebrew also denotes "understanding") is relational and contingent. The Torah addresses itself to reality, to the acts or accomplishments of living men, not to moral abstractions. The so-called dignity of the individual smacks of reification or idolatry. Because man is created in the image of God, a person's merit (*zchut*) is logically proportional to his study and observance of the Torah. A person merits honor to the extent that he reveals the infinite wisdom, power, and kindliness of his Creator in every aspect of existence, physical, moral, and intellectual. But in honoring that person, we are really honoring the Torah from which true honor is ultimately derived.

It cannot be too strongly emphasized that whereas the dignity of the individual is an absolutistic concept divorced from reality, honor as delineated by the Torah is existential and addressed to the real differences among men. The contrast may be seen even more clearly by examining cases of Jewish law involving humiliation. In such cases, the assessment of compensation, says Maimonides, "depends upon the relative status of the one who causes the humiliation and the one who is humiliated. Humiliation caused by an insignificant person cannot be compared with the humiliation caused by a great and eminent person. The humiliation caused by the lesser individual is greater." For example:

If one humiliates an imbecile, he is exempt, but if one humiliates a deaf-mute ... or a slave, he is liable. If one humiliates a minor, the rule is as follows: If the minor feels ashamed when insulted, the offender is liable; if not, he is exempt. Nevertheless, there is no comparison between one who humiliates a minor and one who humiliates an adult. ... If one insults [ordinary persons] in speech ... he is exempt, but the court should institute preventive measures in this matter [for derogatory speech is culpable in the judgment of Heaven]. ... If [however,] one humiliates a scholar, the offender must pay him full compensation [i.e., thirty-five denar in gold], even if he humiliates him merely in speech.[13]

Now, as noted above, the Hebrew word for "honor," *kavod*, also denotes understanding, above all, of the Torah. Thus, to humiliate a scholar is to depreciate the Torah, just as to honor a scholar is to honor the Torah. The personal dimension is secondary. If, therefore, a person is compensated for humiliation, it will not be because he falls under that abstraction called the "dignity of the individual," but because his mind is mature enough to render him susceptible to shame. But shame, the other side of honor, involves understanding. Is it not clear that the only solid foundation for "human dignity" is man's creation in the image of God?

Laws prohibiting slander and pornography should be viewed (or reformulated) in this light. To defame an individual, or to present a degrading and reductive picture of man, is tantamount to disparaging God in Whose image man was created. Given the primacy of man's intellect which, together with free will, distinguishes him from beasts, to insult a scholar is especially heinous, for it is through his intellect and intellectual freedom that God's creation and glory can be known and disseminated to mankind. By relating these matters to man's Creator, we avoid arbitrariness and minimize personal acrimony.

Also, by discarding the notion of the intrinsic dignity of the (abstract) individual, we rid ourselves of a hypocritical platitude that levels intellectual and moral distinctions and blurs the real merit of real men. Here I shall substitute for this obsolete, religious concept the more tangible idea of man's unique character, which is empirically obvious even to many secularists who remain ignorant of the Torah (thanks, in part, to the obscurantism of many religionists).

Now, to facilitate the perfection of man's unique character, the Torah prescribes a minimum code of conduct for all mankind, the Seven Noahide or Universal Laws of Morality. It bears repeating that this code prohibits murder, stealing, unchastity, and cruelty. All men are creatures of God. Each individual is a center of purposes known to God alone. Hence we must be duly concerned about men's lives, their property, and their honor. The Noahide laws also forbid idol worship and blasphemy. Such is the unique character of man—again, he alone is endowed with intellect and free will—that only God is worthy of his worship. To desecrate the Name of God is therefore to degrade humanity as well. For when man denies his Creator, he not only denies the source of human perfection; he undermines the supreme development of man's mental faculties. Stated another way, when man turns away from his Creator, he ends by worshipping himself, be it the creations of his own mind, like some utopian ideology, or the product of his own will—all of which eventuates in bestiality, as history so amply illustrates. Or when men deny that God is the ultimate reality, they end by genuflecting to matter or energy or chance as the ultimate reality.

Finally, given the fallibility of man's intellect as well as the freedom of his will, the Torah requires the establishment of courts of justice. Here there is no trial by ordeal or combat. A person is presumed to be innocent until proven guilty, and not by circumstantial evidence, but only on the oral testimony of righteous eyewitnesses meticulously examined in open court by judges of impeccable character. (Of this, more in Chapter 11.) Moreover, in criminal cases, self-incrimination is inadmissible, if only because one may not speak ill of himself, created as he is in the image of God. (Unlike procedures in other legal systems, voluntary confessions are not admissible in a Jewish court of law.)

Having examined the only real and rational source for the idea of limited government, namely, that men are creatures of and belong solely to God, the ground has been prepared for deriving the cardinal principles of democracy from the Torah.

NOTES

1. In introducing the Virginia Plan at the Constitutional Convention, Governor Edmund Randolph declared: "Our chief danger arises from the democratic parts of our [state] constitutions. It is a maxim which I hold incontrovertible, that the powers of government exercised by the people swallow up the other branches. None of the constitutions have provided sufficient checks to the democracy." Cited in my *The Philosophy of the American Constitution*, p. 42.

2. Exod. 23:2 actually refers to judicial proceedings in criminal cases. The plain meaning of the verse is, "Do not go with the [bare] majority to do evil [i.e., to convict, but otherwise] incline toward the majority." On this verse, see *Hirsch Commentary*.

3. Although the Hebrew word *rov* can be translated literally as "majority," the term "probability" most often conveys its operational meaning. See Louis Jacobs, *The Talmudic Argument: A Study in Talmudic Reasoning and Methodology* (Cambridge: Cambridge University Press, 1986), p. 50. An oft-cited example of the probability principle is the town in which nine butcher shops sell kosher meat and one sells nonkosher meat (*Hullin* 11a). Any meat found in the town is halakhically kosher. What determines the status of the meat is not its physical properties, i.e., whether it was ritually slaughtered, but the supervening halakhic principle under discussion. This corresponds to Einstein's view of physical reality: "it is the theory that decides what we observe," or determines what is real. Cited and elaborated in my *Jersualem vs. Athens*, p. 195.

4. See *Berachot* 37a, *Kidushin* 59b, *Yevamot* 108b, *Gittin* 15a, 47a.

5. Nachmanides, *Commentary on the Torah* 5 vols., trans. C. Chavel (New York: Shilo Publishing House, 1972), I, 25. See also Maimonides, *Guide of the Perplexed* (Chicago: University of Chicago Press, 1963), I, 2; *The Zohar* (5 vols.; London: Soncino Press, 1978), I, 65ff.; Malbim, *Commentary on the Torah*, translated with scientific notes by Dr. Zvi Faier, 5 vols. t.d., (Jerusalem: Hillel Press, 1984), I, 27–28.

6. Ibid.

7. Hobbes, *Leviathan*, p. 46.

8. The author is indebted to Dr. Chaim Zimmerman for this reference.

9. Despite their vast differences, both Aristotle and Hobbes agree that the soul is part of nature, and that the study of the soul is part of physics.

10. Malbim, *Commentary on the Torah*, I, 191–192.

11. Computers do not really think. Nor do they have a sense of shame, of honor, or of justice.

12. Hobbes, *Leviathan*, p. 32.

13. *The Code of Maimonides* (Book of Torts) (New Haven: Yale University Press, 1954), pp. 169–170.

6
Equality with Excellence

A casual glance at the above discussion of Jewish law governing humiliation would seem to indicate that the Torah does not provide the most spacious accommodations for the democratic principle of equality. It must be remembered, however, that one of the aims of the present inquiry is to derive from Jewish law conceptual constraints for equality in order to save this principle from degradation.

Given man's creation in the image of God, the Jerusalem Talmud states with perfectly logical consistency: "If gentiles [surrounding Israel] demand, 'Surrender one of yourselves to us and we will kill him; otherwise we shall kill all of you,' they must all suffer death rather than surrender a single Israelite to them"(*Terumot* 8, 9). According to Jewish law, no individual may be sacrificed for the sake of his society. With respect to human life, therefore, all Jews—learned and unlearned, rich and poor—are equal. This equality is logically entailed, for the soul of each individual (his *Neshama*) is infinite, and his purpose in world history is known only by his Creator.

Consider, too, the principle of equality before the law, which is clearly enunciated in various places in the Torah. For example:

You shall not respect the person of the poor, nor favor the person of the mighty; but in righteousness shall you judge your neighbor. (Lev. 19:15)

When, however, a judge is requested to arbitrate rather than adjudicate a matter, he may, on appropriate grounds, favor the cause of the poor. Also, it is a basic principle of the Torah to demand higher standards of conduct from the leaders of the community.[1] The reason is simple enough: The leaders of the community, especially its educators, possess the power to do great harm as well as great good, for they set the standards for the living and posterity. And so the more elevated a person, the higher is the level of conduct required of him, as may be seen in the following incident recounted in the Talmud (*Baba Metzia* 83a).

Some porters negligently broke a barrel of wine belonging to the scholar Raba ben Huna. In accordance with the strict letter of the law, he confiscated the porters' coats as security for its value. The porters complained to the court, and Rav, the judge, told Raba ben Huna to return the coats. "Is that really the law?" he asked. "Yes indeed," replied Rav, "so that you may walk in the way of good men" (Prov. 2:20). The porters spoke up again: "We are poor men, have worked all day, and are in need; are we to get nothing?" "Give them their wages." Again Raba ben Huna asked, "Is that the law?" And Rav replied, "Yes—and keep to the path of the righteous" (ibid.). This judgment should not be construed merely as "going beyond the letter of the law." As Rav clearly stated, he was in fact applying the law. But in this case the applicable law was the law for a scholar, not for the ordinary man. Another example makes the point even clearer.

In Jewish law, unlike in other legal systems, proven ignorance of the law excuses a criminal in a court of men (though not necessarily in the judgment of Heaven).[2] He can only be held liable for damages. Accordingly, a person may not be punished for a transgression unless he was warned of, and understood, its culpable nature. If, however, the person is a scholar, then, capital cases aside, he may be held responsible for his crimes without having been warned, since warning is only a means of deciding whether one has committed a crime willfully or not (*Sanhedrin* 8b, 41a). It is therefore evident that equality before the law in the Torah does not involve the complete leveling of humanity. Indeed, noblesse oblige is a fundamental Torah principle.

Nevertheless, efforts are made by various Jewish apologists to find in the Torah support for egalitarianism. By egalitarianism I mean an ideology which subordinates all values to the principle of equality, and which therefore tends to level all moral and intellectual distinctions among mankind. Hence it will be necessary to refute the tendentious exegesis of apologists in order to prevent the totalitarian degradation of equality on the one hand, and to redeem what is truly valid and of value in this principle on the other. No greater disservice can be done to democracy and mankind than to so distort the Torah as to reduce it to a democratic charter.

To appreciate the distortions of apologists, consider this oft-misquoted passage from the Mishnah concerning the Sanhedrin's admonition of witnesses in capital cases. False witnesses are answerable for the life of him who is falsely accused. Here is the way the judges impress upon witnesses the gravity of their testimony:

Perhaps you are unaware that ultimately we shall scrutinize your evidence by cross examination and inquiry? Know then that capital cases are not like monetary cases. In civil suits, one can make monetary restitution and thereby effect atonement; but in capital cases he is held responsible for the blood of the accused and the blood of his descendants until the end of time. . . . For this reason was man created alone, to teach you that whoever destroys a single *Israelite*, Scripture imputes to him [guilt] as though he had destroyed a complete world; and whoever preserves a single *Israelite*, Scripture ascribes to him [merit] as though he had preserved a complete world. (*Sanhedrin* 37a)

The censors substitute for "Israelite" the word "soul."[3] True, any gentile can become an Israelite through voluntary conversion, as did some of Israel's greatest Sages. But it is sheer impudence and the height of intellectual dishonesty to transform the Torah into an egalitarian creed based on the dignity of the abstract individual.[4]

Although the principle of equality may rightly be derived from the verse "God created man in His own image," it does not follow therefrom—and no serious person has ever maintained—that men are born equal in their mental faculties. And none but arrant fools would contend that, despite the palpable inequality of men's intellectual and moral endowments, all men should be treated equally in *all* respects. Some people resent the natural inequality among men and hold it against the Creator; but they have yet to show how any society in this world could function under absolute equality. Indeed, if all men were equal in all respects they would cease to be human. They could not experience love, for they could not love one person more than another. And so it would be with all the generous emotions: They would have no preferred object.

May it then be said that all men are equal in the "eyes" of God? Perhaps this is true, but only in the sense that all men are equally nothing in relation to the Creator. Surely God makes a distinction between saints and sinners. Thus: "I loved Jacob, and Esau I hated" (Mal. 1:2–3). On the other hand, the egalitarian doctrine that all men are at birth tainted by "original sin" is contrary to the Torah. "Just as you enter the world without sin, so you may leave it without sin" (*Baba Metzia* 107a).

Now it so happens that one of the gravest of sins is egalitarianism! For as the Talmud states unambiguously, "Jerusalem was destroyed only because the small and the great were made equal" (*Shabbat* 119b), which is to say that Israel was conquered because of the leveling of ranks and the consequent loss of deference to men of learning.[5]

Although equality is a basic principle of the Torah, it is not its primary or distinctive principle. We saw that no person, whether rich or poor, wise or unwise, may be sacrificed for the sake of preserving his community. Contrast, however, the following examples of inequality (bearing in mind the relationship between intellect and sentiment). In procuring their release from captivity, "a Kohane ("priest") takes precedence over a Levite, a Levite over an Israelite, and an Israelite over a bastard. . . . This applies when they are all [otherwise] equal; but if the bastard is learned in the Torah and the Kohane is ignorant of the Torah, the learned bastard takes precedence over the ignorant Kohane" (Mishnah, *Horayot* 3:8). Similarly, under Jewish law "a scholar takes precedence over a king of Israel" (*B. T. Horayot* 23a). Finally, "If a man and his father and his teacher were in captivity [for ransom], he takes precedence over his teacher and his teacher takes precedence over his father, while his mother takes precedence over them all [if only because of her greater vulnerability]" (ibid.).

Clearly, the order of precedence is determined by learning qualified by the thrust of natural inclinations and sentiments, which the Torah seeks to regulate rather than repress or ignore. (It may be noted in passing that if a court has many cases on its docket, then, as Maimonides points out, the case of an orphan is tried before that of a widow, a widow's before a scholar's, a scholar's before an illiterate's, and the suit of a woman before that of a man, because the humiliation is greater in the case of a woman. Feminists may have some difficulty here.)

Having referred to Israelites, Levites, and Kohanes ("priests" is a misleading translation), it should be noted that these three "classes" are hereditary. Nevertheless, the daugher of an Israelite or of a Levite may marry a Kohane and her children will be Kohanes, since "class" status is patrilineal. Hence, even though they have distinct duties and privileges (of which more later), there is no separation of "classes.") Nor is there, as in Plato's *Republic*, a ruling class. Who rules is based, first and foremost, on intellectual and moral qualifications: those who are most learned in the Torah receive the highest honors. And whereas in Plato's *Republic* education is restricted to the guardian class, in Israel education is open to, and even required of, all members of the community.

Josephus, writing in the first century, says that Moses "showed the Torah to be the best and most necessary means of instruction by enjoining the people to assemble not once or twice or frequently, but . . . every week while abstaining from all work, in order to hear the Torah and learn it in a thorough manner—a thing which all other law-givers seem to have neglected." (See Deut. 4:9–10; 6:6–9, 20–25; 31:10–13; Joshua 1:8.)

Thus, thousands of years before any democracy thought of providing (compulsory) education for all its citizens, all the people of Israel were being highly educated as a matter of course (which helps to explain Theophrastus's characterization of Israel as a "nation of philosophers").

Far from separating or stratifying the three "classes," Torah education is the great unifying force of the Jewish people who, we saw, honor scholars more than kings.[6]

Strictly speaking, therefore, a Torah community is devoid of classes in the socioeconomic or political sense of the term. In fact, neither Kohanes nor Levites can own land, a major source of wealth, power, and prestige. Does this mean that a Torah community enjoys "social equality" despite the different privileges and duties of its three divisions? Clearly the term oversimplifies and distorts the rich, pluralistic relationships of a Torah community, in which Kohanes, Levites, and Israelites learn together, pray together, and serve each other in various ways. Outside a Torah-inspired community the desire for social equality springs not only from envious resentment and ambition, but from the recognition that social hierarchy is man-made, artificial and fortuitous. In contrast, no Israelite resents his status vis-à-vis a Levite or Kohane if only because their respective prerogatives are not determined by fallible and self-interested men, but by laws prescribed by an infallible and just God. Besides, he knows that what ultimately distinguishes one person from another is knowledge and observance of the Torah, and in this respect the humblest Israelite can be superior to any Levite or Kohane and be treated as such. Consequently, deference to wisdom modulates the principle of equality in a Torah community, wherein one honors not wise men so much as Him who endowed man with wisdom. Insofar, therefore, as the community manifests social equality, it is not the kind that levels intellectual and moral distinctions. The only way to avoid such leveling is to derive the principle of equality from the Genesis account of man's creation.

Social equality, at least in democratic societies, more or less parallels political equality. To speak only of democracies, all have laws governing the relative status of native-born citizens, naturalized citizens, and foreign residents. These distinctions may be assimilated to the Torah in order to endow the principle of equality with solid ethical content.[7]

Consider the verse "Do not offend nor oppress the stranger (*ger*), for you were strangers (*gerim*) in the land of Egypt" (Exod. 22:20). The concept of the stranger has been perverted by Jewish egalitarians to include any foreign resident of Israel. But the truth is that the term *ger* means a convert to Judaism. Consistent therewith, the *Book of Education* (*Sefer HaHinukh*) explains that if "a member of the seven nations has converted and entered our faith, it is forbidden for us to shame him, even with words—as it states, 'Do not offend the *ger*.' "[8] Moreover, Leviticus 19:34 declares: "The foreigner who becomes a *ger* [i.e., proselyte] must be [treated] exactly like one who is native born among you. You shall love his well-being as if it were your own, for you were foreigners in Egypt."

Now, to say "You shall love the *ger*, for you were *gerim* in the land of Egypt" (Deut. 10:19) may suggest to some people that a *ger* is indeed a "stranger" because of the parallel verse, "For you were *gerim* in Egypt." But from the great Aramaic translation of Onkelos (circa 90 c.e.), himself a *ger*, we learn: *Uterachmun yet Giori* (and you shall love the *ger*), *arei Dayarin havyotan* (for you were residents) *b'ara d'Mitzrayim* (in the land of Egypt)." Onkelos carefully took the two words *ger* and *gerim* in this verse and translated them differently to avoid the very distortion now current among Jewish apologists. The Jew is exhorted to love the *ger*, which Onkelos translated as *giori*, convert. But the second half of the verse, which refers to the Jews as *gerim* in Egypt, was carefully translated differently: *gerim* was rendered as *dayarim*, residents, to clearly indicate that the commandment to love the *ger* means the stranger who has converted and become a Jew.

For the born Jew and the *ger* or proselyte in Israel there is but one law. Hence the concept of the *ger* provides a moral foundation for the social and political equality of naturalized citizens in any democracy. To be sure, it is reasonable and proper to require, say, a president of the United States to be a native-born American (as prescribed in the American Constitution). This qualification is anticipated in the Jewish "constitution": a convert to Judaism cannot be a king of Israel (although it may be possible for him to be appointed to the Supreme Court).[9]

Now, one purpose in distinguishing between a proselyte and a foreign resident is this. There is an unfortunate democratic tendency to degrade the dignity of citizenship in such a regime by removing virtually all moral and intellectual standards from the naturalization process. This is a direct consequence of the leveling principle of equality (which the present study is trying to salvage). The ultimate good of immigrants or foreign residents is not well served by cheapening the value of democratic citizenship. On the other hand, it should be understood that the rights and well-being of foreign residents can be protected without the boon of citizenship, as will now be seen by returning to the distinction between the proselyte and the foreign resident in Jewish law.

Although the born Jew and the proselyte have but one law, this equality does not extend to a foreigner living in Israel. The same may be said of the status of a foreign resident of any country. Obviously a foreigner must acknowledge the sovereignty of the host country and abide by its laws. In Israel, moreover—and I have been speaking of Israel under a Torah government—a foreign resident must also adhere to ethical monotheism. For example, a Moslem living in Israel is free to practice his religion so long as it does not countenance murder, theft, immorality, and cruelty.[10] Foreign residents may have their own law courts and educational institutions. Not only are they entitled to civil rights, but it is the duty of the government to provide for their poor, their sick, and their aged whenever necessary (Deut. 15:4). To the extent that democracies adhere to such principles, they are practicing Jewish law. In no case, however, may a foreign resident participate in the various offices of the state. Just as foreigners in America, for example, must become Americans to merit the political rights of Americans, so any foreign resident in Israel would have to become Jewish to be worthy of holding any office under the state of Israel.

It cannot be emphasized too often that Judaism is not a religion but a nationality—the way of life of the Jewish nation. As Isaac Breuer wrote in 1922: "The Old Testament, unlike the New, is not the recorded source of a religion but the history of the divine founding of a nation."[11] Indeed, the Jewish people, as no other people in history, remained a nation without a state or land for two thousand years—two thousand years of dispersion and decimation by nations many of which no longer exist or have lost their former grandeur. It was only the Torah that preserved Israel as a nation. Hence, to become an integral part of this nation, to partake fully of its duties and privileges, one must be or become a Jew.

As already suggested, acceptance of Judaism in a Jewish commonwealth is what naturalization is in any modern state. Without such a requirement the democratic principle of political equality would lack rational justification.[12] Of course, conversion to Judaism is much more profound than the process of becoming, say, a naturalized citizen of America. The prerequisites are more exacting and more exalting. But so they must be if the cardinal principles of democracy are to be derived from a source that gives them a meaning more elevated than that found in secular categories. Moreover, not only are those prerequisites essential for the integrity and existence of the Jewish state, they are also necessary for the ultimate good of humanity, as I now shall attempt to explain.

Uncorrupted common sense clearly indicates that a Jewish state can only be run by those who believe in the validity of the Torah and in the salutary character of Jewish law—logically and historically the sine qua non of Jewish survival. The governors of the Jewish state must be those whose whole life is dedicated to the observance of the Torah. They must be familiar with the elaborate and towering edifice of the Halakha, must know how to apply its specific laws to a vast variety of facts and changing circumstances. Judaism does not proselytize. It presents its way of life as an example for mankind, but without fanfare or importunity. Still, whoever wishes to accept this way of life, no matter to what race or nation he may belong, can join the people of Israel and participate in the running of its government.[13] Those who do not accept the Torah are not entitled to have any hand in shaping the basic policies of the state. They can live in Israel and enjoy all the rights and privileges accorded them in the spacious and generous provisions of Jewish law.

This kind of discrimination is perfectly just and reasonable. Conversely, it is both unjust and unreasonable to accord to non-Jewish residents the rights and privileges of Jews, the more so inasmuch as non-Jews do not have the duties incumbent on members of a Torah community. On the other hand, it should be borne in mind that not only non-Jews, but nonobservant Jews are not qualified to hold office under a Torah government. Even secular democracies sometimes eliminate from high office persons who have violated basic ethical standards, derived, incidentally, from the Torah. Obviously the Torah must prescribe the highest standards for Israel if it is to serve as the light of the nations. Thus:

You shall be holy, for I the Lord your God am holy. (Lev. 19:2)

I have separated you from the nations that you should be mine. (Lev. 20:26, and see Deut. 7:6, 32:8–10)

Lo, it is a people that shall dwell alone and shall not reckon itself among the nations. (Num. 23:9)

This people have I created that they may relate My praise. (Isa. 43:21)

This setting apart of Israel is absolutely essential for the ultimate perfection of mankind as a whole.[14] As Leo Jung has so eloquently written:

Had Judaism been entrusted to all nations, it would have lost color and intensity. As everybody's concern it would have remained nobody's concern. . . . Ideals are better entrusted to minorities as their differentiating asset, because of which they live. . . . Judaism, given at once to the shapeless multitudes of the world, would have become a meaningless phrase . . . Hence it was bestowed upon one nation as its heirloom, as the single reason for its existence, as the single argument of its national life, as the aim and end of its struggles and labors. The Jewish people thus received a charge that was to inspire its life, but the benefit of which was to accrue to all the world. At the beginning of Jewish history, Abraham, the first Jew, received the universal call, 'And thou shalt be a blessing to all the nations of the world.' For the consummation of this ideal, Israel is to walk apart. It will not be counted among the nations . . . Guided exclusively by the will of God, living by His commandments and dying if need be for the sanctification of His name, Israel is to present the example of a whole nation elevated, ennobled, illumined by the life in God and encouraging thereby a universal *imitatio Dei*.[15]

But what has the separateness of the Jewish people to do with democracy and the subject of this chapter? This question may be answered by clarifying the Hebrew word *Kodesh* translated as "holy."[16]

The translation is utterly unJewish, otherworldly or spiritualistic, and cannot but repel the secular mind, especially in a world where holy men are not too conspicuous. The noun form of *Kodesh* is *Kedusha* ("holiness").

Unfortunately, the concept is not translatable. Nevertheless, like thought or mentality, which also defies space-time description, the term can be somewhat clarified by reference to its manifestations and functional relationships.

To separate oneself from what is vulgar, to abhor deceit and dissimulation, to shun violence and bloodshed—these are negative manifestations of *Kedusha*. To love peace, to be consistent in word and deed, to dedicate one's heart and soul with all one's might to God so that even the humdrum tasks of life are elevated and performed with joy—these are positive manifestations of *Kedusha*. *Kedusha* therefore prompts Judaic man to seek unity and wholeness, to be sincere and gracious. It enables him to overcome the dichotomies and contradictions that beset mankind. It liberates his mind, indeed, it is itself a mind-like quality.

Accordingly, in Jewish law a house of learning has more *Kedusha*, hence a higher status, than a synagogue. It is therefore permissible to convert a house of prayer into a house of learning, that is, to raise it to a higher level of *Kedusha*, whereas it is forbidden to convert a house of learning into a house of prayer, which is to lower its *Kedusha*. The intellectual dimension of *Kedusha*, as opposed to the moralistic notion of "holiness," is obvious. And it is precisely because of the creativity of the intellect that renders a house of learning more creative than a house of prayer. Indeed, to be "holy." as God is "holy," is to be creative in a finite way as God is creative in an infinite way. This is not to suggest that prayer is an emotional outpouring. Quite the contrary, as the term signifies in Hebrew, to pray is "to rectify one's judgment, to get clear about one's relationship to things in general, and of one's obligations." Still, prayer does not involve the intellectual creativity that takes place in a Torah academy dedicated to revealing the infinite wisdom, power, and kindliness of God in every domain of existence. And so there is nothing more mystical about *Kedusha* than there is about creativity. (Neither can be measured in spatiotemporal terms.) This should dispose of the excessively moralistic and spiritualistic rendering of this fundamental Torah concept. But there is more to the concept of *Kedusha* that may appeal to the secular mind if it is not entirely closed.

Thus anyone who studies the logical system and jurisprudence of the Talmud will see why Judaism has been called the religion of reason as well as the religion of law. But this can be misleading. Since the Torah is properly understood as the Tree of Life, reason and law must (1) preserve life and (2) facilitate the creative thrust of life without loss of rooted order. Regarding the first, all the commandments of the Torah may be suspended to save life, excepting those prohibiting idol worship, sexual crimes, and of course murder. (See Lev. 16:34; *Yoma* 88b; *Sanhedrin* 74a.) Regarding the second, in any academy inspired by the Sages of the Talmud, inquiry and learning embrace every aspect of existence, every field of knowledge, but in a way that renders the mind more discriminating, more capable of developing new methods of understanding the interrelatedness of all creation, and more concerned to bring to fruition the ethical values of creation in the everyday life of man.

Viewed in this light, the *Kedusha* or life-thrust of the Jewish people counters two extreme tendencies of the generality of mankind: intellectual and moral stagnation, or tyranny; and intellectual and moral anarchy, or entropy. Both involve the leveling of distinctions and the degradation of human life. Making logical distinctions and relating them to the different aspects and levels of existence are of the essence of the Talmud, which does justice to the ordered multifariousness of creation.

Sympathetic gentile philosophers have often been puzzled by the excellence and creativity of the Jewish people, which have flourished throughout the ages despite the ravages of the nations. What has made the Jews unique was of course their unqualified acceptance of the Torah at Mount Sinai (see Exod. 19:5–8), by virtue of which they were endowed with *Kedusha*, whose ultimate purpose is to reveal the truth of the Torah in every domain of existence.

This inherited endowment may be acquired by any human being who chooses to become a member of the Jewish people through halakhic education and practice. The process is a thoroughly rational one; it is no more mystical than the process of becoming a member of one of the learned professions, be it teaching, medicine, or law. Interestingly, if the members of the learned professions are to win our respect and confidence, they must maintain higher ethical and intellectual standards than that of people in general. We therefore expect them to be especially concerned about the well-being of others, and yet to stand somewhat apart in order to perfect themselves and their profession. This aspect of the learned professions is not *Kedusha*, but it may suggest the quality of the Jewish people that renders them "distinct" and "separate," that prompts them to preserve their own identity or individuality, to be concerned about the good of others, and yet to strive for self-perfection.

Now, just as it is in the best interest of any democracy for its learned professions to set an example of moral and intellectual excellence to society at large, so it is in the best interest of mankind that there be a nation wholly dedicated to the same end. This is Israel's world-historical function, which it betrays when it merely imitates the nations, just as a teacher or doctor or lawyer betrays his calling when he becomes just another seeker of prestige, wealth, and power. He will then become more equal than the ordinary fellow, but he will have further removed himself from the human essence described in Genesis.

The above analogy between the character of the learned professions and the nation called Israel should make it easier to dispel the prejudice that a Jewish state is a "theocracy." Clearly the Torah does not prescribe a theocracy if by that term is meant a state ruled by a priestly caste.[17] A Jewish state is ruled by men schooled in, and constrained by, God-given law, that is, the Torah, which is accessible to human reason and wholly applicable to the entire range of human concerns. In a properly constituted Jewish state, the law is not the preserve of any professional class or jurists; it is the property of all the people (see Exod. 21:1). For notwithstanding the Sanhedrin (of which, more later), all members of a Torah community are more or less learned in the Law. It cannot be emphasized too strongly that, from the Torah point of view, no group of men, be it of the few or of the many, has a right to make laws governing the lives of others unless these are consistent with the laws of God. (This principle, by the way, is clearly implied in the American Declaration of Independence, a document that was incorporated into many of the early American state constitutions.)[18] To put the matter another way, no secular state—not even a constitutional democracy, can be rigorously consistent with the idea of a "government of law and not of men." Such a government, the best hope of mankind, can only be realized when both rulers and ruled alike are subordinate to a veridical system of laws, laws whose obligatory character is not dependent on the transient and arbitrary will of whims of men. Finally, and as will be seen later, neither kings nor "priests" nor judges can lord it over the people in a Torah community; indeed, the Torah imposes limits even on God!

The Torah is a covenant to which God, as a party, subordinates Himself. In other words, here the King of Kings subordinates Himself to the Law of which He is the creator. How different from the Latin maxim *Princeps legibus solutus est*—The ruler is not bound by the law—a relic of which will be found in modern Israeli law: "No act of legislation shall diminish the rights of the State, or impose upon it any obligation, unless explicitly stated" (Interpretation of Ordinance, section 42). Contrast the Jerusalem Talmud:

A human king issues a decree. He may choose to obey it; he may choose to have only others obey it. Not so the Holy One, praised be He. When He issues a decree, He is the first to obey it, as it is stated: "And they shall observe My observances, I am the Lord," I am He who was the first to observe the commandments of the Torah. (*Rosh Hashanah* 1:3a)

The rule of law ultimately requires the crystallization of infinite intelligence, which alone makes possible the reconciliation of permanence and change.[19] Only an eternal and immutable yet viable body of laws can provide conceptual constraints on the discretion of those who deliberate and act in the name of the laws. Without such constraints, the democratic principle of equality becomes a formula for the reign of quantity, of majoritarian willfulness and arrogance. When, however, the laws under discussion constitute the living heritage of a people—a people who study the laws and their elaboration and application through the vicissitudes of time—one can more readily expect their rulers, who are but servants of the law, to pursue justice and kindness, always guided by reason and truth. This principle applies to any nation, Jewish and non-Jewish alike.

It will be evident from the foregoing discussion that the Torah presents a complex view of equality. While it prescribes hereditary classes, these are not absolutely closed, and the prerogatives of any class are qualified by knowledge of the Torah. What the Torah envisions, therefore, is an aristocracy of learning open to all mankind.

This bears comparison with the principle of equality of opportunity. The principle requires that no station in life and no privilege that society may confer can rightly be denied to any person on grounds other than merit. If the notion of "merit" included some of the virtues of the Torah man to be discussed later, a regime based on the principle of equality of opportunity might well be called a "universal aristocracy." Democratic equality would then cease to be a merely quantitative or leveling principle. It would become, instead, the qualitative and elevating principle deeply implied in the Genesis account of man's creation. The alternative is all around us: Equality of opportunity has transformed society into a big shopping center in which democratic man roams around and chooses objects at will. He is drowned in trivia and transcience. Surely the principle of equality can be more edifying.

If all men were created truly equal, it would be a most monotonous and even impossible world. The Torah will not have it so. It has man created in the image of a just and gracious God but endowed with unequal faculties or potentialities. This inequality, obvious in any classroom, is not simple. Exactly what are an individual's potentialities at birth only God knows. In addition, men are raised under unequally propitious circumstances for which they are also not responsible. It may therefore be said that an individual's worth and reward depends on the use he has made of his potentialities and circumstances, but which only an Infinite Intelligence can determine. Moses was born with extraordinary intellectual, moral, and physical powers. He had superior forefathers and was favored by an excellent education in the palace of the Egyptian monarch. He understood that he was not responsible for these advantages. Of course, he recognized that on the all-encompassing question of how man should live, he was superior in knowledge and judgment, say, to Sandlar the sandal-maker. But without knowing the sandal-maker's original endowments and circumstances, there is no way of knowing whether Moses made greater use of his own resources, and therefore whether he was worthy of greater reward in the judgment of Heaven.

To illustrate the principle, imagine a ladder of 100 rungs.[20] One person may start out in life on rung 80 and, with effort, ascend to rung 81. Another person may start out on rung 20 and, with effort, ascend to rung 21. Both advance one step, to which extent they are equal. For what counts is their struggle to take that one step upwards, that one step that distinguishes the vertical striving of man from the horizontal peregrination of beasts. And so, while men are born unequal in absolute terms, they may be equal in relative terms. Indeed, one person, absolutely inferior to another, may become, relatively speaking, his superior in God's infinite judgment. Viewed in this light, equality and inequality may be called complementary principles of the Torah.

Nevertheless, it must be admitted that excellence itself implies inequality. Nor is this all. Without inequality there can be no freedom. For while freedom presupposes choice, choice necessitates qualitative as well as quantitative inequality. Underlying this simple fact is an ontological principle, that of asymmetry. There is, indeed, a primordial asymmetry in existence without which change and therefore the freedom essential to human life would be impossible. To this freedom I now turn.

NOTES

1. This was a principle in American constitutional law until *Garrity v. New Jersey*, 17 L. Ed. 2d 562 (1967), and *Spevack v. Klein*, 17 L Ed. 574 (1967).

2. The technical Halakhic term for "judgment of Heaven" is *Dinei Shamayim*. The term is discussed in Chapter 11.

3. See, for example, the Soncino edition of the Babylonian Talmud.

4. On the other hand, the Torah categorically opposes the modern, democratic notion of Hobbes that "the public worth of a man, which is the value set upon him by the community, is that which is commonly called DIGNITY."

5. The sequel of the cited passage reads, "And it shall be, like people like Kohane"; which is followed by, "The earth shall be utterly emptied" (Isa. 24:2, 3). And later still: "Jerusalem was destroyed only because scholars [i.e., men learned in Torah] were despised therein. . . ." (The author is indebted to Dr. Chaim Zimmerman for this reference to *Shabbat* 119b.)

6. It follows from these considerations that the term "hierarchy," as applied to a Torah community, is misleading, and should only be used to distinguish such a community from an egalitarian society. So far is the Torah from being egalitarian that it conceives of every realm of existence as "hierarchic." Thus, different metals have different levels of value. Scripture uses the metaphors of gold and silver, copper and iron, to signify qualities of purity and impurity, of strength and durability. See *Collected Writings of Rabbi Samson Raphael Hirsch*, III, 169–173, a volume that is replete with evidence that the Torah is not a human product.

Similarly, Jewish law takes cognizance of "hierarchy" in the vegetable and animal kingdoms. Finally, considering the "holy" days and the different levels of "holiness" associated with the Land of Israel, it will be apparent that "hierarchy" governs the domain of time as well as of space. (On this, more later.)

7. According to Dr. Chaim Zimmerman, the concept of "citizenship" is foreign to the Torah, a fact that should interest thoughtful cosmopolitans who regard all nations as artificial.

8. *Sefer HaHinukh* (*The Book of Education*) (Jerusalem and New York: Feldheim, 1978), p. 253.

9. See Rabinowitz, *The Jewish Mind*, 209–210.

10. Islam has a questionable record in these matters. It is known that well over 90 percent of the Moslems living east of the Jordan River openly support the PLO, a terrorist organization that is not only dedicated to Israel's destruction, but that also serves as a client of the Soviet Union to facilitate the demise of the United States, Israel's main ally. The murderous activities of the PLO can easily be traced to Islamic doctrine. See Mordechai Nisan, "PLO Messianism: Diagnosis of a Modern Gnostic Sect," *Terrorism: An International Journal*, vol. 7, no. 3 (1984); Y. Harkabi, *Arab Attitudes to Israel* (Jerusalem: Keter Publishing House, 1972), throughout; D. F. Green, *Arab Theologians on Jews and Israel* (Geneva: Academy of Islamic Research, 1976).

11. Breuer, *Concepts of Judaism*, p. 29.

12. This contradicts Israel's Declaration of Independence of 1948, a thoroughly secular document that guarantees "complete equality of social and political rights to all its inhabitants irrespective of religion. . . . " For a critique of the Declaration, see my "Foundations of the State of Israel: An Analysis of Israel's Declaration of Independence," *Judaism* (Fall 1987), pp. 391–399. The author has in view for the future a new interpretation of the Declaration that will establish within it a hierarchy of principles. Inasmuch as the document confirms Israel's *raison d'être* as a Jewish state, clearly that fact must take precedence over the principle of equality if, as a result of demographic imbalance, contradiction is to be avoided.

13. It is therefore the height of mischievous fatuity to accuse Judaism of racism. Not only will most races be found in the Jewish nation (there are black Jews, Chinese Jews, and Arab Jews), but any one of these may become a king of Israel.

14. There is a subtle tension here. On the one hand, Israel is to be distinct and separate; on the other hand, it is to set a vivid example to mankind as a Torah nation. The tension is intensified by Israel's strategic location. Geographically situated at the crossroad of three continents, Israel is exposed to the ambitions and untoward influences of the nations. Thus situated, however, Israel, guided by the Torah, has the grand opportunity to foster among nations the love of truth and justice. The question is whether Israel will herself succumb to the ways of nations and join in the old struggle for power.

15. Jung, *Judaism in a Changing World*, pp. 15–16.

16. See Zimmerman, *Torah and Reason*, ch. 9, for a most profound discussion of *Kedusha* and Israel.

17. Commenting on the scriptural verse "You will be a kingdom of priests and a holy nation unto Me" (Exod. 19:6), Eliezer Berkovits writes: "This kingdom of priests is not a society in which a priestly caste rules over an unpriestly populace in the name of some god. A holy nation is a realm in which all are

priests. [Note the misleading translation of the term *kohanim*, better rendered as "servants"]. But where all are priests, all are servants and God alone rules. 'A kingdom of priests and a holy nation' is not a theocracy, but a God-centered republic." *God, Man and History* (New York: Jonathan David Publishers, 1965), p. 136. This idea calls to mind the Puritans, who not only rejected the English Church or ecclesiastical authority, but identified themselves with the children of Israel, and transplanted Hebraic laws and institutions to the New World.

18. See the author's *On the Silence of the Declaration of Independence*, pp. 4–5; *The Philosophy of the American Constitution*, Appendix II.

19. Synthesis of permanence and change is symbolized by the gold and acacia wood used to construct the Ark containing the Tables of the Law. The gold represents immutablity for all that is true and good; the wood, i.e., the tree, represents growth or development. The Torah requires both. (See *Hirsch Commentary*, Exod. 25:10–11.)

20. The author is indebted to Professor Dale Gottlieb for this illustration.

7

Freedom with Virtue

The primordial source of freedom has already been anticipated. In fact, the principle of freedom can be derived more obviously from the Genesis account of man's creation than the principle of equality. This may be confirmed in two ways.

First, unlike freedom, equality is not a faculty or power of the mind. This is why a democracy based on the primacy of equality is more entropic or further removed from the Torah than a democracy based on the primacy of freedom. (It is also why tyranny is the worst regime.)

Second, the *imitatio Dei* emphatically entails the freedom involved in creativity. Just as God is creative in an infinite way, so man can and should be creative in a finite way. And just as God's freedom manifests order, justice, and graciousness, so man's freedom should exhibit order, justice, and graciousness.

By thus deriving freedom (as well as equality) from the Torah's account of man's creation, this cardinal principle of democracy will have conceptual constraints necessarily consistent with man's unique character and conducive to his perfection. It may even be said that examination of mankind's history would reveal that the Torah provides the only solid rationale for the freedom and equality that democracies cherish, but that they inevitably abuse at home and too often betray abroad.

Freedom is one of the most precious jewels of the Torah. Again and again the Torah refers to the deliverance of the children of Israel from Egyptian bondage. But the freedom attained in the Exodus was not merely freedom from Egyptian servitude, which is negative, so much as the positive freedom to serve God. (See Exod. 7:16, 8:16, 21–22.) Consistent therewith, the deliverance of the Jews from Egyptian bondage is repeatedly associated with God's Ineffable Name (*YHVH*), as in the First Commandment, signifying the ultimate source of freedom but also of eternal laws of morality. Finally, apropos of the Passover commemorating the Exodus, it should be noted that this Festival of Freedom is not only one of the three major festivals of the Jewish people; it is also the grateful acknowledgment of God's graciousness. Freedom without such gratitude is unknown to any serious Jew.

Nevertheless, while the Torah celebrates freedom, it also seems to countenance "slavery." This has led superficial critics to contend that the Torah's conception of freedom is limited to the community in contradistinction to the individual.[1] The previous chapter clearly refutes this contention. Only recall that no individual may be sacrificed for the sake of the community. As for the concept of "slavery," like so many other concepts that degrade and confuse mankind, it is foreign to the Torah. Before discussing this issue, however, the meaning of freedom must be clarified.

FREEDOM UNDER JEWISH LAW

Having derived man's intellectual-volitional character from the Genesis account of his creation, it follows that genuine freedom does not consist in the absence of obstacles to the realization of one's desires, or living as you like. Nor is freedom to be found in the interstices of the law, such that one may do whatever the law does not forbid. Nor, finally, does freedom consist in obedience to laws in whose formulation one has merged his will with the will of others. Quite the contrary: true freedom is the voluntary and rational observance of laws that are independent of human volition.

Man is free because he is created in the image of God, Who alone is absolutely free. To understand and willingly obey the laws of God is the height of human freedom, for only the laws of God are wholly just and rational. This is why it has been said that where justice and reason reign, " 'tis freedom to obey."

In Judaism "He who is commanded and does stands higher than he who is not commanded and does" (*Avoda Zara* 3a). It requires a more powerful will and intellect to intelligently obey the will of God than to obey one's own will, which is but to follow one's natural inclinations. Contrary to Kant and modernity, the Torah does not exalt the "autonomous" man.[2] "Do God's Will as you would do your own will, so that He may do your will as if it were His" (*Ethics* 2:4). What does this mean?

Each individual is, by definition, a unique creation, endowed with a unique combination of characteristics and capacities. Hence King Solomon could say: "Train a child according to his way" (Prov. 22:6), but obviously within the great framework of the Torah (*Avoda Zara* 19a). The only way to achieve self-actualization and genuine freedom is to fashion one's life within that all-comprehensive framework. (See *Ethics* 6:2.) In other words, only by becoming a servant of God can you overcome all other forms of servitude—be it to your own passions and prejudices or to those of others—and thus ascend to your highest level of freedom and perfection. For a person at that level, the laws of morality become equivalent to the laws of nature, except that, unlike mindless nature, he freely obeys what he knows to be the crystallized thought of God. Freedom then becomes necessity, and the will becomes thoroughly rational.

Just as man is endowed with the freedom to turn away from God, so is he endowed with the power of "repentance." "Repentance" is an inadequate rendering of the Hebrew word *teshuva*, which means "to return," to return to the ways of the Torah. *Teshuva* is not merely a feeling of contrition and reform; it is an act of restoration having profound legal and social significance. For in Jewish law, and apart from cases involving manslaughter, all criminals who have paid the penalty for their misdeeds and have done *teshuva*, are not only qualified to resume their former occupations, honors, and offices, but are eligible to be appointed or elected to new ones for which they are qualified.[3]

This is a most remarkable commentary on the freedom or power of man's will as well as on the magnanimity of Jewish law. Indeed, such is the power of the human will that a habitual sinner, through *teshuva*, may become righteous (and vice versa).[4] Through *teshuva* a person can reverse the past, which exists only in the present, by altering the future.[5] That the future is not simply determined by the past is a fundamental principle of the Torah and is even implied in the divine name *Ehyeh Asher Ehyeh*, "I shall be that which I will be" (Exod. 3:14).[6] All creatures other than man are that which they have to be, for they do not transcend the repetitiveness of nature. But because man is created in God's image, his freedom is a reflection, as it were, of God's absolute freedom. Hence man is not simply a creature of habit, let alone a mere stimulus-response mechanism.

The law of *teshuva* maximizes human freedom by enabling a human being to create his life anew. "I have set before you this day life and good, death and evil . . . therefore choose life" (Deut. 30:15, 19). There can be no freedom, however, without law, physical and moral. Freedom necessitates predictability; it requires the future to bear some resemblance to the past. Without a large measure of determinism both in nature and in man, the universe would lapse into chaos, and freedom would be reduced to self-defeating randomness. On the other hand, that determinism is not complete is as palpable as the fact of change. Hence there can be no freedom without some measure of indeterminism. This suggests an analogy with quantum physics.[7]

It is a marvelous fact that the notion of statistical law actually synthesizes determinism and indeterminism. It is well known that whereas the behavior of matter waves is deterministic and predictable by the laws of wave mechanics, these waves govern only the overall statistical behavior of electrons, leaving their individual behavior quite unpredictable. More familiar is the random decay process of radionnuclides and their rigidly determined half-lives. This randomness or indeterminism prompted Einstein's remark that God does not play dice with the world. The truth is more complicated: God does play dice with the world, only the dice are loaded. The wonderful thing is that statistical laws of nature attest to the superordination of design over chance. This is why it was said above that quantitative laws of existence are only statistical manifestations of qualitative laws of existence. It is the Creator Who made these laws and Who ensures their stability (the stability of the mean). Strictly speaking there are no immanent, eternal, and absolute laws of nature. A law of nature, recall, is nothing more than God's oath or promise that He will not change some stable form or predictable regularity of existence. God allows the world to function within the limits or constraints of the laws He has created, although He Himself is not bound by these laws.[8] His being absolutely unbounded is the guarantee of man's freedom, a freedom that enables man to transcend his probabilistic inclinations.

It is hardly an exaggeration to say that the will of man, so long as he is conscious and his brain has not been tampered with, has an absolute freedom of decision. No earthly power can subjugate his mind, for no being except God is above him.[9] The most cruel torture cannot break his will without a decision on his part to surrender.[10]

No matter who his parents are, no matter the character of the society in which he is raised, the individual can liberate himself from Plato's cave, can rise above the determinism of his environment. This is the teaching and the example of that "pillar of the world," Abraham, who left the cave of the Chaldeans, having discovered by himself the cosmological and ethical principles of the Torah—all this more than thirteen hundred years before Plato, with the help of Socrates, left the cave of Athens, only to construct a more cosmopolitan cave of his own, one from which modern men have yet to extricate themselves.

It was said above that freedom involves the power to fulfill one's purposes. It is common knowledge, however, that the purposes or goals of an individual may be nothing more than conceits leading to psychic frustration, mischief, and social disorder. But whether they are conceits or not, the goals of any individual inevitably compete and clash with each other as well as with those of other individuals. It is this undeniable fact that issues in the classical and modern dichotomies subsumed under the conflict between individual and society: freedom versus authority, rights versus duties, reason versus law. As will be seen more clearly in

Part IV, all these dichotomies are dissolved by the Torah. Under the Torah obedience to law is obedience to reason. Here obedience to law eliminates the internal contradictions and external restraints that stifle individuality and impoverish the community. Here obedience to law brings into mutual coordination and intensification the good of the individual and the good of the community.

"SLAVERY" UNDER JEWISH LAW

I turn now to the concept of "slavery." Contrary to appearances, this concept is extrinsic to Torah jurisprudence. The Hebrew word *eved*, usually rendered as "slave," really means "servant." Nevertheless, let us use the mistranslation and show, by a discussion of Jewish law governing "slavery" (*avdut*), that the concept *eved* has no counterpart in the non-Torah world.[11]

There is no corporate slavery in the Torah. In fact, no Jew can make another human being a slave. He can only acquire, by purchase, someone who had already become a slave, de facto or de jure. He might purchase a Canaanite slave, say, from Egypt. Or he might purchase a Hebrew who had been declared a "slave" by a Jewish court as a result of his having committed a theft for which he was unable to make restitution to his victim.

The most remarkable thing about the Canaanite slave is that he cannot be retained in a Jewish household unless he fulfills all the negative commandments of the Torah as well as all those positive commandments which do not depend on time for their performance. (If he refuses to fulfill these precepts, he is released after a maximum probationary period of one year.) One may say, therefore, that a Canaanite slave is half Jewish. Moreover, if his master should inadvertently inflict upon him some palpable blemish, the slave is not only automatically emancipated, but he must be accepted into the community as a Jew (*Kidushin* 24a, b).[12]

Although a Canaanite slave cannot liberate himself, he may be emancipated through the agency of others (ibid., 23a). On the other hand, his master may not sell him to a non-Jew or even to a Jew outside the land of Israel. (In either case the slave would go free.) Finally, the Halakha prohibits the extradition of a non-Jewish slave who had fled from his Jewish master living abroad. Nothing like this can be found in any other ancient code. In the Code of Hammurabi, which is the product of a well-advanced civilization, harboring or aiding a runaway slave was a crime punishable by death. The Torah commands: "You shall not deliver a slave to his master who has escaped from his master to you. He shall dwell with you in your midst in the place which he shall choose within one of your gates (towns) which he likes best" (Deut. 23:16–17, and see *Gittin* 45a). Indeed, the runaway Canaanite slave must be given a certificate of manumission and be accepted into the Jewish community, where he attains the full rights of a Jew. This law clearly tends in the direction of the virtual abolition of slavery.

Consider, now, the slavery of a Jew for theft.[13] A Jew who cannot restore the value of his theft to his victim is sold into servitude by the court—he is not imprisoned—to help him make this restitution. Such sale is imposed only on male thieves, not females. In no case is the period of service to exceed six years, and even during this period the "slave" may at any time acquire his freedom by paying off the proportionate value of the remaining period of his service. The only kind of work that can be demanded of him by his master is that which had been his usual occupation, be it as a cobbler or as a woodchopper. (In fact, if the amount of his theft is less than the value of six years of service in his normal occupation, he cannot be sold into servitude, and he still cannot be imprisoned. Of course, the victim of his theft may be compensated by confiscation of the malefactor's property, so long as this does not leave him destitute or incapable of earning an honest living.)

In any event, the case of the Hebrew "slave," writes Rabbi Hirsch, *"is the one and only case* in which the Torah orders deprivation of freedom as a punishment [if punishment it may be called]":

[The Torah] orders the criminal to be brought into the life of a family as we might order a refractory child to be brought under the influence of Jewish family life. How careful it is that the self-confidence of the criminal should not be broken, that, in spite of the degradation he has brought on himself, he should still feel himself considered and treated as a brother . . . [Moreover, the Torah] insists that he may not be separated from his wife and family, and . . . that his family should not be left in distress through his crime and its results. In depriving him of liberty, and thereby the means to provide for his dependents, the Torah puts the responsibility of caring for him, or those who, for the duration of his lack of freedom, have the benefit of his labor.

Punishments of imprisonment, with all the attendant despair and moral degradation that dwell behind prison bars [where criminals become even more hardened], with all the worry and distress that it entails for wife and child [the wife usually divorces her husband], are unknown in Torah jurisprudence.

During his service the Halakha requires complete equality of the slave with his master and the rest of the household in food, clothing, and bedding. (In fact, the "slave" must be fed before his "master"!) And after his term of service has been completed, he must be liberally provided for by his master so that he is not returned to independence empty-handed but is instead equipped to earn an honest living. Hence the popular saying, "Who buys a Hebrew slave for himself has bought for himself a master" (*Kidushin* 22a).

It should thus be evident that, although servitude for theft is theoretically permissible under the Torah, its practical tendency is toward desuetude. In fact, it ceased with the rise of the Second Commonwealth. (See *Arachin* 29a.) It may even be said that the terms of slavery under Jewish law are so restrictive on the master and so protective of the "slave," that this institution was partly intended to rehabilitate certain malefactors, to bring them within the saving and generous embrace of the Torah.

FREEDOM IN HISTORY

To be sure, the idea of one man serving another is abhorrent in democratic times, and rightly so. But perhaps the reason is not because democracies honor human nature so much as because in democratic times hardly any person is worthy of being served by a human being. Chattel slavery can never be justified. But it is a provincial conceit to think that democracy enables men to achieve the heights of human freedom. The heights of freedom cannot be achieved without inner freedom and social harmony, both of which require given laws and leisure devoted not to trivia, but to virtuous deeds and learning.

No less a friend of democracy than Alfred North Whitehead has written—and this was before the soul-shattering and moronizing effects of television: "So far as sheer individual freedom is concerned, there was more diffused freedom in the City of London in the year 1663, when Charles the First was King, than there is today in any industrial city in the world."[14] Postindustrial democracy breeds its own kind of bondage.

Here I am reminded of those celebrated words of Rousseau's *Social Contract*: "Man was born free, and yet we see him everywhere in chains. . . . How did this change come to pass? I do not know. What can make it legitimate? I believe I can resolve this question." It follows from this insight into man and society that all existing regimes are illegitimate, that is, unjust! Rousseau does not promise to break the chains of civil society but rather to make them *legitimate*. Virtue is necessary to civil society, but the man who acts from considerations of duty does so at the expense of his sweetest natural sentiment, that of freedom. The constraints of morality, though necessary for civilized life, are contrary to nature, to the feeling of freedom, man's highest good or happiness. Rousseau quite knowingly does not solve this dilemma.[15] The great philosopher of democracy thus admits that, although democracy leaves some space for freedom—for the few who, like bohemians, live on the fringes of society—it is nonetheless another form of servitude. How is this servitude to be understood in the broad outlines of a Torah theory of history?

Although human servitude in the past was not, in all instances, the unmitigated evil it is made out to be, its abolition was certainly justified.

But the basic causes leading to the abolition of slavery have escaped the researches of democratic historians.[16] Paradoxical as it may seem, the demise of slavery was not the result of moral progress so much as the result of moral decline. True, there had always been masters unworthy of having slaves. Nevertheless, when individuals were historically important, were of the caliber of a King David or even of a Plato, it was fit and proper that they should be served by lesser men. Indeed, it was an honor to serve such great personages, to behold their demeanor, to imbibe their words of wisdom.

But when the virtue and importance of individual leaders declined and they were no longer worthy of human servitude, divine providence (i.e., laws of history) brought about the rise of democracy and science on the one hand, and the eradication of slavery on the other. The process was of course gradual. The less men merited slave labor, the more they had to rely on animal and hired labor. Eventually, mankind sank to so low a level as to be unworthy even of animal labor. (Only consider how the learned began to exult in tracing their genealogy to apes and to be offended by the idea of a higher origin!) Providence therefore accelerated the development of science and technology so that animals could be replaced by machines, progressively automated (and now very much geared to the gratification of paltry desires). In other words, given the increasing selfishness and hedonism of modernity, man no longer merits being served by any living thing.[17]

Concomitant with the moral decline of the individual, there has been an outward improvement in the character of society. This dichotomy is not paradoxical. Recall Machiavelli's separation of morality from politics and the consequent liberation of the acquisitive instincts. As already indicated, the progress of science and technology, the hallmark of Western civilization, was actually the result of egoism or moral decline. Rousseau writes in his *First Discourse*, "Our souls have been corrupted in proportion to the advancement of our sciences and arts toward perfection."[18] Rousseau was not merely referring to the moral depravity of his own times, the peak of the "Enlightenment." He regarded the relationship between corruption and the progress of the arts and sciences as if it were a law of history, a phenomenon, he says, that "has been observed in all times and in all places."[19] By corruption Rousseau had in mind the decline of civic virtue, of dedication to the common good, in other words, the ascendancy of egoism.

Rousseau aside, the egoism he deplored can only be harnessed and yield material abundance if moderated by political and institutional checks and balances that prevent any class, rich or poor, from gaining a monopoly of power. Such institutions also enable men to resolve, through compromise, their competing interests. Also required, however, is institutionalized charity to alleviate the condition of the poor, lest ambitious demagogues incite the masses to insurrection. Enter the welfare state. To be sure, such charity is praiseworthy even if it is not motivated by concern for the individual or human dignity so much as by the desire to preserve public order. Similarly, the rushing of aid to victims of natural disasters all over the world is also meritorious, even though it is animated less by compassion for the individual than by the desire for national influence and prestige. (See Prov. 12:10.)

These seemingly cynical conclusions are borne out by the failure of the democracies to make any sacrifices or undertake any risks on behalf of small nations subverted and ravaged by mafiosos trumpeting some Marxist or other ideology.[20] Hundreds of thousands of people from Biafra were massacred in full view of the democratic world. Add to this the indifference of the democracies to the carnage in Cambodia, Ethiopia, Zimbabwe, Mozambique, Lebanon, and other countries of the Third World. Consider, too, how democracies, committed to freedom, appease and arm Islamic despotisms bent on Israel's destruction; how they even honor a terrorist organization responsible for the murder of their own citizens and diplomats.

CONCLUSION

I mention this tragic record of democratic infirmity only to indicate that the concept of democratic freedom is flawed, that it is tainted by egoism. This was inevitable given the Machiavellian severance of morality from politics that brought on to the stage of world history Secular Man. Thus, while secularists boast of their humanism, we see the result of their pride: the dehumanization of man. Secularized freedom has yielded pornographic vulgarity at home without curbing obscene violence abroad. Removed from the conceptual and ethical constraints of the Torah, its only true source, freedom can only lead to bondage. Indeed, it is only by virtue of modulations from that source that the West can still speak of human dignity and resist, however feebly, the encroachment of tyranny.

Let me repeat: humanism has led to the dehumanization of man. At the same time, however, we are granted the opportunity to redefine man, to develop a model of human perfection surpassing anything thus far offered by Western civilization. Such a model will be developed in the next two chapters.

NOTES

1. See, e.g., Georg W. H. Hegel, *The Philosophy of History* (New York: Dover Publications, 1956), pp. 196–197, whose inane understanding of "Judea" is

laughable. Hegel confirms the adage that great intelligence and great stupidity can coexist under the same hat.

2. See Breuer, *Concepts of Judaism*, pp. 53–81, for a brilliant essay on "The Philosophical Foundations of Jewish and Modern Law." This essay, by the way, shows how an orthodox Jewish philosopher (and jurisprudent) can surpass the Straussian understanding of modernity.

3. See *Hirsch Commentary*, Num. 35:28.

4. For the Christian theologian, however much the sinner may repent and mortify himself, remission of sins, hence the efficacy of his repentance, depends on the miraculous intercession and grace of God. For the Jew *teshuva* depends solely on one's own rational will and effort, so that the worst sinner can attain purity (*tahara*) without the intercession of any transcendent and incomprehensible being.

5. See my *Jerusalem vs. Athens*, p. 278, and Soloveitchik, *Halakhic Man*, pp. 114–116, 121–122.

6. See my *Jerusalem vs. Athens*, pp. 29–32, on the concept of time.

7. See ibid., pp. 209–215 for an elaboration of this and the following paragraph.

8. See Zimmerman, *Torah and Reason*, pp. 137–141.

9. See ibid., p. 167.

10. Consider the decade-long ordeal of Natan (Anatoly) Shcharansky in the Soviet Gulag. Contrast Flavius Josephus who writes of the Jews: "It is no new thing for our captives, many of them in number, and frequently in time, to be seen to endure racks and deaths of all kinds upon the theaters, that they may not be obliged to say one word against our laws and the records that contain them; whereas there are none at all among the Greeks who would undergo the least harm on that account. . . . " *Complete Works*, 4 vols., trans. Haverman (New York: Bigelo, Brown & Co., n.d.), *Contra Apion*, I, 8.

11. The following analysis should be compared with Thomas More's discussion of slavery and of punishment for theft in *Utopia*. See note 13 below.

12. See *Hirsch Commentary*, Exod. 21:26–27.

13. The following discussion is partly based on *Hirsch Commentary*, Exod. 21:2–3 and Deut. 15:12, 23:16. See also Isaac Herzog, *The Main Institutions of Jewish Law*, 2 vols. (London: Soncino Press, 1936), I, 45. After reflecting on the laws of the Torah regarding servitude for theft, the reader should contrast the perverse, not to say slanderous, treatment of Jewish law by Thomas More in his *Utopia* (New York: Crofts Classics, 1949), p. 12, who surely must have known better. Indeed, contrast his discussion of the utopians' policy on punishment for theft (pp. 23–24) with the infinitely more humane and enlightened policy of the Torah. Contrast, too, the utopians' harsh policy toward slaves, p. 56.

14. Alfred North Whitehead, *Science and Philosophy* (New York: Philosophical Library, 1948), pp. 165–166.

15. See Allan Bloom, "Jean-Jacques Rousseau," in Leo Strauss and Joseph Cropsey, eds., *History of Political Philosophy*, 2d. ed. (Chicago: Rand McNally, 1972), pp. 532–537.

16. See Zimmerman, *Torah and Reason*, pp. 147–151, on which this historical view of slavery is based.

17. See de Tocqueville, *Democracy in America*, II, 104, who attributes the spread of selfishness to democratic individualism:

Individualism is a novel expression to which a novel idea has given birth. Our fathers were only acquainted with *egoisme* (selfishness). Selfishness is a passionate and exaggerated love of self, which leads a man to connect everything with himself and to prefer himself to everything in the world. Individualism is a mature and calm feeling, which disposes each member of the community to sever himself from the mass of his fellows and to draw apart with his family, so that after he has thus formed a little circle of his own, he willingly leaves society at large to itself. Selfishness originates in blind instinct; individualism proceeds from erroneous judgment more than from depraved feelings; it originates as much in deficiencies of mind as in perversity of heart.

Selfishness blights the germ of all virtue; individualism, at first, only saps the virtues of public life, but in the long run it attacks and destroys all others and is at length absorbed in downright selfishness. Selfishness is a vice as old as the world, which does not belong to one form of society more than to another; individualism is of democratic origin, and it threatens to spread in the same ratio as the equality of conditions.

18. Jean-Jacques Rousseau, *First Discourse*, in *The First and Second Discourses*, ed. R. D. Masters; trans. J. R. Masters (New York: St. Martin's Press, 1964), p. 39.

19. Ibid., p. 40.

20. American intervention in Vietnam was primarily motivated by fear of Soviet expansion into Indochina, from whence it could readily close off the Malacca Straits, the passageway to the Indian Ocean and the Persian Gulf for both the U.S. Seventh Fleet (stationed in the Philippines) and Japanese oil tankers. Unfortunately, the U.S. government failed to inform the American people of this strategic concern. Had it done so, say at the time of its initial intervention in 1963, when the United States had overwhelming nuclear superiority over the USSR, a tremendous slaughter could have been avoided both in Vietnam and in Cambodia. For a further analysis, see the author's *Beyond Détente: Toward an American Foreign Policy*; (LaSalle, Ill.: Sherwood Sugden & Co., 1977), p. 180, and *Jerusalem vs. Athens*, p. 363 n.40.

III

A "New" Model of Man

8

Four Types of Men

We have seen that Jewish law secures individual freedom, holds the principles of equality and inequality in dynamic equilibrium, and thereby ensures intellectual and moral excellence.

Outside that jurisprudential framework the free will of man, acting upon the inequality of our natural endowments, renders the differences among mankind mutually obstructive rather than mutually supportive. The free will with which men are endowed by their Creator, and which distinguishes them from beasts, is precisely the force that splinters mankind into its profusion of regimes whose behavior is so often subhuman. Let his intellect become the instrument of his passions and man, although created in the image of God and born utterly innocent, can become not only the bloodiest of beasts, but the most stupid of animals.

Barbarism is as old as mankind, but today it is armed with technique. Stupidity is as old as humanity, but today it is thoroughly computerized. Never has man been more dangerously muddled, for now he has weapons of mass destruction as well as media of mass stupefaction.

Despite great advances in brain research, man has never been so far removed from himself. The mind of contemporary man, at least in democratic or pluralistic societies, is buried beneath countless layers of civilization. No mere archaeologist or paleontologist can excavate and restore the essence of man from the debris of a thousand and one diverse cultures, mythologies, religions, philosophies, ideologies, and pseudosciences under which the poor creature is buried.

Desperately needed is a model of man and mentality that can lead humanity out of the secular and religious jungles of our time. To develop such a model—the task of this and the following chapter—it will be necessary to get beneath the centuries of accumulated "isms" that obscure the human essence and reduce the profusion of mankind to clearly defined types of human beings.

ESAVIAN MAN

However various mankind, there are only four basic types of human character that affect the peace and prosperity of nations. A most concise and penetrating view of the subject will be found in (the previously cited) *Ethics of the Fathers*, which is included in most Jewish prayer books and is studied by youngsters in Torah academies even before they reach the age of ten. Here is how that tractate of the Mishnah defines the four types of human character:

He who says "What's mine is mine and what's yours is yours" is the ordinary type, although some say this is the Sodom-type [those who are callous or morally insensitive]; he who says "What's mine is yours and what's yours is mine" is the fool; he who says "What's mine is yours and what's yours is yours" is the godly or gracious type; he who says "What's yours is mine and what's mine is mine" is wicked (5:13).[1]

Many brilliant commentaries have been written on this deceptively simple passage, for here, as elsewhere, the simple is profound.

The first character type—"What's mine is mine and what's yours is yours"—is obviously animated by egoism, usually of a moderate form. His attitude, if generalized, would favor the rich. The second character type—"What's mine is yours and what's yours is mine—is also animated by egoism, still moderate but deceptive. His attitude, if generalized, would favor the poor.

Clearly, no political community or regime can be founded exclusively on either of these character types. Regarding the first: No regime can exist without some common property, such as public buildings, public roads, hence a public treasury. Regarding the second: Contrary to the obvious fact that no regime can exist without some private property, the principle of "What's mine is yours and what's yours is mine" logically extends to wives and children (recall Plato's *Republic*), as well as to public functions to which particular individuals must be assigned and for which they must be held individually responsible. The second type of character (the paragon of Plato's best regime!) is indeed a fool, and if his attitude were translated into political terms, the result would be utterly preposterous, not to say destructive (as Plato surely understood). Hence the first or ordinary type of character will usually be preferable to the second. To form a political community, however, the attitudes of both types must fuse or coexist in some proportion. If the proportion leans toward the first, it will be a capitalist or liberal democracy; if toward the second, a socialist democracy. Still, it should be borne in mind that socialism as well as capitalism is animated by common egoism, which militates against the political preeminence of wisdom and virtue.[2]

Turning from the second to the fourth character type, the attitude "What's yours is mine and what's mine is mine" obviously represents the most extreme form of egoism, combining as it does the egoistic elements of the first two types. A regime based on such egoism would be a tyranny, which means that tyranny combines the worst character-istics of capitalist and socialist democracies.[3]

The three preceding elaborations of the mine-thine distinction may be regarded as a taxonomy of what I shall call the "Esavian" world of politics (from Esau, who symbolizes the primacy of force and fraud).[4] This is exactly the world portrayed in Chapter 3, especially in Elie Wiesel's and Eliyahu Amiqam's devastating commentaries on mankind—secular, democratic, and religious. All Esavian regimes, whatever their ideolo-gies, are in practice animated by varying degrees of collective egoism. As for their ideologies, these consist of secular and religious myths, fabrications, and half-truths which serve to legitimize power and to facilitate the pursuit of gain and glory. Consider more closely, however, those subtle kinsmen of modernity, socialism and capitalism.

Socialism (or Marxism) may be called the opium of the intellectual who self-righteously exploits the envy and grievances of the poor against the greed and exploitations of the rich (both magnified by capitalism). Admittedly, envy—"the rottenness of the bones" (Prov. 14:30)—is the more corrosive vice, as well as the more dangerous when it becomes organized by the ambitious. But it is the avarice of the rich that often ncites the envy of the poor. It is the rich who tend to set the example for society at large.

In any event, in domestic affairs, the avarice and leveling tendency of capitalism yields external freedom and psychic insecurity—say public liberty and private misery. Meanwhile, the envious and more leveling character of socialism generates what Nietzsche called the "last man," men devoid of aspiration, of any sensitivity to what is noble and what is base.

As for their foreign relations, Esavian regimes may be described as follows. Tyrannical states (religious as well as secular) are instruments of force and fraud designed to facilitate expansion and conquest. Their diplomacy conforms to the precept "What's mine is mine and what's yours is negotiable." In contrast, liberal and social democratic states are designed to facilitate self-indulgence and "peace" (recall Munich), which may require one democracy to sacrifice another. Esau sacrificed his birth-right for potage. Today the democracies would sacrifice Israel for petro-leum.

The reader would err if he should think that the preceding is written with polemical intent. That all states are primarily animated by material interests is the unanimous conclusion of political theorists from Plato to the present. What contemporary political scientist does not echo Hobbes, who naughtily declared, "money is the blood of the commonwealth"? I need only add the following. Having given themselves their own laws—laws dependent on the shifting opinions, passions, and interests of men—it is only natural for Esavian nations to engage in frequent conflict with each other, and to succumb, so easily, to hatred of the one nation that did not give itself its own laws.

To be sure, a distinction must be made between the behavior of Esavian nations and of the individuals composing them. The behaviors of individuals and nations are subject to statistical laws analogous to those that govern microphysical and macrophysical entities. Whereas the individual is free, the behavior pattern of a nation is statistically determined. (To simplify the exposition, I shall ignore revolutions, wars, and catastrophes, which may transform a nation's political character.) Of course, consistent with the notion of statistical or probabilistic law, it is possible for a nation to turn away from evil, as was the (transient) case of Nineveh. Nevertheless, the sociological characteristics of a nation are very stable despite the diversity that may obtain among its individual members. Although Esavian individuals are free, there are always enough common characteristics among such individuals to ensure the stability of the mean—the laws or behavior patterns of the nation. (Still, as every yeshiva student knows, Esau was the son of exemplary Jewish parents; King David, Israel's greatest monarch, was a descendant of Ruth, a Moabitess; and some of Israel's greatest Sages were proselytes.)

THE GRACIOUS MAN

If all men and all nations were cast in the Esavian mold, it would be absurd to speak of man's creation in the image of God. Let us therefore hasten and repair to the man who says, "What's mine is yours and what's yours is yours." These words are those of an extraordinary and profound human being whom the Mishnah calls the godly or Gracious Man, a man whose cup runneth over, who gives even to the underserving and does so out of a knowledge that dissolves all egoism.

To say "What's mine is yours and what's yours is yours" is to say, in effect, that nothing is really mine. The equivalent of this will not be found in the philosophic tradition, a tradition that denies creation from nothing (*creatio ex nihilo*). In contrast, a Torah-educated person knows that nothing in a created universe can be "mine," metaphysically speaking. The Torah translates this abstract principle into living reality, especially in the observance of the Sabbath Day and the Sabbath Year of the Land. Every seventh day and every seventh year the Jew is to refrain from exercising his own mastery over any of God's creatures or creations.[5] What thus appears to be a moral attitude—"What's mine is yours and what's yours is yours"—is actually the derivative of a cosmological principle. This may be seen most vividly and profoundly in the life of Abraham, the first Jew and the father of the Jewish people.

Abraham is not only a world-historical individual. He is the supreme personification of a qualitative law of existence, that of *Hesed*, which manifests itself in different ways and degrees in the conduct and character of humanity. Often translated as "loving-kindness," but better rendered as "graciousness," *Hesed* is a qualitative law that prompts us to be concerned about the good of others. (The complementary law of *Gevura* or "severity," personified by Isaac, prompts us to be concerned about our own good, which includes not only self-preservation but self-perfection.) To grasp the intellectual foundation and moral significance of Abraham's graciousness, it will be necessary to reexamine the biblical narrative of the first Patriarch.

To comprehend any biblical narrative, one must think of its leading characters, especially the Patriarchs and Moses, as consciously participating in a world-historical program, the unfolding of which required the formation of a unique nation. In this program, Abraham is to be viewed as the successor of the original Adam. Whereas Adam, as a result of his transgression, was driven out of the Garden of Eden, a place of perfection, Abraham, as a result of his righteousness, was urged by God to leave Chaldea, a place of sophisticated corruption, and go to a land that in time would become a new Eden. Thus: "For your own sake, go away from your land, from your birthplace, and from your father's house, to the land that I will show you. And I will make of you a great nation, and I will bless you and make your name great...." (Gen. 12:1–2). Significantly, the narrative begins after the dispersion of the people of Babel. Unlike Babel, a nation that sought to glorify or make a name for itself, Abram, a solitary individual, sought to glorify God. And it was because he did not seek to make a name for himself that God changed his name to Abraham, a name revered down through the ages by countless millions of people. Let us see why.[6]

Abraham is probably the most original thinker that ever lived.[7] So far as is known, he was the first to discover and speculate upon the great concept of the unity of God and the principle of creation *ex nihilo*, the principle that has so vexed and offended the intellectual pride of philosophers since the pre-Socratics. Without any teacher, and in opposition to his generation, he discovered, through reason and observation, that this vast, multifarious universe is an integrated whole created by one supreme and transcendent Being of infinite wisdom and power (Gen. 14:22). Abraham also discovered the providential kindliness of God and deduced therefrom His code of conduct for mankind (Gen. 26:5). He saw in the interrelatedness of heavenly and earthly phenomena something that neither Plato nor Aristotle saw some fourteen hundred years later, namely, that the world was designed for man's use and happiness, hence that man is the purpose of all creation. He reasoned that since the Creator showed nothing of Himself but only his deeds, then it is His will that men should know Him by the graciousness of His deeds, an attribute they ought to emulate in their relations with one another (for example, in anonymous charity). Abraham also reasoned that it is proper for men to be grateful to their Benefactor by speaking of His graciousness and by consecrating their lives to His service.

Accordingly, Abraham devoted all his thoughts and labors to the glorification of God's Name. He disciplined himself by unrelenting effort until he learned absolute self-control (Gen. 15:9–11, 17:24, *Nedarim* 32b). No difficulty was too great for him, and the greatest sacrifice did not hinder him. Moreover, in his dealings with men—even enemies—he manifested unequaled hospitality and magnanimity, for which reason he is the exemplar of *Hesed*, that purely voluntary and overflowing kindness that seeks neither reward nor recognition (Gen. 14:22, 18:1, 23). Over the course of years thousands of people gathered about him, listened to his teachings, and became part of his household. Such was his greatness as a teacher and leader of men that he was called a "Prince of God" (Gen. 23:6). Yet, despite his greatness, he was ever humble, regarding himself as "mere dust and ashes" (Gen. 18:27). (How different was this Jew from humanists who proudly speak—so often with self-concern—of human dignity.)

In short, Abraham developed in himself superior intellectual and moral qualities which became part of his being and were transmitted to his posterity (*Megilla* 13b).

Yet this most gracious of men, who pleaded with God to spare the wicked inhabitants of Sodom, readily acceded to God's request to sacrifice his own son Isaac! "Take (*kah na*) your son, your only son, whom you love—Isaac—and go to the land of Moriah; and offer him there for a burnt-offering upon one of the mountains which I will tell you of" (Gen. 22:2). I have here followed the conventional translation which erroneously renders the two words *kah na*, as a command, "take," rather than as a request, "please take" (*Sanhedrin* 89b). The request indicates that Abraham would have suffered no tangible harm had he declined to sacrifice his son. Nevertheless, he knew in the fullness of his being that God is the Maker or Owner of heaven and earth (Gen. 14:22). Knowing this he knew what was to be proclaimed a thousand years later by his descendents: "Behold, all souls are Mine" (Ezek. 18:4), and what is more profound, "My thoughts are not your thoughts" (Isa. 55:8).

Both utterances are logical conclusions from the principle of creation *ex nihilo*.

And so, such was the depth of Abraham's knowledge on the one hand and the boundlessness of his love of God on the other—a love rendered rational and unsurpassable by his profound comprehension of how to stand before the Creator—that the father of the Jewish people found in his heart the humility and unequaled courage to make that unforgettable journey to Mount Moriah. For three days he walked alongside his son to the mountain on which he would perform the "greatest act, most remote from nature," indeed, most foreign to his own nature. For as emphasized earlier, Abraham's distinctive trait, corresponding to one of the pillars of creation (Ps. 89:4), was graciousness, enough to say kindness. His readiness to sacrifice his son was therefore completely contrary to the grain of his character.[8] This is why the Binding of Isaac was the ultimate test of Abraham's love of God, or rather, of the essence of that love, a test rendered the more awesome precisely because it required the Patriarch to transcend his own nature. He had to act cruelly toward his son (hence to his wife as well) and yet remain what he truly was, a man of unsurpassable graciousness.

At the same time, he would have to violate, in a most terrible manner, the godly way of life he had long taught men to imitate and in virtue of which he was admired by so many of his contemporaries. By slaughtering his son (from whom alone his posterity was to issue) he would be misunderstood, despised, and vilified; and his work of a lifetime, of creating a people who would turn mankind away from paganism, human sacrifice,and superstition to enlightenment, graciousness, and the worship of the true God, would be nullified.

Clearly, no man of emotion could have ascended Mount Moriah, there to perform Abraham's incomparable sacrifice. All the emotions involve self-concern, or at least, in the case of love and kindness, some element of satisfaction and pleasure. Nor was it some Kierkegaardian leap of faith that governed Abraham's unique journey.[9] Rather, it was his intellectualized love of God, rooted in his cognitive awareness of God as the Creator of heaven and earth. (This is exactly what Maimonides refers to in his *Mishneh Torah*: "No one loves the Holy One . . . except by means of the knowledge with which he knows Him. The love will be according to the knowledge: if it be small, the love will be small; if it be great, the love will be great.")[10]

The intellectual character of Abraham's love was foreshadowed in his remonstrance with God on behalf of Sodom. He could not have so argued on behalf of Isaac. Nor could he have offered his own life for that of his thirty-seven-year-old son. Isaac, the personification of *Gevura*, nonetheless transcended the most powerful of man's natural instincts, that of self-preservation, and willingly offered himself as a sacrifice for God. For Abraham, that kind of self-sacrifice would have been relatively easy. It would not have required him to rise above his own character. But what is more significant, it would have placed emotion (or the body) above the intellect, hence the merely human above the divine.

The Binding of Isaac represents a most fundamental principle, namely, that man stands above nature (contrary to classical political philosophy), and even above self-love (so contrary to modern political science). Indeed, Abraham embodies the teaching that, only let a person be wholehearted in his love of God, and he will be capable of activating a power within him that is more than human.[11]

It will not have escaped the reader's attention that in the Binding of Isaac, Abraham activated within himself the very character trait of his son, severity, or *Gevura*. We are to understand, therefore, that the Gracious Man, the man who says "What's mine is yours and what's yours is yours," is capable of the greatest severity, foremost against himself, but also against his nearest and dearest—all out of the fullness of his recognition that everything in this universe, a universe created *ex nihilo*, belongs to God. Here I touch upon the fundamental conflict between Judaism and the philosophic tradition, say between Jerusalem and Athens.

The philosopher insists that creation out of nothing involves a contradiction in terms. This is correct, but only because traditional logic is limited by inescapable spatial and temporal categories. Twentieth-century physics, however, is no longer limited by the old-fashioned notions of space and time, hence by what constitutes a "thing" or "no-thing." Besides: (1) it is impossible to prove by empirical means that the universe is eternal; (2) it is illogical to say that the universe created itself;[12] (3) though not illogical, it is unbelievable that any rational system can be the product of chance; and (4) it is conformable to both reason and experience to posit a designer of things that exhibit design.

The first Patriarch drew similar conclusions. Recall his referring to God as the Maker or Owner of heaven and earth. Contrast Adam. God warns Adam not to eat from a particular tree in the Garden of Eden. Adam disobeys. This disobedience, tantamount to a denial of God's ownership of heaven and earth, is equivalent to the denial of creation *ex nihilo*. In other words, Adam's disobedience dramatically symbolizes the philosophical tradition of an uncreated or eternal universe elaborated in Athens. This tradition rejects the idea of God's infinite power over nature as well as His supervision over history. The inevitable consequence is to deny God's existence or human relevance, or to identify Him with the forces of nature (as in paganism and pantheism).

In contrast, the God of Abraham is a providential and personal God. He created not only the quantitative laws of nature, but also the qualitative laws of history. Hence we belong entirely to Him. To Him do we owe, in loving gratitude, our highest loyalty, for all good things, life included, come from His infinite care and munificence. The words "Behold, all things are Mine" simply echo the Binding of Isaac, the world-historical deed that has borne a people through almost 4,000 years of trial, tragedy, and triumph.

CONCLUSION

Viewed from the vantage of cosmology, that is, of a created universe, the mine-thine attitudes of the three Esavian character types falsify existence and eventuate in regimes that deny the absolute proprietorship of God. Put another way, the separation of church and state or of religion and politics, which is characteristic of democratic regimes, is inconsistent with the idea of creation and of God's absolute unity and sovereignty.[13] But this bifurcation of the sacred and the profane reflects the inadequacy of religion as well as of politics and political philosophy. Needed is another conception of man and of the universe in which he lives.

The Binding of Isaac is the earthly confirmation of a cosmological insight, of Abraham's discovery of creation *ex nihilo*. Therein is the cognitive source of his unequaled love of God. At the same time, that extraordinary act at Mount Moriah symbolizes the supremacy of the intellect and free will over nature or the emotions. Abraham's love transcended the eros of the philosopher, an eros which, in the final analysis, is a refined form of narcissism or of intellectual pride. The philosopher lacks what the Torah calls *anava*, a quality without which mankind cannot achieve the heights of knowledge and of human perfection. But what is this *anava*? In the answer to this question Judaism goes beyond the secular mind and points the way to transcending Western civilization.

NOTES

1. See my *Jerusalem vs. Athens*, ch. 8, on which the following analysis is based.

2. Nietzsche exposed the lie of socialism after revealing the truth about modern individualism. Here are his penetrating remarks:

Individualism is a modest and still unconscious form of the "will to power"; here it seems sufficient to the individual to get free from an overarching domination by society (whether that of the state or of the church). He does not oppose them as a person but only as an individual; he represents all individuals against the totality. That means: he instinctively posits himself as equal to all other individuals; what he gains in his struggle he gains for himself not as a person but as a representative of individuals against the totality.

Socialism is merely a means of agitation employed by individualism: it grasps that, to attain anything, one must organize to a collective action, to a "power." But what it desires is not a social order as the goal of the individual but a social order as a means of making possible many [mediocre] individuals. This is the instinct of socialists about which they frequently deceive themselves. . . . The preaching of altruistic morality in the service of individualism: one of the most common lies of the nineteenth century. (*The Will to Power*, trans. W. Kaufmann [New York: Random House, 1967], pp. 411–412.)

3. Aristotle (*Politics* 1210b16) describes tyranny as a combination of the worst characteristics of democracy and oligarchy.

4. See Gen. 27:22, 40. This is the only world with which Machiavelli was familiar, the world that justifies his exclusion of justice from his enumeration of qualities for which rulers are praised or blamed (again, in Chapter 15 of *The Prince*). See also *Jerusalem vs. Athens*, p. 21 n, for an explanation of Jacob's (or Rebecca's) attempt, seemingly to deceive, but actually to undeceive, Isaac.

5. See *Hirsch Commentary*, Exod. 23:10–11. See also Gottlieb, *The Inescapable Truth*, pp. 128–132, who includes the ordinance of the sabbatical year as one of nine proofs that the Torah is not a human product.

6. The following paragraph is largely indebted to Avigdor Miller, *Rejoice O Youth* (New York: privately published, 1968), pp. 73–78.

7. Josephus quotes from the ancient Chaldean historian Berosus the statement that "in the tenth generation after the Flood, there was among the Chaldeans a man righteous and great, and skilled in astronomy." (Flavius Josephus, *Complete Works, Antiquities*, I, 7.2). The reference is to Abraham, who taught the Egyptians mathematics and astronomy when he sojourned in the land of the Nile.

8. See *ArtScroll Tenach Series, Bereshis*, 6 vols. (Brooklyn, N.Y.: Mesorah Publications, 1970), II, 601–606 throughout, R. Nossom Scherman's overview, to which the remainder of this and the next paragraph is indebted.

9. See Soren Kierkegaard, *Fear and Trembling*, trans. W. Lowrie (New York: Doubleday Anchor Books, 1954), who says of Abraham: "He believed by virtue of the absurd . . ." (p. 46).

10. Maimonides, *The Book of Knowledge*, trans. M. Hyamson (Jerusalem: Feldheim, 1974), Repentance, 10.6. Conversely, the more a person loves the Creator, the more he will want to sing His praises, which is an incentive to acquire knowledge of His creation.

11. "For it is implanted in man that in all things touching the glory of God, he has the capacity of being merciless to his own body and its emotions and to show no compassion [even] for his wife and children." Malbim, *Commentary on the Torah*, I, 246. See Lev. 10:1–3.

12. The contention that the universe created itself is also contradicted by the first law of thermodynamics, that of total energy conservation.

13. Now, without intending any offense, it should be noted that although Islam acknowledges the absolute unity and sovereignty of God, its attitude regarding religion and politics is opportunistic both in theory and in practice. Following al Ghazzala, Islam's leading theologian of the Middle Ages, Moslems sacralize the principle of national cohesion around whoever happens to seize or gain control of state power, usually a military commander or the head of some party. To this extent, therefore, religion is subordinate to politics, but under a facade of theological purity. Of course, the facade does impose some religious constraints on the *imam*, the head of state, who may sometimes have to appease the *ulamas*, the Muslim clerics. But it is a mistake to regard an Islamic state as a theocracy per se. The truth of the matter is that an Islamic state is or tends to be a clerical state, a state that has an official religion, but that is actually under the control of a political head. Stated another way, a clerical state is one in which the official religion has been politicized, which means that those who run the state use religion for political ends.

Reinforcing this phenomenon in Islam is the well-known fact that the *jihad*, or holy war is a religious obligation. This religious obligation raises into prominence and into eventual political preeminence the military, i.e., a profession whose religiosity tends to be superficial. In other words, the bellicose character of Islam makes it a political-military religion, one which stands in stark contrast to the apolitical character of Christianity. Whereas the latter preaches "love your enemy," the former teaches the contrary. Indeed, scholars have noted that "the mutilation, dismemberment, and ritualistic uses of slain enemies are widespread among Arab peoples." See Gil AlRoy, *Behind the Middle East Conflict* (New York: Capricorn Books, 1975), p. 93. In this connection, consider the following report in the *Jerusalem Post*, Magazine Section (Oct 21, 1983), p. L: "In a ceremony marking the 10th anniversary of the Yom Kippur War, Syrian militia trainees [men and women] put on a show for Syrian President Hafez Assad. Martial music reached a crescendo as Syrian teenage girls suddenly bit into live snakes [some four feet long], repeatedly tearing off flesh and spitting it out as blood ran down their chins. As Assad applauded, the girls then attached the snakes to sticks and grilled them over fire, eating them triumphantly. Others [militiamen] then proceeded to strangle puppies and drink their blood." This televised spectacle was monitored in Israel. The present writer witnessed the snake ceremony on Israel TV. The puppy ceremony was not broadcast because of its more gruesome character. The ceremony's symbolism is fairly obvious. But all this is unexceptional among Moslems and suggests that Islam has not entirely overcome paganism, despite its own contribution to the elimination of primitive idolatry in Africa and Asia.

Finally, let it be noted that there is reason to believe that the great Arab philosophers of the Middle Ages, Alfarabi, Avicenna, and Averroes, were really Greeks in Muslim dress. See *Alfarabi's Philosophy of Plato and Aristotle*, trans. M. Mahdi (Ithaca, N.Y.: Cornell University Press, 1969), pp. 6–9. *Averroes on Plato's "Republic"* (Ithaca, N.Y.: Cornell University Press, 1974).

9

Beyond the Secular Mind

It is a remarkable fact that the Hebrew word *anav*, usually translated as "humble" or "meek," is the only adjective used in the Bible of Israel to describe the man Moses.[1] The word appears in Numbers 12:3. "Now the man Moses was very humble (*anav*), above all the men that were on the face of the earth."

It is strange that the Torah uses no other adjective to characterize a man so extraordinary as Moses. After all, though supremely humble, Moses has also been called the wisest man that ever lived—and not only by Jews.[2] Yet we find in the Torah of Moses not the lofty adjective "wise" but only the lowly *anav* to characterize this greatest teacher and lawgiver of mankind.

One might conclude from the foregoing that humility ranks above wisdom in the Torah order of values. The trouble is that such words as "humility" or "modesty" fail to capture the meaning of *anava*, a concept that radically distinguishes Judaism not only from Christianity, but from Hellenism. Moreover, a brief survey of the status of "humility" in the philosophic tradition, beginning with Socrates, will reveal that the soul of modern man is still rooted in ancient Athens. Indeed, it is no exaggeration to say that Jerusalem versus Athens remains as ever the paramount issue of mankind, an issue that may be illuminated by the almost unknown concept of *anava*.

Humility is commonly believed to be a precondition of wisdom. This opinion has been rejected by the philosophic tradition at least as early as the Platonic Socrates. True, in the *Apology*, as in other Platonic dialogues, Socrates readily professes ignorance regarding the most important questions of human life. But this is not *anava* so much as modesty couched in Socratic irony and rooted in restrained skepticism. Upon his death as portrayed in the *Phaedo*, Socrates is described as the "noblest," "wisest," and "most just" man of his time. No Greek would be praised for being humble.

To the contrary, Aristotle extols pride—*megalopsychia*—or magnanimity as the adornment of the virtues. The magnanimous man is one who deems himself worthy of great things, especially honor, and not out of vulgar conceit but from a just estimate of his merit and deserts. He deserves much because he "possesses greatness in every virtue." Aristotle's ideas about the magnanimous man may be summarized as follows:

The object with which the magnanimous man is particularly concerned is honor. Great honors accorded by persons of worth will afford him pleasure in a moderate degree; he believes he is receiving only what belongs to him, or even less, for no honor can be adequate to the merits of perfect virtue. Honors rendered by common people he will utterly despise. In fact, he does not care much even about receiving honor, which is the greatest of external goods. Rather, he is fond of conferring benefits, but ashamed to receive them.

It is also characteristic of the magnanimous man to be haughty toward men of position and fortune. Furthermore, he cares more for truth than for what other people think. Hence he will speak frankly and openly, since concealment shows timidity. As a consequence, he is bound to make enemies. Nevertheless, he does not bear a grudge, for it is not the mark of greatness of soul to recall things against people, especially wrongs they have done you, but rather to overlook them.

Clearly, humility has no place in the soul of Magnanimous Man, whose description may be taken for that of the philosopher. Indeed, for the Olympian philosopher, humility is a vice.

Consider, now, the modern attitude toward humility, an attitude which supposedly originates with Machiavelli, but which is actually rooted in the pagan philosophers of Greece. We have already seen that Machiavelli omits humility from the qualities for which men, especially rulers, are praised or blamed. Humility is the virtue of the weak. Hobbes goes further: he substitutes for humility "dejection," to which he opposes pride or "vain-glory." Significantly, Hobbes defines "dejection" as "grief, from opinion of want of power."[3] He thereby prepares the way for Spinoza's conception of humility.

In his *Ethics*, Spinoza writes: "Though dejection is the emotion contrary to pride, yet the dejected man is very nearly akin to the proud man."[4] Before considering his explanation of this remarkable statement—the likes of which might be found in Freud—it should be made explicit that, for Spinoza, "Humility is not a virtue, or does not arise from reason" (Prop. LIII). Humility is pain accompanied by the idea of one's weakness or one's power of activity being thwarted. Inasmuch as "pain," according to Spinoza, "is a transition of a man from a greater to a lesser perfection" (Prop. LIX, Def. III), humility, far from being a virtue, is an obstacle to human perfection.

This perhaps startling but logically unavoidable conclusion may also be deduced from Spinoza's conception of what he calls "self-approval." "Self-approval may also arise from reason . . ." (Prop. LII). It is "pleasure arising from a man's contemplation of himself and his power of action" (ibid., Proof). To this extent, and to this extent only, Spinoza's definition of self-approval is consistent with Aristotle's understanding of pride. This may be called "rational" as opposed to "nonrational" pride because Spinoza defines pride as "pleasure arising from man's overestimation of himself" (Prop. LVII, Proof). But given his definition of pleasure as "the transition of a man from a lesser to a greater perfection," it follows that nonrational pride is conducive to human perfection! Surely Spinoza does not intend such a conclusion. Hence it would be wise to assume that when he speaks of self-approval, he is using the term as a euphemism for pride.

Bearing this in mind, we read: "Self-approval is in reality the highest object for which one can hope. For . . . no one endeavors to preserve his being for the sake of any ulterior object, and, as the approval is more and more fostered and strengthened by praise . . . fame becomes the most powerful incitement to action . . ." (Prop. LII, Note). Viewed in this light, humility is contrary to human nature, that is, to what is truly human.

This seemingly paradoxical conclusion requires for its clarification some understanding of Spinoza's secularized conception of virtue on the one hand, and of human nature on the other, both of which he largely derives from Machiavelli and Hobbes. Like Machiavelli, Spinoza identifies virtue with power. "By virtue (*virtus*) and power I mean the same thing; that is . . . virtue, in so far as it has the power of effecting what can be understood by the laws of that nature" (Def. VIII). For Spinoza (like Hobbes) the fundamental law of nature is self-preservation.[5] "The effort for self-preservation is the first and only foundation of virtue" (Prop. XXII, cor.). Accordingly, "the more a man endeavors, and is able to preserve his own being, the more endowed with virtue, and, consequently in so far as he neglects his own being, he is wanting in power" (Prop. XX). By preserving one's own being Spinoza means more than physical self-preservation. He has in view nothing less than the contemporary notion of self-actualization. Thus was developed the philosophic doctrine of egoism, a doctrine utterly opposed to *anava* and to its superficial renderings such as humility or modesty.[6]

We can now understand why Spinoza regards the dejected man as very nearly akin to the proud man. "For inasmuch as his pain arises from a comparison between his own infirmity and other men's power or virtue, it will be removed, or, in other words, he will feel pleasure, if his imagination be occupied in contemplating other men's faults . . ." (Prop. XVII, Note). Humility may therefore be understood as pained or frustrated pride, which means that there is no such thing as genuine humility.[7]

From Spinoza's understanding of humility it follows that the very quality that the Torah explicitly regards as most distinctive of Moses is irrational, contrary to man's nature and to human perfection. Moses' humility, it would then seem, resulted from lack of power, from an inability to enhance his own being, that is, to achieve self-actualization. His humility, the skeptic would conclude, was nothing more than thwarted pride or ambition, a facade for a frustrated ego. Clearly, either Spinoza's conception of human nature as a whole is distorted, or we are in need of a very different understanding of *anava*. A very different understanding of *anava*, however, may lead us to a conception of human nature, in comparison with which Spinoza's, viewed without prejudice, will appear commonplace, not to say narrow or parochial.

An incisive treatment of humility is to be found in the twelfth-century work of Bachya ben Joseph ibn Paquda, *Duties of the Heart*.[8] Unlike Spinoza, Bachya distinguishes three types of humility. The first is common to man and certain species of animals: patient endurance of injuries which are borne only because the sufferer lacks the intelligence to avert them. The second type of humility "is that exhibited by an individual toward other human beings who dominate him or who lack aught of what others possess and is in need of" (73). Notice that these two types of humility conform to Spinoza's view of the subject: the first does not spring from reason, while the second results from impotence. Neither type, for Bachya, represents true humility so much as ignorance and spiritual poverty. From this Torah man's perspective, Spinoza was dealing with counterfeit currency, attacking straw men. Writes Bachya: "Humility in the true sense is that quality which comes into being after the soul's exaltation, when it has raised itself from the condition which it shares with brute creatures and their low qualities, and when, on account of its superior wisdom, spiritual nobility and definite knowledge of qualities that are good and those that are ignoble, it is too elevated to be put in the same class with the dispositions of the lower classes. When, finally, to this superiority, humility and lowliness have been added, this humility is a praiseworthy quality" (75). For Bachya true humility is a result of superior wisdom and spiritual nobility. The superior wisdom involves recognition of God and knowledge of His creation; the spiritual nobility follows therefrom, that is, from an understanding of man's exalted role in creation. Here we touch upon the third and highest type of humility, which is humility toward the Creator (77). What this humility ultimately consists in will be discussed later.

Although humility for Bachya involves self-depreciation, this self-depreciation coexists with intellectual and moral superiority, but not self-approval. We have here a much more complex and subtle conception of human nature than that found in Spinoza as well as in Aristotle (indeed, in the Greco-Christian tradition). Let us see.

It is common knowledge that the greater a person's intelligence, the greater his ego or the more difficult it is for him to be humble. The reason is simple enough. The power of man's intellect is what most distinguishes him from brute creation. And because intelligence is generally deemed superior to any other virtue, it receives the most praise and honor.[9] Pride of intellect is the human vice par excellence. The coexistence of great intelligence and pride is therefore rather common; the coexistence of great intelligence and humility is very rare. Spinoza's *Ethics* is tailored for ordinary and conceited men. We are in quest of *anava*.

Suppose a distinguished professor of philosophy were to say: I'm a mental pygmy compared to Aristotle. This might be indicative of modesty—although comparing himself to such an intellectual giant as Aristotle smacks of conceit—but it would not be *anava*. On the other hand, suppose an obscure rabbi were to say: I know that Aristotle is one of the greatest minds in history. I have read all his extant treatises on logic, natural science, psychology, metaphysics, ethics, politics, and of course his rhetoric and poetics. I know these may be regarded as the first systematic treatments of their respective subjects. Nevertheless, and quite apart from any subsequent progress that may have been made in these disciplines, I must confess that I found Aristotle's knowledge of man and the universe rather superficial. Hardly anyone would mistake such a claim for humility or modesty; yet it might not be inconsistent with *anava*.

The Torah conception of humility, or rather of *anava*, differs fundamentally from that of the philosopher as well as from the Christian view that was under attack by Machiavelli and Spinoza. Like Aristotle's magnanimous or great-souled man, the man of *anava* knows his true worth or value: He may know that he is the wisest or greatest of men.[10] But unlike Aristotle's paragon of virtue, not only does he not want or seek honor for his wisdom or greatness—although he knows that others are obliged to honor him—but he does not even regard himself as ultimately deserving any credit for his wisdom or greatness. This self-depreciation does not stem from a lack of power or inability to achieve self-realization. It is not symptomatic of pain resulting from a frustrated ego—Spinoza's view of Christian humility. It originates not in any emotion but in the cognition or apprehension of certain facts accessible even to ordinary men so long as they have not been corrupted or misled. Let us return to Bachya.

Bachya raises the question of how humility may arise in men. Let us summarize his exposition (89–93). He begins by reminding us that a human being originates in a malodorous drop. "Lord, what is man, that You should regard him" (Ps. 144:3)? Surely it is enough to make a man humble when he reflects upon the trials to which he is subjected while on earth—hunger and thirst, cold and heat, sickness and accidents, grief and anxieties, from which he is relieved only upon death. Or let him consider the transient character of his existence, how swiftly death comes, how his desires and hopes are cut off in the grave, the light of his countenance gone, his body turning into corruption. As King David wrote: "But I am a worm, and no man" (Ps. 22:7). So will he feel when he observes the reverses in human affairs, how nations rise and fall, and how peoples perish: "Like sheep they are laid in the grave" (Ps. 49:15). Finally, when he compares what he knows with the vastness of the unknown, humility would seem to be more natural to man than to any animal, and therefore a consequence of what is distinctively human—reason. Nor is this all.

Again, the wise man who possesses *anava* neither seeks nor desires any credit for his wisdom. He knows that he did not create language, without which he would understand nothing. He knows that without the accumulated knowledge transmitted to him by tradition, by his parents and teachers, he would be less than a savage or an ignoramus. It may be objected: But surely the wise man deserves credit for utilizing his resources, studying diligently, and subordinating everything to the pursuit of truth. Perhaps; but the question of whether he deserves any credit for his wisdom is known only to God, Who alone can evaluate the use he has made of his potentialities. Because he cannot determine the extent of the latter, he cannot know whether he deserves any credit for his intellectual and moral accomplishments. Recognizing this, the wise man is humble even with respect to those who are manifestly his inferiors—humble with them yet knowing they are obliged to defer to his wisdom. In this *anava* between man and man, Moses had no equal. In fact, the verse wherein he is described as the most humble man on the face of the earth occurs immediately after Miriam and Aaron inveigh against his having separated himself physically from the Cushite woman (Num. 12:1–2). In the sequel, after God defines the unique and superior character of Moses' prophetic power and afflicts Mirian with leprosy, the wisest and humblest of men pleads with God to heal her.

We have arrived at one of the two basic sources of *anava*: ignorance of the measure of our God-given potentialities and therefore of whether we have used them to the fullest extent possible. (The other source is the awareness that we cannot know our Creator.) This knowledge of ignorance (which, contrary to Spinoza, springs from reason) should render us doubly humble with respect to others, for we are also ignorant of the natural endowments of others and the use they have made of them. Recognition of natural inequality requires us to defer to our superiors in wisdom; yet our superiors cannot rightly claim any credit for their wisdom. "If you have learned much Torah, do not claim any credit for yourself, because you were created for this purpose" (*Ethics* 2:9).

The wise man who possesses *anava* does not need praise or honor from others. To this extent he is more independent than Aristotle's magnanimous man. What then shall we say of him in comparison with Spinoza?

Let us recall two related aspects of Spinoza's teaching: (1)"self-approval is the highest object for which one can hope," such that (2) "fame becomes the most powerful incentive to action." The man of *anava*—the Torah man—would see in this an absurd incongruity. On the one hand, the statement that self-approval is the highest object for which one can hope is a tacit denial of God, the Supreme Judge, a denial leading to self-deification. On the other hand, inasmuch as this attitude of auto-intoxication cannot be sustained by men of flesh and blood, the desire for fame will be activated and will render Spinoza's egoist pathetically if not pathologically dependent on the approval or good opinion of others. This leads to the kind of social or democratic psychology fore-shadowed by Hobbes. The following passage was anticipated earlier:

The *value*, or WORTH of a man, is as of all other things, his price; that is to say, so much as would be given for the use of his power [and knowledge, for Hobbes, is power]: and therefore is not absolute; but a thing dependent on the need and judgment of another. . . . And as in other things, so in men, not the seller, but the buyer determines the price. For let a man, as most men do, rate themselves at the highest value they can; yet their true value is no more than it is esteemed by others.[11]

Hobbes calls this man's "DIGNITY." This kind of psychology or concep-tion of human nature may in the end be more conducive to humility than to pride, but certainly not to *anava*. It discourages the pursuit of any wisdom devoid of value in the marketplace or unresponsive to the law of supply and demand. As the Torah man would see it, Spinoza's philosophy, like that of Hobbes, short-circuits the intellect or closes the mind.

Leaving aside the esoteric distinctions between "wisdom" (*hokhma*) and "understanding" (*bina*), two prerequisites of "knowledge" (*da'at*), the Torah view is that wisdom is not less a precondition of *anava* than is *anava* a precondition of wisdom.[12] According to the Talmud, before one can attain to *anava*, one must undergo rigorous intellectual and moral discipline. *Anava* is achieved only after study, precision, external purity, abstemiousness, internal purity, and holiness (*Avoda Zara* 20b). Once achieved it leads to the intellectual apprehension of truths inaccessible to those who lack *anava*. Lacking *anava*, a person could no more grasp these truths than could countless Ph.D.'s master quantum mechanics without knowledge of mathematical physics. The more *anava* a man has, the more wisdom he acquires, and the less importance he attaches to his intellectual accomplishments. Because he desires, and recognizes that he deserves, neither praise nor honor for his wisdom—thanks to his *anava* he needs neither self-approval nor the approval of others— he becomes psychologically receptive to other dimensions of wisdom.

Indeed, the psychological consequences of *anava* are profound. Desiring no credit for his knowledge, deeds, and efforts, an *anav* person has no ego problem. He readily acknowledges and defers to men of superior wisdom. No one is better disposed and more prompt to admit error, to surrender long-held and deeply cherished convictions once they are shown to be inadequate or erroneous. (Plato regarded this as the mark of the philosopher [*Republic* 503c].) It was with alacrity that Moses accepted Aaron's correction regarding certain sin-offerings (Exod. 31:3). And how readily Moses hearkened to the advice of Jethro, his father-in-law, when the latter suggested the delegation of judicial power to expedite the dispensation of justice (Exod. 18:13–25). "Reprove a wise man, and he will love you. Give to a wise man, and he will be yet wiser" (Prov. 9:9). Precisely because the man of *anava* wants no credit for his wisdom, he is the least dogmatic and the most receptive to learning. At the same time, because he desires neither praise nor honor, he will not be afraid to tell people the truth even at the risk of arousing their resentment. Courage and wisdom unite in the *anav* man.[13]

The Torah man regards his wisdom as a special gift bestowed upon him by his Creator, a gift but also an obligation. As Bachya observes, while the man of *anava* is obliged to increase his rational and received knowledge, he is also obliged to transmit it to others. He is a receptacle but also prolocutor of truth. Because he reveres God and is grateful for the exceptional talent with which he has been endowed, he cultivates loftiness of soul while looking upon his own accomplishments as petty. And so he strives for something higher (101). The problem arises: Can humility and pride coexist?

Bachya distinguishes two kinds of pride. "One sort is a man's pride in his body and conditions, or in all things that further its well-being. The other kind is pride in one's spiritual qualities, in wisdom employed and good deeds performed in the service of God. Any pride that has its origin in physical excellencies drives humility out of the heart, and it is impossible that they should dwell together, being mutually repellent" (113).

Now, with Spinoza in mind, consider what Bachya says of pride in spiritual excellencies. This kind of pride "falls into two divisions—one blameworthy, the other praiseworthy. Despicable it is that a person should pride himself on his wisdom, or a righteous man on his good work. The result is that his wisdom or righteousness becomes magnified in his sight, so that he is satisfied with what he has already accomplished in these regards and thinks that the good name and praise that he has gained among his fellow-men are enough for him" (113). Not only will this lead to complacency, but it "will induce him to despise human beings, abhor and speak disparagingly of them, depreciate the wise and the great of his generation, and glory in his colleagues' limitations and ignorance" (ibid.). Here the proud man who takes pleasure in the limitations of others corresponds to Spinoza's dejected or humble man who takes pleasure in contemplating other men's faults. Bachya would say that Spinoza's dejected man is not truly humble, that his humbleness is akin to a despicable form of pride. Clearly, Spinoza's understanding of both qualities is very narrow in comparison to that of Bachya. We now have to examine the praiseworthy form of pride.

"Laudable is the pride of the wise man in his wisdom or the righteous man in his work, when it is an expression of his gratitude for the Creator's great goodness in conferring these favors upon him, and of his joy therein, and when it induces him to increase these endowments and be zealous in their (right) use" (ibid.). This kind of pride can coexist with humbleness or *anava* because the proud man who possesses *anava* will "rejoice with his colleagues, be solicitous about the honor due them, speak in praise of them, love them, defend their cause and be heedful to show them respect. All his own good deeds will seem to him but a few, and he will always be laboring to increase them" (115). True pride and true humility can coexist in the same soul because both result from the knowledge that all good things come from the Creator. No more beautiful expression of the Jewish synthesis of humility and pride will be found than in these words of King David:

Lord, our Master . . .
When I behold Your heavens, the work of Your fingers,
The moon and the stars, which You have established,
What is man's worth that You should be mindful of him? . . .
Yet you have made him a little less than God.
You have crowned him with dignity and majesty.
You have made him the ruler of the works of Your hands.
You have put everything under his feet and control . . .
Lord, our Master,
How powerful is Your Name and Glory in this world (Ps. 8:4–
   10).[14]

Let us consider these words most carefully.

"When I behold Your heavens, the work of Your fingers, / The moon and the stars"—these words do not glorify nature (as in Greek philosophy) but the Creator of nature. Moreover, King David is not comparing man to the moon and the stars. When he says to the Lord (referring to the Ineffable Name, not to *Elohim*), "You have made him a little less than God," he thereby affirms that man is the most important essence in the universe; for having been created in the image of God (*Elohim*), man possesses intellect and free will, the highest qualities in creation. King David could therefore say: "You have crowned him with dignity and majesty. / You have made him the ruler of the works of Your hands." But when he adds, "Lord, our Master, / How powerful is Your Name and Glory in this world," we are here given to learn that the glory of the Creator is manifested through the intellect of man.[15] This noblest synthesis of *anava* and pride reveals how Judaism extols the intellect without succumbing to its deification, the highest tendency of the secular mind, more precisely, of the philosophic tradition originating in Athens. But then, as we saw in Bachya, true *anava* presupposes man's exaltation, specifically, the exaltation of man's intellect, the ultimate heights of which can be achieved only by the Torah man.

CONCLUSION

The comparison in this chapter between the mentality of the Torah man and that of some of the world's greatest philosophers has revealed the psychological and intellectual limitations of the secular mind. Together with the previous chapter's study of the Patriarch Abraham, a model of man has been constructed that transcends Aristotle's paragon of virtue, the Magnanimous Man, in comparison to which modernity has nothing to offer.

With that model in mind, it will be easier to reveal the limited rationality of the classics, to say nothing of the moderns. This will be done by showing how the Torah transcends the contradictions of mankind.

NOTES

1. The following analysis is based on *Jerusalem vs. Athens*, ch. 2. Note that the noun form of *anav* is *anava*. See Exod. 2:2 where the infant Moses is called "good," and Exod. 11:2 where Moses is referred to as "very great in the land of Egypt. . . ."

2. Numenius of Syria, a gentile philosopher of the second century and a forerunner of the neo-Platonic school, regarded Moses as the first and greatest of the philosophers. See Isaac Herzog, *Judaism: Law and Ethics*, pp. 101–102.

3. Hobbes, *Leviathan*, pp. 36, 46.

4. Benedict de Spinoza, *Ethics*, trans. R. H. M. Elwes (New York: Tudor Publishing Co., n.d.). Part IV, Prop. LVII, Note. Unless otherwise indicated, all

further references to the *Ethics* are from Part IV and will be cited between parentheses in the text.

5. See Benedict de Spinoza, *Works*, 2 vols., trans. R. H. M. Elwes (New York: Dover Publications, 1951), vol. 1, *Political Treatise*, ch. 3. sect. 18, which is drawn largely from Hobbes's *Leviathan*.

6. One should not be misled by Spinoza's saying that "the mind's highest good is knowledge of God, and the mind's highest virtue is to know God" (Prop. XXVIII). Spinoza's God is nothing more than nature, if not merely a reflection of his own ego. Perhaps not even congenial Holland would have tolerated atheism unless garbed in pantheism. Suffice to point out one of Spinoza's many deliberate contradictions on the subject. Thus, on the one hand he writes, "Love toward God is the highest good we can seek under the guidance of reason" (V, Prop. XX, Proof), while on the other hand he rejects reverence, along with humility and repentance, as a virtue (Prop. LIV). Finally, when Spinoza says that "the love of God toward man, and the intellectual love of the mind toward God are identical" (V, Prop. XXXVI, cor.), one must conclude that the so-called God-intoxicated philosopher was auto-intoxicated.

7. This is precisely the skeptical position taken by Hume, *Treatise of Human Nature*, Part III, sect. ii. Spinoza's rejection of humility and repentance as irrational anticipates Freud's view of guilt as pathological.

8. Bachya ben Joseph ibn Paquda, *Duties of the Heart*, 2 vols., trans. M. Hyamson (Jerusalem: Jerusalem Publishers, 1970). The Hebrew text was translated from the Arabic by Ibn Tibbon, who uses the word *hakhnaa* for humility, rather than *anava*. All further references to Bachya's work are to Vol. II, with page numbers appearing between parentheses in the text.

9. See Chaim M. Luzzatto, *The Path of the Just*, 2d ed., trans. S. Silberstein (Jerusalem: Feldheim, 1980), p. 285.

10. Here as elsewhere I am indebted to the eminent Torah scholar Dr. Chaim Zimmerman.

11. Hobbes, *Leviathan*, p. 57.

12. See Rashi on Exod. 31:3. According to Dr. Zimmerman, *hokhma* (wisdom) involves creative insight, new ideas. *Bina* (understanding) involves the logical (or mathematical) development or application of such ideas. *Da'at* (knowledge) refers to a cognitive decision that such an idea is true. But inasmuch as these are not finite (or quantifiable) concepts, their boundaries are necessarily vague, i.e., they shade into each other.

13. The above exposition accords well with the following statement of Rabbi J. B. Soloveitchik: "Halakhic man does not quiver before any man; he does not seek out compliments, nor does he require public approval. If he sees that there are fewer and fewer men of distinguished spiritual rank about, then he wraps himself in his mantle and hies away to the four cubits of the Halakhah" (*Halakhic Man*, p. 89).

14. This rendering is adapted from Chaim Zimmerman, *Torah and Reason*, pp. 160–161.

15. Ibid.

IV

BEYOND THE CONTRADICTIONS OF MANKIND

10

On the Limited Rationality of the West

THE CLASSICS

Reflecting on the universe and man, philosophers from the pre-Socratics to the present have been bedeviled by various contradictions that they have sought to overcome, in vain. These contradictions are rooted in a single error, namely, that the universe is uncreated. Today this ancient error, to which the failure of secularism may be ultimately traced, is dividing mankind between random and regimented individuals.

One of the most important contradictions in question is that between theory and practice.[1] Consider, again the distinction between the best regime in theory and the best regime in practice referred to in Chapter 1. This has ever been the central theme of political philosophy, as well as the despair of serious men.

When Aristotle inquired into the best regime in theory, he did not have in view some utopia. He raised the intelligent question of what is the best regime that reasonable men can reasonably wish for. Such a regime would of course require wise and virtuous rulers, as well as a deferential people disposed to moderation and justice. It would require fertile land with adequate natural resources. (The object here is self-sufficiency, minimizing intercourse with foreign nations.) The land should also have easily defensible borders so that no large standing army would be necessary. For the primary concern of the best regime in theory is internal perfection, not external glory; peace, not war, would be its foreign policy. Nevertheless, Aristotle sanctions war for the purpose of acquiring slaves of good quality. Though not hard-hearted, Aristotle was no sentimentalist. He presupposed, as a more or less permanent condition of man, an economy based on scarcity. Slaves would therefore be necessary to perform household chores and other menial tasks to enable gentlemen of leisure, the rulers of the best regime, to cultivate intellectual and moral excellence. Therein is the reason why persons engaged in manual occupations (the large majority) are excluded from citizenship in Aristotle's best regime—kingship or aristocracy—which alone can cultivate men of high quality as a matter of public policy. (How different from the "nation of philosophers" described by Aristotle's disciple, Theophrastus.)

Now one can better understand why Aristotle thought that the coming into existence of the best regime in theory would depend very much on chance. Aristotle had modest expectations of mankind. He deplored radicalism. So did Plato, despite his having written the most radical work on politics, *The Republic*. Read with care, *The Republic* is an anti-utopian book. It reveals, in a most subtle and profound way, the limitations of political life. The aim of political life is justice. But injustice among men will never be overcome until philosophers become kings or kings become philosophers. Unfortunately, not only do genuine philosophers abhor the idea of devoting their lives to politics, ruling the unwise, but the unwise will never defer to wisdom.

Consequently, if the best regime or city is to come into existence, then, as already noted, philosophers must be compelled to rule on the one hand, while those over the age of ten must be expelled from the city on the other.[2] This hardly conforms to justice. Besides, justice requires complete dedication to the common good. Such dedication cannot be achieved unless the mine-thine distinction is eliminated. Hence Plato's communism, his fantastic community of wives and children; for the mine-thine distinction begins with the private family. But not quite: It originates with the body, the ultimately private. You can share your thoughts with others; you cannot share your arms and legs, your heart and brain. Plato's best regime, his "city in speech," is not only impossible, it is meant to be seen as such by careful readers. Such readers may be brought to the recognition that political life is base compared to the life of philosophy.[3]

Here one may discern the link between Hellenism and the other worldliness of religion. For the Greeks, man is not the highest thing in the universe. This is why practical wisdom or politics, which is concerned with things human and variable, is inferior to philosophic wisdom.[4] Therein is the dichotomy between the *vita activa* and the *vita contemplativa*, prompting certain sensitive types to abandon humanity for a more refined world. This dichotomy is foreign to the Torah, wherein man not only stands at the pinnacle of creation, but is charged (in Gen. 2:28) with the duty of improving and perfecting it.

Clearly the inevitable disparity between the best regime in theory and the best regime in practice is rooted in Plato's and Aristotle's denial of a providential God. As cosmopolitan denizens of a decayed city-state, they could not conceive of a God-created and God-bearing nation whose ultimate purpose is to unite "theory" and "practice," law and life. Speculation about their meetings with Jews aside, it was beyond Plato's and Aristotle's great intellects to see how the free-willed acts of men and the multifarious practices of nations are dynamically and logically interrelated in a world-historical program.[5] And no wonder: such a conception of history runs contrary to the classical cosmology of an uncreated, finite, and therefore cyclical universe in which are to be found, on planet earth, eternal species, including man—a rational animal going nowhere.

It follows from this (now untenable) cosmology that human history is endlessly repetitive. This is exactly what Ecclesiastes indicates in saying there is nothing new under the sun—but in a book of the Bible wherein only the divine name of *Elohim* appears, the name associated with nature.[6]

Borrowed from the East, the cyclicality of the Athenian cosmology renders human history meaningless or absurd. Plato goes so far as to intimate, in his allusion to the myth of Sisyphus at the end of the *Apology*, that there is an ineluctable injustice in the universe: Socrates will again and again have to take hemlock for betraying a philanderer like Zeus rather than philosophy.

This helps to explain what philosophy and history (which correspond to theory and practice) mean to the classics. Philosophy alone enables Cognitive (i.e., Secular) Man to transcend the meaningless cyclicality of history. Whereas history involves the particular and the coming into being and passing away of things, philosophy enables man to grasp the universal and the immutable. This is why philosophy (even poetry) is higher than history, why theory is superior in dignity to practice. Yet it is precisely because of their one-sided longing for the universal and the immutable that the classics have no place for individuality and creativity.

In contrast, individuality and creativity are of the essence of Judaism. Indeed, not only is the individual the highest thing in creation, but as noted earlier, he is called upon to be creative in a finite way as God is creative in an infinite way. Of course, I am speaking of the righteous individual, whose creativity consists in revealing, in new ways, the infinite wisdom, power, and kindliness of God in every aspect of creation. It is a fundamental principle of Torah Judaism that the universe was created for the righteous man who is not only pious—there are pious ignoramuses—but a man of supreme intellect. For as was seen in Psalm 8, God's greatness is made known only through the intellect of man. It needs to be emphasized, however, that the centrality of the individual in the Torah is inseparable from the idea of a personal and providential God, the God Who not only created laws of nature, but laws of history. Consistent therewith, man was created not only to master and perfect nature, but to master and perfect himself such that human history would exhibit joyful wisdom rather than miserable folly, justice and peace rather than wickedness and war. That human folly and wickedness will nonetheless serve a felicitous end by virtue of the (infinite transformation) laws of history is a basic tenet of Judaism. "The wicked will prepare and the righteous shall wear" (Job 27:17).

The classical mind was closed to this awesome idea. Put another way, a teleology of history was foreign to classical mentality. Plato and Aristotle made nature purposeful while making history purposeless. From this compounded error and contradiction all the inadequacies of classical political philosophy follow. Both philosophers praised justice, but neither had any grounds for justice, as Machiavelli discerned and made public.

It also follows that Plato and Aristotle, exemplars of Cognitive Man, are not the highest exemplars of rationality. The rationality of these greatest secular philosophers was limited by their failure to discover or recognize the God of Abraham.

THE IRRATIONAL CHARACTER OF MODERNITY

In contrasting the modern view of theory and practice, it will be necessary to ignore distinctions that are almost as various as the number of philosophers. Only the main thrust of things will receive attention.

Unlike the classics, the moderns subordinated theory, or what professes to be theory, to practice. They accepted the dogma of an uncreated universe, but thanks to Galileo's mathematization of nature they no longer saw the universe as finite.[7] The reason is this. When Galileo writes of mathematics, he means Euclidian geometry. Unlike Riemannian space, which is curved, Euclidian space is flat (and homogeneous). Hence, if "the book of nature is written in geometrical characters," the universe is infinite.[8]

Now it so happens, and as the classics understood, an infinite universe—infinite in the conventional sense—is irrational.[9] In such a universe the center would coincide with the circumference, straight with curvilinear, motion with rest. The world-image of any observer would depend on his place, and no place would have any privileged position. Everything would be relative to everything else. Not only would the earth no longer be the center of the universe, but the terrestrial world, regarded contemptuously by Plato and Aristotle, would have the same status as the heavenly spheres. All this was irrational and intolerable to the deified intellect of the classics.

For the moderns, however, an infinite universe opens the door to infinite possibilities, to a new conception of man and history, to unlimited creativity and individuality, indeed, to the radical idea of progress.

In an infinite universe endless novelty is possible rather than endless repetition. Moreover, an infinite universe does not entail eternal species. In a curious turn of thought, the moderns accepted the biblical account that man had an origin in time, but denied that his original state was one of paradisaical perfection. Not only did man begin his career on earth as a primitive savage, but he had to work by the sweat of his brow, enslaved to the vicissitudes of a penurious nature. Man's progress is to be attributed to various natural disasters, such as famine and drought, acting upon his instinct of self-preservation, prompting cerebral exertion, leading to the invention of tools, thereby facilitating survival and, for the few, leisure. Thus did arts develop, and later philosophy and science. But now that we have insight into man's naturalistic origin, human progress need no longer be fortuitous, the result of blind necessity.

To be more precise: We now see—or so moderns are wont to believe—that human nature is a product of history, of external, mechanical causes. Far from being fixed and permanent, human nature is plastic, infinitely malleable and perfectible. Could there be a greater affirmation of the possibility of unbounded individuality and creativity? But given this insight into history and human nature, it should be possible to control man's environment and liberate mankind from natural necessity and historical accident. And so it appeared. For in modern science and technology, human reason, it seemed, had reached a level of development such that man could look forward to mastering nature and shaping his own destiny. This means that reason can not only design the fully rational and just *political* order, but it can also bring this order into existence here and now.

Thus did the thinking of Rousseau and Marx inspire, respectively, the French and Bolshevik Revolutions. Thus did the so-called rationalism of the Enlightenment spawn totalitarianism, the greatest enemy of individuality and creativity!

The only kind of totalitarianism having philosophical pretensions is of course communism, and no other need be considered here. (In what follows, however, the concept of totalitarianism will be used independently of any scholarship on the subject.)[10]

The wicked motives of men aside, totalitarianism is an attempt to overcome the dichotomy as well as the disparity between the best regime in theory and the best regime in practice. This attempt may be traced to the Enlightenment. The Enlightenment transformed philosophy and science into handmaids of society for the purpose of eliminating human misery and injustice. To this end it was necessary to eradicate superstition, meaning religion, and to establish society on the basis of atheism. The religion of God was replaced by the religion of man, that is, humanism. All venerable beliefs and customs were to be relegated to the dust heap of history. At last man had come of age.

It has been called the Age of Reason. In fact, however, it was the age of democratic reason. The age promised *liberté*, *égalité*, and *fraternité*. The promise was engraved in solemn charters, such as the Declaration of the Rights of Man and of the *Citizen*. But note the distinction between the rights of man and the rights of the citizen. Marx did, and he saw that "the rights *of the citizen* are only the rights of the *member of civil society*, that is, of egoistic man, man separated from other men and from the community."[11] But so long as there is egoism there can be no fraternity.

Communism is the attempt to dissolve egoism and therefore the mine-thine distinction. Hitherto it was thought that the mine-thine distinction was a reflection of an unalterable characteristic of human nature, that of self-preference. But if human nature is malleable, as Rousseau maintained in his *Second Discourse (On the Origin of Inequality)*, it should be possible to eliminate self-preference. Rousseau did not go this far because, as noted earlier, the one thing he exalted in human nature was freedom, but which, he saw, would ever be in tension with virtue, meaning dedication to the common good. In other words, there would always be a tension between the individual and society, between happiness and morality. This is an inevitable dilemma of democracy, of which he was the candid philosopher. Rousseau was afraid to draw the ultimate logical conclusion of malleable man.

Marx was not. Ostensibly, he eliminated the dichotomies mentioned in the previous paragraph by singling out what for him was the unique and paramount characteristic of otherwise malleable man, namely this: man is the only animal possessing a "species consciousness," meaning a capacity to identify with mankind.[12] Egoism is merely a consequence of the scarcity of nature operating on the animal instinct of self-preservation. This scarcity will eventually be overcome by the scientific conquest of nature on the one hand, and by revolutionary violence on the other. History itself is the process of overcoming the dichotomy and disparity between theory and practice, a process issuing in universal communism.

Now, to reject the traditional view of a permanent human nature is to regard contemporary man as a transitional being more or less tainted by egoism. The only rational objective (given history's meaning) is to eliminate this egoism and usher in a world order where all men will be wholly animated by altruism. But inasmuch as there is nothing sacrosanct in the present, imperfect state of human nature, any and all means may be used to hasten mankind's conversion. The "best regime" in theory—a communist society—may thus be imposed on any people regardless of their beliefs, customs, and material circumstances. Not only Machiavelli, but history, impersonal and progressive, sanctions unmitigated violence and terror.[13]

Thus did terror or terrorism receive a license from historicism, the doctrine mentioned in Chapter 2. Marxist communism is a form of historicism. It has often been called an inverted religion, more specifically, an inversion of Christianity. There is some truth to this view, but it is misleading if not unjust. To be sure, like Christianity, communism is a proselytizing creed that spreads by means of propaganda and, when necessary and expedient, by coerced "conversions." But whereas Christianity deifies a human being as the agent of mankind's salvation, communism deifies a fraction of a human being by offering, via history, an economic solution to human suffering.

Couched in pseudoscientific language, communism is a form of secular mysticism. Its program of salvation through material abundance by means of scientific technology has no empirical foundation. In fact, it is falsified by the experience of mankind.

As was seen in Chapter 3, science and technology have not elevated the moral character of the nations wherein these pursuits have flourished. Nothing in mathematical physics has imbued men with concern for humanity or steeled them against tyranny.[14] (Certainly the Nazis and their accomplices, no small number of whom were scientists, showed little evidence of Marx's "species consciousness.") So long as the sciences are ethically neutral, they prompt men to serve any convenient master. Indeed, science makes tyrants all the more dangerous.

It would be a great mistake, however, to regard communist tyranny or totalitarianism as a thing-in-itself. The disastrous attempt of communism to overcome the dichotomy between theory and practice needs to be understood as a consequence of the intrinsic shortcomings of Western civilization in general, and of its present democratic dispensation in particular. As previously indicated, democracy has accentuated the dichotomies of individual and society, of church and state, of freedom and morality. The Marxist attempt to escape from these dichotomies has produced regimented men. The democratic entanglement in these dichotomies is producing random individuals, T. S. Eliot's "hollow men."

THE SUPREME RATIONALITY OF THE TORAH

We have seen that the classical dichotomy between theory and practice was based on the cosmology of an uncreated and finite universe. This cosmology reduces human life and history to endless repetition, a veritable tragicomedy. (Here I am reminded of Plato's *Symposium*, where Agathon, the tragedian, Aristophanes the comic poet, and of course the ironic Socrates are the only banqueters to remain awake and sober after the night-long festivities of that arcane dialogue.)

We also saw that the modern attempt to overcome the dichotomy under discussion is rooted in the cosmology of an uncreated and infinite universe. This cosmology liberates the individual and then enslaves him, either to his own passions or to those of others. It leads to random and regimented men.

If we adopt, however, the cosmology of a created universe, the cosmology of the Torah, all the antinomies heretofore mentioned are dissolved, and the path is opened to a new era of human greatness.

Given the Genesis account of creation, man is the only creature on earth that is endowed with intellect and free will. Whereas intellect makes theory possible, free will makes action or practice possible. Although theory seems to have a higher dignity in Judaism, it is only because learning is more likely to lead to practice than practice to learning.[15]

Nothing is more difficult than to cultivate the habit of independent and logical thought aimed at comprehending the truth regarding man and the universe. On the other hand, man is concerned not only with the true but with the good. The good is also true, but it is the true that should be. The true that should be is the proper object of man's will, the will to translate knowledge of the good into practice. No necessary dichotomy can exist between theory and practice because man is created in the image of God. The Torah, let us recall, "is something very close to you . . . so that you can do it." God, in His infinite graciousness (*Hesed*), would not give laws that cannot be readily fulfilled. Indeed, the laws of the Torah "are ways of pleasantness, and all her paths are paths of peace. She is a tree of life to them that lay hold upon her, and happy is everyone that holds her fast" (Prov. 3:18–19). These two verses deny the inevitability of two debilitating tensions of the philosophical tradition: truth versus civic virtue or morality, and morality versus happiness. A Torah view of the subject is necessary.

Long before Rousseau, Plato had indicated that the arts and sciences emerge from the vices of the soul, especially from the desire for unnecessary comforts. But the phenomenon was already anticipated and better explained in the biblical account of Cain's commercial and technologically oriented descendents, who exalted the works of their hands rather than the Creator of heaven and earth.[16] In any event, Rousseau focuses upon the subject in his *First Discourse*. The society dominated by the arts and sciences is riven with inequality, primarily because the talents needed to pursue them become grounds of distinction among men. Great sums of money and large numbers of mechanics, menial laborers, and traders are required to support such a society, whose life is one of vanity, egoism, and injustice.[17]

Discernible here are the two tensions in question. The first is the apparent conflict between the needs of science or the pursuit of theoretical knowledge on the one hand, and the needs of society on the other.[18] Science, including social science, requires the questioning of all received beliefs and values, for the aim of science is universal truth. In contrast, society requires the more or less unquestioned acceptance of its particular beliefs and values.

Now, social scientists see that nations have given themselves their own laws and institutions, that their ends or values are human creations that have no objective or universal validity. However, by broadcasting this truth they cannot but undermine moral conviction or those shared values without which societies disintegrate from within or are destroyed from without. (People do not readily fight and die for what they can no longer believe to be true or intrinsically just, that is, for what some thoughtless social scientists call "myths.")

Of course, these social scientists do not see the exception, the one nation that did not give itself its own laws and institutions. Without any scientific investigation on their part, they dogmatically reject the idea that the Torah is the standard for determining the relative truth and justice of all other laws and institutions.

The second tension, that between civic virtue and happiness, involves the supposed demoralizing influence of the wealth-producing arts or luxury. Israel itself was warned of the temptations of wealth and luxury in the land it was to inherit:

When the Lord your God shall bring you into the land . . . to give you large and good cities . . . and houses full of good things . . . and wells . . . and vineyards and olive trees. . . . Then take heed lest you forget the Lord your God . . . not to keep His commandments . . . lest you eat and be satiated, and you build and dwell in good houses; and your cattle and sheep increase, and your silver and gold increase. . . . And your heart will become haughty, and you will forget the Lord your God . . . and you will say in your heart: "My strength and the power of my hand have procured me all this wealth." (Deut. 6:10–12, 8:11–17)

Nevertheless, the Torah flourished together with the arts and sciences during the period of the First Temple, as well as in other periods of Jewish history. (See Exod. 36:1, *Berachot* 58b–59b.) It was only when the Jews deviated from the Torah and imitated the ways of the nations that Israel went into exile. (See II Kings, 17:7–8, 23.) The idea that a necessary contradiction exists between material abundance and virtue is a religious and philosophic myth. Some of Israel's Sages were very wealthy men, and they were revered leaders of their communities.

The Prophets were also wealthy. They did not regard wealth and fidelity to the Torah as incompatible. Wealth enlarges the scope of private charity, the greatest act of virtue. (Recall the example of the Gracious Man.) That the Prophets sometimes excoriate people and personages for running after riches and failing to fulfill their obligations is easily misunderstood. For the Prophets judge others by the incomparably high standards of the Torah, the slightest deviation from which by Israel requires condemnation if only because of her world-historical function as the light of the nations. Now we shall better see how the Torah precludes the dichotomies in question.

THE EDUCATION OF A TORAH NATION

The Prophets were especially sensitive to the principle that all Jews are responsible for each other. This principle has been misunderstood by various religionists. The principle of collective responsibility applies not in the courts of men, which try only individuals, but in the court of Heaven. (Recall the error of confusing the general and particular laws of divine reward and punishment.) In other words, even though each individual is judged by his own deeds or misdeeds, it is a basic law of the Torah that "all Israel are sureties one for another" (*Shevuot* 39a). All the more reason for the commandment "You shall rebuke your neighbor, and not bear any sin because of him" (Lev. 18:17). If a Jew fails to reprove wrongdoing on the part of his neighbor, he is himself held accountable for the transgression, but again, only in the judgment of Heaven. It is in this light that one is to understand the censorious language of the Prophets.[19]

Of course, there are laws and rules governing the admonition of others. Here are some of the salient ones discussed by Maimonides:[20]

If one observes that a person committed a sin or walks in a way that is not good, it is a duty to bring the erring man back to the right path and point out to him that he is wronging himself by his evil course. . . . He who rebukes another, whether for offenses against the rebuker himself or for sins against God, should administer the rebuke in private, speak to the offender gently and tenderly, and point out that he is only speaking for the wrongdoer's own good. . . . If the latter accepts the rebuke, well and good. If not, he should be rebuked a second and a third time. And so one is bound to continue the admonitions, till the sinner assaults the admonisher and says to him "I refuse to listen." Whoever is in a position to prevent wrongdoing and does not do so, is responsible for the iniquity. . . .

At the same time, however,

It is forbidden to put an Israelite to shame, especially in public . . . whether he be young or old. . . . If one has been wronged by another [and] does not wish to rebuke or speak to the offender because the latter is a very common person or mentally defective, and [if, moreover] he has sincerely forgiven him, and neither bears him ill-will nor rebukes him—he acts according to the standard of the Gracious Man. All that the Torah objects to is harboring ill-will.[21]

Clearly, these laws and rules of not harboring ill-will and of reproving one's neighbor without bringing him to shame cannot but have a most salutary influence on the mental and moral character of the individual and the community. This is, of course, the plain purpose of the biblical verse in question.

The verse appears in that portion of Levitious called *Kedushim*, where Israel is exhorted to be "holy," to transcend the ways of the unrefined multitude. Accordingly, everyone is commanded to fear his mother and father (that is, to conduct himself with their judgment of things always present in his mind); to observe the Sabbath, to avoid idolatry, to leave corners of his field to the poor; not to steal, lie, or commit perjury; not to oppress his neighbor nor to put a stumbling block before the blind (i.e., not to lead the ignorant astray); not to favor the person of the poor nor to favor the person of the mighty, but to exercise righteous judgment; not to go up and down as a talebearer; not to stand idly by the blood of your neighbor; to rebuke your neighbor, not to bear any grudge against him, but to love your neighbor's good as your own.

These are only a minute fraction of the laws that are designed to promote not only fraternal feeling and justice but psychic and physiological well-being. (The salutary influence of these laws has been clinically tested and confirmed by an eminent scientist.)[22]

Mention should also be made of the laws governing marriage, for these are not only the most conducive to wholesome family life, for which the Jewish people are famous, but to public virtue and public happiness, which the philosophers have vainly sought or promised. The Torah precludes the classical and modern dichotomy between civic virtue and personal happiness.[23] Precluded, too, is the related tension between the individual and society. Such a tension is extrinsic to the nation that was created to exalt God's Name, that is, to relate how His wisdom is manifested in creation (Isa. 43:21). The perennial tension between individual and society results from the fact that no human legislators, be they ever so wise and virtuous, can frame a body of laws that is equally conducive to the good of each individual member of the community. Given the great differences among men, all man-made laws cannot but eventuate in no small measure of injustice and unhappiness. Only an Infinite Intelligence can design laws that avoid this inevitability.

No laws are more important than those concerning the relationship between teachers and students, for these affect the attitudes of young people toward truth, wisdom, learning, and authority on the one hand, as well as their habits of attentiveness, diligence, clarity, integrity, and reverence on the other. Maimonides elaborates.[24] A student is under an obligation to honor his teacher to a greater extent than his father. As noted earlier, if his father and teacher are in captivity, he should first ransom his teacher (unless his father is also a scholar, even of lower rank). Concerning man, there is no reverence profounder than that which is due to the teacher. A disciple is forbidden at all times to give decisions in his teacher's presence. When a teacher and a colleague dispute with one another, he must not interpose his opinion as to who is right. (In Torah Judaism, where truth, learning, and modesty prevail, not everyone is entitled to voice his opinion.) He may question his teacher but not contradict him. It is his duty to rise before his teacher and not turn his back toward him upon leaving. By thus honoring his teacher he is honoring the Torah.

As for the teacher: "Let the honor of your students be as dear to you as your own" (*Ethics* 4:15). The teacher should take an interest in his students and love them, for they are his spiritual children. Students increase the teacher's wisdom and broaden his mind. "Much wisdom have I learned from my teachers, more from my colleagues; from my students, most of all."

Apropos of Maimonides, contrast some of the pedagogical principles of a medieval syllabus, *Hukkei HaTorah* (*Laws of the Torah*), outlining the character and various stages of education for a seven-year institute for advanced talmudic study.[25] The syllabus stresses the absolute primacy of education. But here education means the perfection of the individual's soul, his rational faculties and moral character. Required is the utmost dedication to learning on the part of both teachers and students, and in a setting that removes the student from the daily concerns and distractions of society for a period of seven years. It should be understood, however, that this isolation of the students is also intended to serve the ultimate good of the community. Consistent therewith, students are tested for their occupational aptitudes. Classes are small to facilitate individual attention. Moreover, the classes are graded so as not to stifle individual progress. Students are examined at short- and long-term intervals to determine the accuracy of their comprehension. Furthermore, the teacher is urged to encourage free debate and discussion among the students. Above all, he must be totally committed to his profession.

All this conforms to traditional rabbinic learning. Sustained and uninterrupted Torah study develops in the student extraordinary powers of concentration, logical acuity and conceptual clarity, and the ability to systematize vast and diverse areas of knowledge. (Recall what Nietzsche said about the superior rationality of the Jews.) At the same time, this discipline of mind produces intellectual independence and integrity, contempt for idle chatter and worldly pleasures, moral purity, and a devout sense of mission. And of course, as any Talmudist knows, learning with precision is facilitated by wit and humor, by a proper blend of warmth and rigor, by strengthening and then demolishing the opponent's point of view, but above all, by sincerity, or rather, by that wholeness that communicates to the student the consistency of thought, action, and passion exemplified by the Prophets and Sages of Israel.[26]

Here, a brief digression. Recall Chapter 2 and those subjectivist and relativistic doctrines that render philosophy a "species of autobiography" and place men "beyond good and evil." These doctrines appear rather sophisticated to the modern mind. And yet the essence of such doctrines has been known for millennia by any thirteen-year-old lad who has been studying Torah with his father or in a Jewish academy! (Bear in mind that he starts studying the Mishnah at the age of ten if not sooner.) Hence it is no exaggeration to say that every properly educated Jewish child learns that without the Torah, man becomes the author of good and bad, and that what he calls "good" and "bad" will be as variable as his impulses and circumstances. Having studied the history of Cain, he does not have to read Plutarch to know that a fratricide was the founder of a city. Indeed, given his knowledge of Hebrew, he will know from the plain meaning of Cain's name and of the names of Cain's descendents that acquisitivenesses or self-aggrandizement is a primordial passion of human nature (the same passion that Machiavelli took such pains to impress upon his adult readers, only to exalt the commonplace to the level of a "new" political science). This is why the Mishnah teaches our youngster that one should "Pray for the welfare of the government, since were it not for the fear of it men would devour each other alive" (*Ethics* 3:2). Tutored in the Mishnah, he knows that the very qualities that make some men godlike—reason and free will— make others beastlike. He sees that, without the Torah, "every man does what is right in his own eyes" (Deut. 12:8); so that he need never hear the word "relativism" to know of its perniciousness. He learns enough about history, about the calamities of his own people and of others, to say with the Prophet, "Woe unto them that call evil good and good evil" (Isa. 5:20). He has studied enough of the faults of his own great ancestors—never covered up in the Torah—for him to be a sober realist. Having read about paganism recounted in the Torah, he would be amused to learn of how philosophers like Hobbes and his twentieth-century descendents have discovered that man is nothing more than a clever beast—amused, moreover, because, having also studied Ecclesiastes (which he does at least once a year), he knows that this "discovery" is less than trivial: "For that which befalls the sons of men befalls beasts: . . . as one dies, so does the other; yea, they have all one breath; so that man has no pre-eminence above a beast, for all is vanity" (3:19). But this is not all.

Even before he has entered manhood he has become a skilled logician through study of the Talmud. He has learned to differentiate between wisdom (*hokhma*) and logical reasoning (*bina*). Our thirteen-year-old did not have to take a course in logical positivism (or in its wayward step-child, analytical philosophy) to know that knowledge of good and bad cannot be obtained by mere ratiocination or by logical inference from facts of experience. Such knowledge can only be obtained from wisdom, as embodied in the Written and Oral Torah. Logical positivists are therefore correct insofar as they deny that reason, either by itself or supplemented by empirical observation, can ascertain what is good and bad. What they fail to recognize, however, is that the deductive faculty, which operates through logical relationships or through chains of analogy and comparison, does not exhaust the powers of the human intellect. The great intuitions of an Einstein or a Newton did not arrive on the heels of logic; logic (*bina*) was only the vehicle of their elaboration. Nevertheless, although one cannot reach wisdom through reason alone, one can test the deliverances of wisdom by means of reason and observation. This is expected of every lad who enters a Torah academy. Such a lad, therefore, will have learned about the ethical and epistemological limitations of the philosophic tradition without having taken a single course in philosophy.

It will be evident from the preceding that a Torah academy, unlike a secular university, synthesizes moral and intellectual discipline. A student who lacks good character is not admitted to a house of study unless he reforms. It cannot be emphasized too strongly that Torah education refines the student's character. It imbues him with a critical and self-critical attitude, prompting him to translate noble ideas and ideals, that is, the Law, into living reality. He can philosophize without being an academic philosopher, and do so more seriously. For learning is not an end in itself; it must issue in good deeds. "Anyone whose deeds exceed his wisdom, his wisdom shall endure; anyone whose wisdom exceeds his deeds, his wisdom shall not endure" (*Ethics* 3:12; and see ibid., 3:22). Again, "He who learns in order to teach will be granted adequate means to learn and teach; but he who learns in order to practice will be granted adequate means to learn and to teach, to observe and to practice" (ibid., 4:6).

This is very different from the Greco-Christian tradition. Whereas the Greek philosophers emphasized knowledge over practice, their Christian imitators emphasized faith over deeds—thus fostering hypocrisy and subjectivism, along with petty as well as immense crimes of passion and violence.[27] In the philosophic tradition the moral virtues constitute no more than a probabilistic precondition for the cultivation of the intellect. Accordingly, unlike in Judaism, in which higher standards of moral conduct are required of men of superior intellect, one finds in the

West the tradition that men of genius ought not be censured for moral lapses. Machiavelli even encourages rulers to indulge their vices so long as they do not incur hatred or contempt. But no less than the author of *Faust*—a modern Olympian—offers us this tempting plum of political wisdom: "The man of action is always unscrupulous; it is only the observer who has a conscience." It would seem that the dichotomies of theory and practice, of individual and society, of freedom and authority, of happiness and virtue, are manifestations of a basic flaw in Western civilization, one that fosters moral laxity and eventuates in social disintegration.

Of course the West knows better, as may be seen in Chesterton: "It is considered more withering to accuse a man of bad taste than of bad ethics." And Jonson: "Good men are the stars, the planets of the ages wherein they live, and illustrate the times." People learn by example, especially by the example of their political and cultural elites. Not brilliance of intellect so much as exemplary moral character is the cement of society and the foundation of public and private happiness. Besides, where passion enters, wisdom departs.

CONCLUSION

Consider the antiquity of Jewish law along with its logical and comprehensive character, its immutability and applicability under the most various of human conditions. If one considers, moreover, the absence in the Torah of any of the dichotomies mentioned above, one cannot but wonder why no philosopher—not even Nietzsche—has allowed available knowledge of the Jewish people and of Judaism to qualify his basic principles or conclusions regarding mankind. I mention Nietzsche because no gentile philosopher had a deeper understanding and respect for Judaism, polemical statements to the contrary notwithstanding. Allow me to quote at length from *The Dawn of Day*, where he speaks of "The People of Israel":

In Europe they have gone through a school of eighteen centuries, such as no other nation can boast of, and the experience of this terrible time of probation has benefited the community much less than the individual. In consequence whereof the resourcefulness in soul and intellect of our modern Jews is extraordinary. In times of extremity they, least of all the inhabitants of Europe, try to escape any great dilemma by a recourse to drink or to suicide—which less gifted people are so apt to fly to. Each Jew finds in the history of his fathers and grandfathers a voluminous record of instances of the greatest coolness and perseverance in terrible positions, of the most artful and clever fencing with misfortune and chance; their bravery under the cloak of wretched submissiveness, their heroism in the *spernere se sperni* [despising their despisers] surpass the virtues of all the saints.

Nietzsche continues:

People wanted to make them contemptible by treating them scornfully for twenty centuries, by refusing to them the approach to all dignities and honorable positions, and by pushing them all the deeper down into the mean trades—and, indeed, they have not become genteel under this process. But contemptible? They have never ceased believing themselves qualified for the highest functions; neither have the virtues of all suffering people ever failed to adorn them. Their manner of honoring parents and children, the reasonableness of their marriages and marriage customs make them conspicuous among Europeans. Besides, they know how to derive a sense of power and lasting revenge from the very trades which were left to them (or to which they were abandoned). . . . Yet their vengeance never carries them too far, for they all have that liberality even of the soul in which the frequent change of place, climate, customs, neighbors, and oppressors schools man; they have by far the greatest experience in human relationships. . . .

Now Nietzsche concludes his encomium:

Where shall this accumulated wealth of great impressions, which forms the Jewish history in every Jewish family, this wealth of passions, virtues, resolutions, resignations, struggles, victories of all sorts—where shall it find an outlet, if not in great intellectual people and work? On the day when the Jews will be able to show as their handiwork such jewels and golden vessels as the European nations of shorter and less thorough experience neither can nor could produce, when Israel will have turned its eternal vengeance into an eternal blessing of Europe: then once more that seventh day will appear, when the God of the Jews may rejoice in Himself, His creation, and His chosen people—and all of us will rejoice with Him![28]

What Nietzsche does not make explicit in this penetrating sketch of the extraordinary virtues of the Jews is the formative and sustaining power of the Torah, which they have ever exalted both in word and in deed. Consider, therefore, this aphorism from Nietzsche's *Beyond Good and Evil*:

In the Jewish "Old Testament," the book of divine justice, there are human beings, things, and speeches in so grand a style that Greek and Indian literature have nothing to compare with it. With terror and reverence one stands before these tremendous remnants of what man once was, and will have sad thoughts about ancient Asia and its protruding little peninsula Europe, which wants by all means to signify as against Asia the "progress of man." To be sure, whoever is himself merely a meager, tame domestic animal (like our educated people of today, including the Christians of "educated" Christianity) has no cause for amazement of sorrow among these ruins—the taste of the Old Testament is a touchstone for "great" and "small"—perhaps he will find the *New* Testament . . . rather more after his heart. . . . To have glued this New Testament, a kind of rococo taste in every respect, to the Old Testament to make *one* book, as the "Bible," as "the book par excellence"—that is perhaps the greatest audacity and "sin against the spirit" that literary Europe has on its conscience."[29]

Here Nietzsche ignored the fact that what is called the "Old Testament" has always been new, has always been a living tradition inspiring generation after generation of Jews, including men of the highest intellect, men unknown to the non-Torah world. Of course, Nietzsche was ignorant of the theoretical principles underlying the practical dimensions of Jewish law.[30] Knowledge of these theoretical principles on the one hand, and steadfast adherence to the Law on the other, are exactly what made Jewish scholars of the past the leaders of their communities, whether in Asia Minor, Africa, or Europe. These men are historical refutations of Plato's oracle that there has never been nor will there ever be a city or nation ruled by philosopher-kings.

Strange that this great philosopher, while residing in Athens or when travelling abroad, never heard of Israel, never came into contact with a Jew who could recount the glorious reigns of King David and King Solomon, to mention only two of Israel's philosopher-kings. Had he consulted a Jewish sage he would have learned of a nation that had united wisdom and power as well as power and consent. This that nation could do because its Torah transcended the dichotomy of reason and law, hence of law and justice. To this subject I now turn.

NOTES

1. To simplify the exposition, I shall ignore the Nietzschean position taken earlier that philosophy is a manifestation of the will to power, a view that places in question the dichotomy between theory and practice.

2. Contrast Moses's reluctance to accept the leadership of the children of Israel (Exod. 3:11, 13, 19; 4:1, 10, 13) and their forty-year wandering in the desert.

3. For Aristotle, "it would be strange to think that the art of politics, or practical wisdom, is the best knowledge since man is not the best thing in the world" (*Nicomachean Ethics*, 1141a 20–30).

4. " . . . philosophic wisdom is scientific knowledge, combined with intuitive reason, of the things that are [eternal and immutable, hence] highest by nature " (Ibid., 1141b 1–5).

5. For compelling evidence, see Daniel Michelson, "Codes in the Torah," *B'Or Ha'Torah* No. 6 (in English) (Jerusalem: "Shamir," 1987), pp. 7–39.

6. See the author's *Jerusalem vs. Athens*, pp. 310–312.

7. Nietzsche, by the way, remained wedded to the cosmology of a finite and eternal universe, hence his doctrine of the Eternal Recurrence of the Same.

8. For elaboration, see *Jerusalem vs. Athens*, p. 162.

9. See George Gamow, *One Two Three . . . Infinity* (New York: Bantam Books, 1971), for the scientific view of infinity.

10. See the author's *Beyond Détente: Toward an American Foreign Policy*, ch. 4,

and "Karl Marx and the Declaration of Independence," *Intercollegiate Review*, 20:1 (Spring/Summer 1984), pp. 3–11, printed in the *Congressional Record*, House of Representatives, June 5, 1985.

11. L. Easton and H. Guddat, eds., *Writings of the Young Marx on Philosophy and Society* (New York: Doubleday, 1967), p. 235.

12. Ibid., pp. 293–295, 306–307.

13. The forced conversions and inquisitorial practices of communism represent the ascendancy of ideology over political philosophy. Political philosophy made allowances for the frailties of men as an inevitable aspect of the human condition. In fact, Aristotle had another meaning for the "best" regime, viz., the best for a particular people, something that was therefore relative to a people's character and material circumstances. Aristotle was anything but doctrinaire. The term "doctrinairism" actually describes the attempt of ideologists to discard the distinction between theory and practice.

In contrast, the Torah, which dissolves the dichotomy between theory and practice, forbids proseletyzing and accepts the existence of diverse non-Torah nations which do not violate the seven Noahide or universal laws of morality. Hence, so far as the Torah is concerned, it is perfectly acceptable for a people to live under a kingship, a republic, or a mixed regime, and to have a capitalist, a socialist, or a mixed economy.

14. Consider the Nazi purge of Jewish scientists from the universities after Hitler came to power in 1933. At none of these universities did any of the non-Jewish scientists publicly protest. The great majority of Germany's most distinguished physicists collaborated with the Nazis from the very outset of Hitler's regime, that is, even before he gained unchallenged power. See Joseph Haberer, *Politics and the Community of Science* (New York: Van Nostrand, 1969).

15. "Study leads to action" (*Kidushin* 40b). See Maimonides, *Mishneh Torah: The Book of Knowledge*, "Laws Concerning the Study of the Torah," ch. 3, p. 3: "Of all precepts, none is equal in importance to the study of the Torah. Nay, study of the Torah is equal to them all for study leads to practice. Hence study always takes precedence over practice."

Compare this Responsa (*Hatham Sofer Chosen Mishpat*, 164): "If people come for instruction or litigation during the time set apart for study, the scholar had to instruct or pass judgment without receiving remuneration; nor could he refuse his service because it interfered with his study; for the service one renders his fellowmen is of greater importance than one's own advancement in scholarship."

16. See Rabbi Samson Raphael Hirsch's brilliant deciphering of the names of Cain's descendants in *Hirsch Commentary*, Gen. 4:16–5:32, discussed in *Jerusalem vs. Athens*, p. 18.

17. See Allan Bloom, "Jean-Jacques Rousseau," in Strauss and Cropsey, eds., *History of Political Philosophy*, p. 533.

18. The West today is wracked by the dichotomy between ethics and ethically neutral science. The Torah opposes this dichotomy. The ultimate end of all science is the sanctification of God's Name. Science is not and cannot be ethically neutral.

19. See Miller, *Behold a People*, pp. 167–170, 220, 365, who shows that even when Israel deviated most from the Torah, the conduct of the nation was ethically far superior to all other nations.

20. *Mishneh Torah*, (*The Book of Knowledge*), "Laws Relating to Moral Dispositions and to Ethical Conduct," ch. 6. pp. 7–9.

21. Ibid. On the other hand, "As one is commanded to say that which will be obeyed, so one is commanded not to say that which will not be obeyed" (*Yevamot* 65b). That is, "reprove not a scorner, lest he hate you; reprove a wise man and he will love you" (Prov. 9:8).

22. Professor Henri Baruk, a biologist, psychopharmacologist, psychologist, sociologist, and a member of the Medical Academy of Paris, used Torah laws for both individual and group therapy with remarkable success. Applied with expertise, these laws, he discovered, overcome toxicities, psychopathologies, and intragroup conflict. Having characterized the Torah as "the most complete science of man," Baruk writes: "Though this extensive science has been vulgarized by the religions which have sprung from it, it still remains little known and even misunderstood. The[se] religions . . . took mainly from its moral principles with, moreover, various modifications which left out Hebraic Law, Hebraic biology, Hebraic sociology, etc.—in a word, the concrete and material parts of the Torah. Complete and scrupulously exact study of the Torah is indispensable if one is to capture its spirit. Then again the Torah forms an indivisible whole, and one cannot study it in borrowed versions or excerpts without completely falsifying its meaning and spirit" (*Tsedek*, pp. 80, 133–140).

23. Adeimantus interrupts Socrates' elaboration of the just city, saying, "you're hardly making these men happy" (i.e., the guardians who are denied private property). To this Socrates responds: "In founding the city we are not looking to the exceptional happiness of any one group among us but, as far as possible, that of the city as a whole. . . . Don't compel us to attach to the guardians a happiness that will turn them into everything except [righteous] guardians" (*Republic* 419a–421c). Moreover, the guardians are the philosophers who, as previously noted, must be compelled to rule and thereby forsake the contemplative life, the highest form of happiness.

24. *Mishneh Torah* (*The Book of Knowledge*), "Laws Concerning the Study of the Torah," chs. 5–6.

25. This paragraph is adapted from Isadore Twersky, *Rabad of Posquieres* (Cambridge: Harvard University Press, 1962), pp. 25–26.

26. Here mention should be made of the outstanding Torah academy of Rabad (Rabbi Abraham ben David), the great contemporary and critic of Maimonides whom the Rambam greatly admired. Like the celebrated Babylonian schools of Sura and Pumbedita, to which students came from Palestine, Egypt, North Africa, Spain, and Italy, so to Rabad's school at Posquieres students flocked from regions throughout Europe "like doves that wander from one dovecote to another seeking food," i.e., knowledge of the infinite wisdom contained in the Torah. That discerning traveler of the Middle Ages, Benjamin of Tudela, says of Rabad: "He attracts students from distant countries who find abode in his own house and are taught by him; he moreover provides them with all necessaries of life from his own means and private property, which is very considerable." *The Itinerary of Rabbi Benjamin of Tudela*, 2 vols., trans. A. Asher (New York: Hakeshet Publishing Co., n.d.), I, 35. I mention Rabad (concerning whom the reader should consult I. Twersky's study) because I have had the honor and privilege of being associated with an eminent Talmudist in Israel, Dr. Chaim

Zimmerman, who, though he would never compare himself with the renowned Rishon, nonetheless has strikingly similar qualities of mind and nobility of character, and whose home is open every day to students and teachers the world over. This extraordinary scholar is wholly dedicated to Torah learning. He systematically applies its concepts and its logic to the secular sciences, to domestic and international politics, to the concerns of everyday life, such that the Torah is vividly seen as the paradigm of knowledge and of how man should live.

27. In contrast, Islam suffers from an "intoxicating twin-gift of audacious dreaming and executive ineffectiveness." See G. E. von Grunebaum, *Islam* (London: Routledge & Kegan Paul, 1961), pp. 69, 185. The Muslim disregard for mere factuality is notorious, especially concerning their own creed and history.

28. Friedrich Nietzsche, *The Dawn of Day*, trans. J. Volz (London: T. Fisher Unwin, 1903), pp. 203–206.

29. Nietzsche, *Beyond Good and Evil*, Aph. 52.

30. All Nietzsche had to do was to read, in the original German, the brilliant works of his older contemporary, Rabbi Samson Raphael Hirsch, especially his philological analysis of the Pentateuch—Nietzsche, too, was a philologist—and he would have had to entertain at least some doubt that the "Old Testament" is a human product. The profound systematicity of its language alone refutes the vaunted "progress of man."

11

The Law of the Future

LAW V. MORALITY

The dichotomies of Western civilization are not merely philosophical conundrums; they are denials of the God of Abraham. They engender the belief that human history is fundamentally irrational and unjust, a belief that again and again has become a self-fulfilling prophecy.

One of the most palpable and pernicious of these dichotomies is that of law and justice or law and morality. Although rooted in Greek philosophy, this dichotomy dominates Pauline Christianity and is evident in the Christian precept "Render unto Caesar the things that are Caesar's and unto God the things that are God's." The dichotomy involves man in two kinds of relationships governed by different kinds of laws and concepts, one civil or secular, the other moral or religious. This division of civil and religious law into separate spheres is precluded in the Torah. Because the Torah is a covenant based on the relationship "Fulfill your obligations and I will fulfill Mine,"[1] both types of laws, that governing the relationship between man and man, and that governing the relationship between man and God, are embraced within a framework of purely juridical concepts. But to appreciate the Torah's juridical framework, the dichotomy of law and morality needs to be examined first from a traditional perspective.

Morality has been understood to mean principles of right conduct whose validity is independent of human volition and therefore of time and place. These principles were thought to be accessible to human reason reflecting on the nature of man and the requirements of human society. But as seen in Chapter 2, positivism has demolished the pretensions of reason in this context: There are no logical foundations for morality. This conclusion of modern philosophy, recall, is anticipated in the Torah, in the fact that the Torah does not offer reasons to justify its commandments. This also helps to explain why morality is not a Torah concept. To be sure, the Torah overlaps morality insofar as the latter includes valid imperatives. The concept may even be assimilated to the Torah by speaking of laws of morality. It should be understood, however, that moral principles as postulated in the non-Torah world lack conceptual constraints and adequate rules of application. This is not the case with the laws of the Torah, whose logical controls are systematized in the Talmud.

Like the laws of nature, laws of morality are independent of human will, for both of these laws are creations of God. Whereas laws of morality are qualitative laws of existence, the laws of nature are quantitative or statistical manifestations of such laws, for all laws are ultimately qualitative. But whereas quantitative laws are accessible to unaided human reason, even to tyros, qualitative laws require for their precise understanding apprenticeship in the Torah.

Now, if one takes the traditional view of morality as consisting of principles of right conduct whose validity is independent of human volition, hence of time and place, it will be obvious that morality as thus defined is bound to come into conflict with the mutable laws of the secular state. One could of course avoid such conflict by eliminating the concept of morality by way of the doctrine of legal realism. But however much legal realism dominates law schools in the West, the public at large still retains, to its credit, some old-fashioned "moral prejudices"; so that legislators, despite their legal training, are compelled out of political necessity, if not from conviction, to speak the (philosophically refuted) language of morality. And so the dichotomy between law and morality persists.

To illustrate, consider the following question posed by Professor Moshe Silberg, former Deputy President of the Supreme Court of Israel.[2] "What is the attitude of the law toward covenants entered into in opposition to the provisions of the law, or to the accepted moral principles of society?" Referring to English and Roman law, Silberg remarks that "The general principle is that the law does not recognize the validity of a forbidden contract or a contract which runs counter to the claims of morality. In other words . . . it does not see in such a contract a basis for making a civic claim." Nevertheless, examination of actual cases in English law reveals that they are not free of internal contradictions. In certain cases judges have upheld the violated law over against considerations of morality; in others they have upheld morality over against the law. Silberg formulates the problem as follows:

Let us imagine ... a small shopkeeper ... who does not close his store at the hour designated by the municipal ordinance, or on the day so provided, and he sells his merchandise during one of the forbidden hours or days. In the formal terms of the law, he made a contract contrary to the provision of the law. ... Let us further assume that he sells his merchandise not for cash but on credit, and the buyer who has fallen into indebtedness does not pay his debt. Can this "lawbreaker" claim what is due him from the purchaser, or shall here ... apply the familiar principle: *ex turpi causa non oritur actio* [out of an illegal or immoral consideration, an action does not and cannot arise]?

Or to cite another, less extreme, illustration: what is the legal status of a manufacturer who sells his product before receiving the necessary license? ... Shall we say that in all instances the purchaser shall be the gainer and be relieved of paying for the merchandise he received?

Evidently, the juridical position taken toward such questions in English law has not been uniform. Silberg cites two cases that occurred some 150 years ago. The first

involved two Frenchmen who had immigrated to London, and one of them, a priest by profession, had been stricken with syphilis. His colleague cured him through the use of various drugs, and he sued him for twenty pounds as the fee for curing him. The defendant did not deny the facts. He admitted that he had been fully cured, thanks to the attention of the claimant who was an expert. He argued, however, that his colleague was not legally permitted to attend to him because ... no one was allowed to practice medicine in London ... unless he were licensed by the medical association. He therefore claimed that his cure of syphilis was a violation of the law, and that one could not claim to be paid for doing something which transgressed the law, that one had to do it without a fee! The Court did not recognize this argument, and ordered the defendant to pay the full amount of the claim.

In the second instance, which was tried the same day and by the same judge, the claim was for payment of the cost of a certain fabricated article, bricks. The defendant claimed that the bricks did not conform to the size prescribed by law, and that it was, therefore, forbidden for the seller to sell them, and that he could not, therefore, claim their price. The Court accepted the argument and dismissed the claim.

Over one hundred and fifty years have passed since the two decisions were given and no one is clear as to the difference between them except for the relative emotional difference between ... the ingratitude of the person who was cured and a merchant's refusal to pay.

After examining more recent cases of English law bearing on the subject in question, Professor Silberg concludes that "Two mutually contradictory tendencies played on the loyalties of the judges: the desire to defend the validity of the legal proscription on the one hand, and the desire to grant redress to the aggrieved claimant on the other." This contradiction, he sees, "is not accidental, partial, or hidden; it is an inevitable fact of existence and it appears in every instance." The contradiction between law and morality permeates the modern system of English jurisprudence.[3]

Turning to the attitude of Jewish law concerning the validity of illegal contracts, two cases cited by Silberg are sufficient for our purpose. Thus, as the great codifier Rabbi Asher ben Yechiel (1250–1327) states in the name of Rav Hai Gaon:

Where a sale was made in violation of law, such as increasing the price in consideration for waiting for payment [this is equivalent to taking interest, forbidden in Jewish law to both vendor and buyer] . . . and the sale was validated through the usual token of completing a transaction, and the price level did not increase, the sale is valid, and it cannot be voided because it occurred with a violation of the law incidental to it.[4]

"This means," says Silberg, that "the purchaser can demand by law the surrender of the merchandise, the seller can demand by law the payment of the price, but, obviously, up to the level of the excess, or: the principal but not the interest." Maimonides takes the same position: "One who sells or transfers a gift on the Sabbath . . . though he is punished with stripes [for violating the Sabbath], the transaction is valid." And so Justice Silberg concludes:

We see clearly that Jewish law does not establish a causal connection between the commission of an offense and the voiding of a civil contract, or any other legal transaction which occurred incidentally to a violation of the law. The violation of the law or of morality is one thing, and the legal validity of the contract is another to the extent that the fulfilling of the contract itself does not activate the offense (as, for instance, the payment of interest by the borrower to the lender). Precisely because Jewish law does not distinguish between law and morality, and that practically every performance of an obligation is at the same time a fulfillment of a . . . commandment, . . . the non-fulfillment of a contract entered into through a violation of a law will only turn out to be an additional offense to supplement the original one committed by the transgressor.

When, however, the learned justice adds that "there is no legal system in the world, ancient or modern, in which the principles of morality and law are so intertwined as in Jewish law," he is insinuating into the Torah a dichotomy he had just denied. This complex and delicate problem requires careful and candid elucidation.

It was just pointed out that morality is not, strictly speaking, a Torah concept. Commentators gloss over this fact. Perhaps they find it too difficult to handle the talmudic concept for which the term morality is a convenient but misleading surrogate, namely, *Dinei Shamayim*, meaning the laws (or judgments) of Heaven. But all the laws of the Torah are, by definition, *Dinei Shamyim*. Nevertheless, a finite subset of these laws are designated *Dinei Adam*, literally meaning those laws that are fully under the administration of human courts. All other laws of the Torah retain the designation of the set *Dinei Shamayim*. Accordingly, certain acts or omissions that do not entail civil or criminal responsibility in a human court (*Dinei Adam*) may still be reprehensible in the judgment of Heaven (*Dinei Shamayim*). How such transgressions are dealt with by human courts is a matter of judicial discretion, as will be seen in a moment.

The *locus classicus* of the distinction between *Dinei Adam* and *Dinei Shamayim* will be found in the tractate of the Talmud, *Baba Kamma* 56a. Of the many examples given therein, it will only be necessary to cite one as formulated by Rabbi Isaac Herzog. Thus:

A refrained from giving evidence in B v. C. B would probably have succeeded in his claim but for the delinquency of A. The circumstances are such that recovery from C is not possible. B therefore sues A for the recovery of the loss indirectly caused by him. B's claim is dismissed, but A is informed that the higher law *Dinei Shamayim* demands that he shall make good B's loss.[5]

The term "higher law" is equivalent to the term "morality" (and to such classical notions as "natural right" or "natural justice"). But there are no "higher" laws in the Torah, for all are of divine origin. To speak of *Dinei Shamayim* as the "higher law" is to lower the dignity, as it were, of *Dinei Adam* and to insinuate into the Torah a false and mischievous dichotomy.

Recall, now, what was said of humiliation in Chapter 5: "If one insults [ordinary persons] in speech . . . he is exempt [from damages under *Dinei Adam*], but the court should institute preventive measures in this matter [for derogatory speech is culpable under *Dinei Shamayim*]. . . . The court has the discretionary power to censure the delinquent, or it may impose a fine. In the interest of justice, the court may take similar measures against persons who fail to fulfill their duties as witnesses. All of which clearly indicates that the Torah dissolves the dichotomy of law and morality that has ever riven Western civilization. Here a brief digression on moralists will clarify what is at stake in this issue.

Moralists would have moral precepts enforceable in the courts of men. Although this would eliminate the dichotomy of law and morality, the cure would be worse than the disease. In the first place, inasmuch as all moral precepts are of equal rank or are thought to have universal or absolute validity, they cannot but compete with each other for precedence, and with no rational outcome. (There is no gradation of values here, as in the Torah.) For example, unqualified adherence to the precept "tell the truth" would inevitably lead to one's own or another's embarrassment, dishonor, or even destruction. One cannot elicit from the precept itself when, how, and to whom to tell the truth in a particular case. Required is an act of judgment where the moral precept is only one factor among others, including other moral precepts. (In Jewish law, judgment is facilitated by a hierarchical system of rules, such as those involving danger to life, probability, lenience and severity.) Secondly, if moral precepts had the binding character of positive law, there would be constant litigation in view of their indeterminate character and lack of gradation. Indeed, anarchy would reign, for anyone and everyone could champion his "higher law." Thirdly, given the contingencies and necessities of everyday life, the absoluteness of moral precepts cannot but eventuate in hypocrisy or in tremendous coercion and bloody violence, as the "Holy" Inquisition and the Crusades amply indicate. Finally, moral precepts are egalitarian: They level the kinds of distinctions elaborated in the discussion of equality in Chapter 6.

Jewish law avoids the inconsistencies and disastrous consequences of moralism, as well as the harshness that often results from narrow legalism. This was clearly illustrated in the case of Raba ben Huna and his porters. Raba ben Huna was obliged to pay his poor but negligent porters, not because of some vague moral considerations, but because he was a scholar, and the law itself, the Halakha, requires of scholars a higher standard of conduct.[6] The standard, we saw, was duly defined by Rav, but the model harks back to Abraham, the Gracious Man. (See Gen. 14:22.)

THE CONCEPT OF ISRAEL

The dichotomy of law and morality is inseparable from the classical conflict between the polis and the philosopher, which modernity metamorphosed into the tension between society and the individual.[7] Such a tension is precluded in the Torah conception of Israel. What does this mean?

Just as the Torah is an existence that cannot be comprehended under the category of religion, nor indeed by any category extrinsic to itself, so Israel is an existence that cannot be comprehended by any political, social, or philosophical categories, for it, too, is *sui generis*.

"Israel," writes the eminent Talmudist and philosopher Dr. Chaim Zimmerman, "is defined in the *Halakha* as a concept of unity and totality. The collective group is viewed as an individual person, not as a mere aggregate of single individuals."[8] In other words, as concerns Israel and Israel alone, the community is not the mere sum of its individual members, as in liberalism (and unavoidable in transnational Christianity); nor is the community more than the sum of its individual members, as in socialism (and unavoidable in militant and expansionist Islam).

In the non-Torah world, societies are caught up in meaningless diversity or in meaningless monotony. The laws of these collectivities apply indiscriminately to the individuals composing them, giving rise to the tension between the individual and society and the ills proceeding therefrom. In contrast, the comprehensive and coherent laws of the Torah enable the individual to walk on his own path to perfection, reinforced by, while contributing to, the perfection of the community. There can be no necessary conflict between the good of the individual and the good of the community if only because the purpose of both is to reveal the infinite wisdom, power, and graciousness of God in every aspect of creation, which purpose is fulfilled by their joint perfection. The individual, therefore, is not a quantitative part of the total number of members of the community, but a qualitative part whose rights and privileges are distinct from, yet correlated with, the qualitative existence of the community.[9] A single Jew is equal to all Israel.

Because the Jew has a status both as an individual and as a member of the Torah community, the laws governing the one differ from, without contradicting, the laws of the other. This complementarity stands in striking contrast to statistical laws of nature, where there seems to be a contradiction between the random behavior of individual particles and the lawful behavior of mass clusters or groups of the same particles. (This contradiction is analogous to the unsolved conflict between the individual and society intrinsic to all non-Torah nations.) "At times," writes Dr. Zimmerman, "that which would be a shortcoming in the individual is a positive factor in the community." For example, whereas pride is a defect in the individual, it is a virtue in the community. Conversely, whereas humility would be a defect in the community, it is a virtue in the individual.[10]

Consider, now, the inevitable differences among individuals. In his *Guide of the Perplexed* (II, 40), Maimonides notes that the differences among individuals in the human species are far greater than are to be found among individuals in any other species. He gives, as an example, a man who is so cruel in his anger that he would kill his own son, whereas another man is so filled with pity that he would not kill an insect. (Then, of course, there are the vast intellectual differences and inequalities among men.) Maimonides goes on to say that all these differences among mankind are not only natural but necessary, that they are required for the perfection of society. How, indeed, could any society exist without people who are more or less limited (in ability) to the performance of menial tasks? Nevertheless, every Jew may climb Jacob's ladder, as it were: All the learned professions are open to virtue and talent.

Still, given all the differences and inequalities among men, Maimonides adds that the perfection of society requires "multiple points of accord." This is made possible by the Torah, by its various commandments, which all men, high and low, must observe. Indeed, among the three hereditary ranks of Israel, the Levites have more public duties to perform than Israelites, while the Kohanes are held to even higher standards of public service. Moreover, and as noted earlier, neither of these two "classes" can own any land, for their paramount responsibility is to supervise all activities involving public education. The Torah was not given to eliminate inequality (save those resulting from injustice). Rather, it provides a framework of laws by which unequal men can live in genuine and abiding friendship while perfecting their different intellectual and moral endowments.

When people see their leaders acting in accordance with the highest standards of rectitude, not using public office for personal advancement but rather caring for the poor, the orphan, and the widow, friendship will indeed be the bond of the community. And when everyone is taught the unalterable laws of the Torah, laws that define and delimit the duties and privileges of the leaders themselves, leaders who can be called to account by any humble Jew, the envy, discontent, and cynicism that rack all Esavian regimes can gain no foothold in the hearts and minds of men.

The present State of Israel has no such leaders. For as explained with scientific rigor by Dr. Chaim Zimmerman, Israel, after two thousand years of existence in the "wilderness of the nations" (Ezek. 20:35), is only in the physical stage of its restoration or redemption.[11] Nevertheless, from one or another Torah academy, or perhaps from the home of a Torah master, some young men will emerge and hasten the day of Israel's intellectual and moral restoration and mankind's as well. These men will scrap Israel's present institutions, which are but poor imitations of decayed European systems. The model that will guide them will be found in Maimonides' *Mishneh Torah*.[12]

BASIC INSTITUTIONS OF A TORAH GOVERNMENT

The supreme organ of governance under the Torah is the Great Sanhedrin or Supreme Court.[13] (See Deut. 17:11.) Consisting of seventy-one judges, this extraordinary institution combines judicial and legislative powers and may even bring the king to justice on a suit brought against him by any private citizen.[14] When there is no king, the president of the Great Sanhedrin exercises the king's powers. The president excels, and is recognized as excelling, all in wisdom and understanding. He is capable of teaching the whole of the Torah and of deciding any question within its all-embracing domain. This means, among other things, that he has mastered the theoretical principles and methodologies governing the practical Halakha.

What follows applies not only to the president of the Great Sanhedrin, but to its entire membership, in fact, to any Small Sanhedrin (which consists of twenty-three judges).

Every judge must of course be expert in Torah. The judges must be versed in many branches of science, such as astronomy, mathematics, logic, anatomy, and medicine. They must possess knowledge of non-Torah doctrines, superstitions, and idolatrous practices so as to be able to deal with cases requiring such knowledge.

If only to maximize public confidence in their decisions, the judges must be of good lineage: Kohanes, Levites, and Israelites having a reputation for wisdom and reverence. They must be of spotless character (even as youth, so as not to give cause for recrimination). They must be of mature age, imposing stature, good appearance, and free from all physical defects, again to command respect and authority. An extremely old man or a man who is childless cannot be a judge because he is apt to be wanting in tenderness. A member of the Sanhedrin must be kind and merciful. Even in the case of three-man courts, each member must possess the following seven qualifications: wisdom, *anava*, fear of God, disdain of gain, love of truth, a good reputation, and love of his fellow men. The humane and rational character of the administration of Jewish law follows as a matter of course.

Thus, unlike all other legal systems, the administration of Jewish law is not only highly decentralized, but the autonomy of local authority coexists with the sanctions of universal principles. The rulings of a local court are binding for the particular town or community and cannot be challenged by any other court however superior its rank or area of jurisdiction. This kind of "federalism" reflects the idea that the twelve tribes of Israel represent, individually, distinct types of human perfection, and collectively, a complete and self-sufficient totality. The administration of Jewish law thus allows for a great deal of diversity, but a diversity constrained and rendered harmonious by the court's knowledge of the Torah's universal, organizing principles.

Furthermore, when principles of Jewish law are applied to new problems, it is not done by mere fiat. Generally speaking, before a ruling is accepted as authentic and authoritative, that is, consistent with the Torah, it must be endorsed by a majority of the leading scholars. This "legislative" process often occurs independently of any established judicial body. Such is its dedication to truth and justice that a court may sometimes consult and be guided by an eminent scholar (who, incidentally, may be residing in a distant country). Conversely, a particular court may enjoy unquestioned authority by virtue of the recognized superiority of one or more of its members.

This absence of institutional rigidity is a consequence of the fact that the law is not the exclusive preserve of professional jurists or of any ecclesiastical elite, but of the people, including those of humble occupations. "You are standing this day, all of you before the Lord your God: your leaders, your tribes, your elders, and your officers . . . from the hewer of your wood to the drawer of your water" (Deut. 29:9–10). All the people of Israel are to be more or less learned in the laws that, after all, are to guide and elevate the conduct of their everyday life. "This book of the law shall not depart out of your mouth, but you shall meditate therein day and night, that you may do according to all that is written therein" (Joshua 1:8).

One of the reasons why Jewish law is and can be the property of the people is that, in contrast to Western law, it is phrased in concrete and familiar language, and not in abstract and impersonal ideas. For example, Jewish law speaks of damages resulting not from public "hazards" but from the presence of a "pit" or a "fire," or from the action of an "ox" or a "man." Each term symbolizes a general category of entities that can cause damage, respectively: (1) the inanimate but stationary, (2) the inanimate but nonstationary, (3) the animate but nonrational, and (4) the animate but rational. Because Jewish law is rooted in ordinary experience and because the Hebrew language is unequaled in its simplicity, brevity, and clarity,[15] a Torah community does not require a professional class of lawyers. The people themselves are educated in the law, which is the basic reason why the rule of law and hatred of tyranny have characterized the Jewish people throughout history.

Now one can better understand why it is that, whereas in modern jurisprudence the judge is virtually "sovereign" over the law, in Jewish jurisprudence the judge is necessarily the servant of the law, that is, the Halakha. In a Jewish court the judge does not exercise *ab initio* discretion. If discretion arises at all, it is only after a finding of culpability or liability, and the degree of judicial latitude will depend on the category of law under consideration. In fact, the decision of a judge is conceptually identical to that of a doctor. Thus, after juxtaposing his knowledge of the laws of biology with the data obtained by examination of his patient, the doctor makes a medical judgment (diagnosis) and prescribes, if necessary, the appropriate treatment. No less rigorously, after juxtaposing his knowledge of the laws, say of damages, with the facts of a particular case, the judge renders a judicial judgment and awards, if required, appropriate compensation (to the plaintiff). In other words, Jewish law, like science, deals with logically and experientially controlled concepts, concepts that are often subject to quantitative and probabilistic delimitations. Jewish law thereby minimizes judicial arbitrariness on the one hand, and facilitates public understanding and accountability on the other. The simplistic dichotomy of "judicial activism" and "judicial self-restraint" that plagues American constitutional law is foreign to Jewish jurisprudence.[16]

Although judicial arbitrariness, usually a sign of judicial ignorance of the law, is exceedingly rare given the high qualifications of Torah judges, still, it is less dangerous to come before an inferior judge in Jewish law than in other systems of jurisprudence. For if a judge errs in law, his judgment is null and void; and whenever either litigant desires, the case has to be retried. In fact, under certain circumstances, an error in law can render a judge liable for damages. Here it should be noted that Jewish law does not know of any *res judicata*: In a thoroughly rational system of law there is no *finis litium*. When newly discovered evidence or new legal reasoning—not available to the party in need at the time of the trial—is brought to bear on a particular decision, the trial may be reopened at any time and the *status quo ante* restored. Such is the paramountcy of truth and justice in Torah jurisprudence that any decision of the Sanhedrin (Great or Small) can be challenged at any time by a litigant on rational or on evidential grounds. Of course, if he cannot persuade a majority of the judges that they have erred, he must abide by their decision.

It follows that Jewish law is not based on judicial precedent (*stare decesis*). Judicial precedent is respected, but as the great fourteenth-century codifier Rabbi Yaakov ben Asher has written:

It is an error of law not to follow the earlier decision of a great scholar, only where that decision was, in your own eyes, the right decision to take; but even the greatest of scholars, and even of most ancient times, may have arrived at decisions which, for reasons of your own, you would not see fit to take: it is then your duty to decide contrary to their decision, for there is no judge except the one in his own days; and so long as a matter is not settled in the codes, you may build and demolish as you think fit, even contrary to the precedents of the great ancients (*Commentary to Sanhedrin* IV, 6).[17]

From this one should not fall into the trap of legal pragmatism, whereby the law changes with the whims of judges or with the circumstances of society. Not precedent but living reason is the ultimate arbiter in Torah jurisprudence. Thus, in any dispute or controversy, "[you shall go] to the judge presiding in your own time; and when you make inquiry [he] will tell you the sentence of judgment" (Deut. 27:9). In an aristocracy of learning, however, one need repair to a court only in difficult cases. For it bears repeating that the study of Jewish law is intended not only for judges or scholars, but for ordinary people.

Needless to say, in such a universal aristocracy, wise and modest men do not campaign for public office. Supreme Court vacancies are filled by disciples of the Torah masters. In general, however, the Court "used to send messengers throughout the Land of Israel to examine [scholars recommended] for the office of judge. Whoever was found to be wise, sin-fearing, humble, of unblemished character, and enjoying the esteem of his fellow men was installed as local judge. From the local court he was promoted to the court situated at the entrance of the Temple Mount; thence to the Supreme Court."[18] (Anyone familiar with the rigorous logic of talmudic law knows that its experts can be ranked with no less accuracy than experts in mathematical physics.)

Finally, we come to the "chief executive" of the Torah community, the king:

When you come to the land that the Lord your God is giving you, and shall have taken possession of it and have settled therein, you will eventually say: "We would appoint a king, just like the nations around us." You must then appoint the king whom the Lord your God shall choose. You must appoint a king from among your brethren; you may not appoint a foreigner who is not one of your brethren. (Deut. 17:14–15)

Rabbi Hirsch's commentary is most revealing. He notes that, from the beginning,

the appointment of the Jewish king is not for conquering the land and not for safeguarding its possession, altogether not for developing forces to be used externally. It is God Who gives the land to Israel, God under Whose support and help it conquered the land, and under Whose protection it lives safely in it, as this support and assistance is assured again and again in the Torah and which was stressed by Moses again and again in his exhortations preparatory for the conquest of the land. For that, Israel required no king, for that Israel had only to be "Israel", had only to prove itself the faithful dutiful People of God's Torah, had only to win the moral victory over itself to be certain of victory over any external force against it.[19]

The purpose of a king of Israel, and of Israel itself, is not to seek external glory but internal perfection. Unfortunately, however, when the people did demand a king, they wanted to be "like all the nations [so that] our king may judge us [as well as] go out before us and fight our battles" (I Sam. 8:20). Had they asked only for a king, or had they sought him in order to improve their chances in war, then, as Rabbi Nissim of Gerona explains, "no sin would have been impugned to them on this account. On the contrary, it would have been considered a *mitzva*. Their sin lay, however, in having said: 'Now make us a king to *judge us* like all the nations.' That is to say, they wanted 'the judgments' to be undertaken by the king, and not (as hitherto) by the Torah judges."[20] This is why God tells Samuel: "They have not rejected you, but they have rejected

Me, that I should not be King over them" (I Sam. 8:7). For it is by way of the Torah judges that God is King over Israel. As for Israel's earthly king, the Hebrew term *melech* primarily implies a chief "counselor," a president whose intellectual and moral qualities warrant his elevation and authority. The king's paramount purpose is to win the hearts and minds of the people to the Torah by his own sterling example of a man whose every word and deed is inspired by the Law of which he is nothing more than a faithful servant.

Here is should be noted that a king of Israel may be appointed either by the Great Sanhedrin or by the people with the Sanhedrin's approval. Under Jewish law, the Sanhedrin will not appoint a king (or any officer, for that matter) who is not acceptable to the people: "We must not appoint a leader over a community without first consulting it" (*Berachot* 55a; Exod. 35:30). On the other hand, the Court will not confirm any popular choice who is not qualified for the office. We see here the principle of "government with the consent of the governed," but without the idol of popular sovereignty. Only God is sovereign; and it is only by the laws of His Torah that men can overcome the perennial problem of democracy, that of reconciling wisdom and consent.[21]

Not only are the king's powers clearly delineated and circumscribed in the Torah, but the Supreme Court is the final interpreter of his prerogatives.[22] And as already noted, any private citizen may bring a suit against the king before the Court. Furthermore, depending upon the nature of the suit and the unimpeachable evidence of two eyewitnesses, the Supreme Court may strip the king of his office. It is not the king but the Great Sanhedrin that represents the Kingdom of Israel. And no person, even if he is of Davidic descent, can become or remain a king of Israel unless he conforms to the Torah, of which the Supreme Court is the ultimate guardian.

For two thousand years the Jewish people were governed by law— the Halakha—without the coercive agency of any state. This phenomenon is not only unique, but virtually incredible. It confounds and confutes all the political philosophers and political scientists. For ever since Polemarchus and his companions compelled Socrates to join them on the way to the home of Cephalus (in *The Republic*), it has been the unanimous contention of serious students of mankind that coercion, in contradistinction to persuasion, is an essential and inevitable ingredient of political life. This may be construed to mean that authentic Judaism is incompatible with politics (a matter pregnant with significance for the present state of Israel).[23] But that a people dispersed for two millennia should give their consent to the same system of law is profound testimony both to the extraordinary intellectual and moral character of that people and to the extraordinary wisdom, versatility, and graciousness of that system of law.

What great nation is there that has laws . . . so righteous as this Torah? (Deut. 4:8)

When Israel recognizes and lives by the truth of these words, then mankind will be inspired by the example of a nation wherein freedom dwells with righteousness, equality with excellence, wealth with beauty, the here and now with love of the Eternal.

NOTES

1. See *Hirsch Commentary*, Deut. 26:16–19.

2. The following discussion is based on Moshe Silberg, *Talmudic Law and the Modern State*, pp. 70–74, 78–82. Unfortunately, Justice Silberg has a somewhat positivist conception of law on the one hand, and a somewhat subjectivist view of morality on the other. "The one," he writes, "is created by an outside source, by governing authority [i.e., the state]; the other is created within man himself, in the depths of his own heart. The one comes to establish a social order, the other to pacify the mind." Yet he goes on to say that "morality is the ideological basis of the law, and the law is the outer garment, the concretization, of a part of the principles of abstract morality." Although this view of morality lacks philosophical rigor, if not logical consistency, it will not affect the present discussion.

3. It seems obvious to the present writer that had the English judges followed Jewish law in such matters, then, as will be seen in the sequel, the recipient of illegally dispensed goods or services would be compelled to render payment to the aggrieved claimant, but who would then be fined to that (or a greater) amount for violating the law.

4. Rabbi Asher's legal commentaries will be found in virtually every edition of the Talmud. Rav Hai Gaon (939–1038), head of the renowned yeshiva in Pumbedita, Babylon, was the most prominent Jewish figure in his time. His commentary on the Mishnah is included in the famous Romm Vilna edition of the Talmud.

5. Herzog, *Main Institutions of Jewish Law*, I, 383.

6. This is referred in Hebrew as *lifnim mishurat had in*, misleadingly rendered as "going beyond the letter of the law." Here going beyond the letter of the law is acting according to the standard of the sage; but this, too, is defined by law.

7. Although Aristotle was well aware of the intrinsic conflict between the philosopher and the polis exemplified in the trial of Socrates, he nonetheless seems to deny any conflict between the good of the polis and the good of the individual (*Politics* 1324a5). Indeed, he even professes to believe that *"all* are agreed they are the same." It must be borne in mind, however, that the *Politics* is primarily a practical, hence to some extent a rhetorical, work intended to influence would-be statesmen. (For evidence, see my *Discourse on Statesmanship*, pp. 124–130.) Later, the philosopher who fled Athens to avoid the fate of Socrates

avers that "we must . . . regard every citizen as belonging to the state" (*Politics* 1337a25). Finally, when Aristotle says that "he who is without a polis, by reason of his own nature and not of some accident, is either a poor sort of being, or a being higher than man . . ." (ibid. 1253a1), he is alluding, in the second alternative, to the philosopher.

8. Zimmerman, *Torah and Reason*, p. 83.

9. Ibid. p. 83–84.

10. Ibid. p. 84.

11. Zimmerman, *Torah and Existence*, ch. 1.

12. See *Mishneh Torah: Book of Judges*, trans. A. Hershman (New Haven: Yale University Press, 1949), pp. 5–10.

13. My sole concern here is with the theoretical Sanhedrin, not with the historical institution that has occasioned a welter of conflicting opinions, as may be seen in Sidney R. Hoenig, *The Great Sanhedrin* (New York: Bloch Publishing Co., 1953) and Hugo Mantel, *Studies in the History of the Sanhedrin* (Cambridge: Harvard University Press, 1965).

14. To simplify the exposition, I am ignoring the "extralegal" status of non-Davidic kings during the Second Commonwealth.

15. Abraham I. Katsh writes: "For a statistical comparison, on the level of vocabulary alone, while Shakespeare in his voluminous plays employs at least twenty thousand different words, and Milton in his sprawling epics requires ten thousand, the vast panorama of Biblical thought and emotion is conveyed in the 'Hebrew idiom' in little more than six thousand words. This is so because the linguistic economy of Hebrew compacts each word with a wealth of imagery and meaning that the more diffuse modern languages can approximate only by an increased number of words." *The Biblical Heritage of American Democracy* (New York: KTAV Publishing House, 1977), p. 3.

16. See Harry M. Clor. "Judicial Statesmanship and Constitutional Interpretation," *South Texas Law Journal* 26: 3 (Fall 1985), pp. 367–433, for a brilliant but nonetheless futile analysis of the subject—futile because limited by the dichotomies of the philosophic tradition.

17. Although there were no specific courts of appeal, lower courts could take difficult matters to higher courts. See Herzog, *Main Institutions of Jewish Law*, I, 15.

18. *Mishneh Torah: Book of Judges*, p. 9.

19. *Hirsch Commentary*, V, 332.

20. Rabinowitz, *The Jewish Mind*, p. 7.

21. Notice that a Torah community combines different aspects of kingship, aristocracy, and democracy—a "theocracy" to confound all theocracies.

22. Contrast American constitutional law, especially the celebrated case of *Marbury v. Madison*, 1 Cranch 137 (1803), and *United States v. Nixon*, 94 S. Ct 3090 (1974) (The Watergate Case), in which the Supreme Court dismissed President Nixon's claim for an absolute privilege of confidentiality of presidential communications.

23. See Zimmerman, *Torah and Existence*, pp. 355–363.

Selected Bibliography

PRIMARY JEWISH SOURCES

Babylonian Talmud. 18. vols. London: Soncino Press, 1978.
Bereshis (Genesis): Traditional Commentary on the Books of the Bible. Trans. and comm. M. Zlotowitz. 6 vols. t.d. Brooklyn, N.Y.: Mesorah Publications, 1977–81.
The Jerusalem Bible (Masoretic Text). Ed. H. Fisch. Jerusalem: Koren Publishers, 1977.
Midrash Rabbah. 10 vols. London: Soncino Press, 1983.

SECONDARY JEWISH SOURCES

Bachya Ben Joseph Paquda. *Duties of the Heart*. Trans. M. Hyamson. 2 vols. Jerusalem: Jerusalem Publishers, 1970.
Breuer, Isaac. *Concepts of Judaism*. Jerusalem: Israel Universities Press, 1974.
Eidelberg, Paul, ed. *Israel's Return and Restoration*. From a discourse of Dr. Chaim Zimmerman. Jerusalem: Privately published, 1987.
Halevi, Yahuda. *The Kuzari*.
Herzog, Isaac. *Judaism: Law and Ethics*. London: Soncino Press, 1974.
———. *The Main Institutions of Jewish Law*. 2 vols. London: Soncino Press, 1936.
Hirsch, Samson Raphael. *Collected Writings of Rabbi Samson Raphael Hirsch*. 3 vols. t.d. Jerusalem and New York: Feldheim, 1984.
———. *Judaism Eternal*. Trans. I. Grunfeld. 2 vols. London: Soncino Press, 1956.
———. *The Pentateuch*. Trans. I. Levy. 6 vols. Gateshead, England: Judaica Press, 1982.
Luzzatto, Chaim M. *The Path of the Just*. 2d ed. Trans. S. Silberstein. Jerusalem: Feldheim, 1980.
Maimonides, Moses. *Guide of the Perplexed*. Trans. S. Pines. Chicago: University of Chicago Press, 1963.

———. *Introduction to the Talmud*. Trans. Z. Lampel. New York: Judaica Press, 1975.

———. *Mishneh Torah: Book of Judges*. Trans. A. Hershman. New Haven: Yale University Press, 1949.

———. *Mishneh Torah: The Book of Knowledge*. Trans. M. Hyamson. Jerusalem and New York: Feldheim, 1974.

———. *Mishneh Torah: Book of Torts*. Trans. H. Klein. New Haven: Yale University Press, 1954.

Malbim. *Commentary on the Torah*. Trans. Z. Faier. 5 vols. t.d. Jerusalem: Hillel Press, 1984.

Miller, Avigdor. *Behold a People*. New York: Privately published, 1968.

——— *Rejoice O Youth*. New York: Privately published, 1962.

Nachmanides. *Commentary on the Torah*. Trans. C. Chavel. 5 vols. New York: Shilo Publishing House, 1972.

Rabinowitz, Abraham H. *The Jewish Mind*. Jerusalem: Hillel Press, 1978.

Rashi. *Commentary on the Torah*. Trans. A. Isaiah and B. Sharfman. 5 vols. Brooklyn, N.Y.: S.S. & R. Publishing Co., 1949.

Sefer HaHinukh (The Book of Education). Jerusalem and New York: Feldheim, 1978.

Soloveitchik, Joseph B. *Halakhic Man*. Philadelphia: Jewish Publication Society, 1983.

———. *The Halakhic Mind*. New York: Free Press, 1986.

Twerski, Isador. *Rabad of Posquieres*. Cambridge: Harvard University Press, 1962.

Zimmerman, Chaim. *Torah and Existence*. Jerusalem: privately published, 1986.

———. *Torah and Reason*. Jerusalem: HED Press, 1979.

The Zohar. Trans. A. Sperling and M. Simon. 5 vols. London: Soncino Press, 1978.

GENERAL

Alfarabi's Philosophy of Plato and Aristotle. Trans. M. Mahdi. Ithaca, N.Y.: Cornell University Press, 1969.

AlRoy, Gil. *Behind the Middle East Conflict*. New York: Capricorn Books, 1975.

Aristotle. *Metaphysics*.

———. *Nicomachean Ethics*.

———. *Physics*.

———. *Politics*.

Averroes on Plato's "Republic." Trans. R. Lerner. Ithaca, N.Y.: Cornell University Press, 1974.

Baruk, Henri. *Tsedek*. Binghamton, N. Y.: Swan House Publishing Co., 1972.

Benjamin of Tudela. Trans. A. Asher. *The Itinerary of Rabbi Benjamin of Tudela*. 2 vols. New York: Hakeshet Publishing Co., n.d.

Berkovits, Eliezer. *God, Man and History*. New York: Jonathan David Publishers, 1965.

Bloom, Allan. *The Closing of the American Mind*. New York: Simon & Schuster, 1987.

Buber, Martin. *Two Kinds of Faith*. Trans. N. Goldhawk. New York: Harper Torchbooks, 1961.

Burckhardt, Jacob. *Force and Freedom*. New York: Meridian Books, 1955.

Clor, Harry. *Obscenity and Public Morality*. Chicago: University of Chicago Press, 1969.

Davies, Alan T. *AntiSemitism and the Foundations of the New Testament*. New York: Paulist Press, 1979.

Descartes, René. *Discourse on Method*. Trans. L. Lafleur. Indianapolis: Bobbs-Merrill Co., 1956.

Easton, L., and Guddat, H. eds. *Writings of the Young Marx on Philosophy and Society*. New York: Doubleday Anchor Books, 1967.

Eidelberg, Paul. *Beyond Détente: Toward an American Foreign Policy*. LaSalle, Ill.: Sherwood Sugden & Co., 1977.

———. *A Discourse on Statesmanship: The Design and Transformation of the American Polity*. Urbana: University of Illinois Press, 1974.

———. *Jerusalem vs. Athens: In Quest of a General Theory of Existence*. Lanham, Md.: University Press of America, 1983.

———. *On the Silence of the Declaration of Independence*. Amherst: University of Massachusetts Press, 1976.

———. *The Philosophy of the American Constitution*. New York: Free Press, 1968. Lanham, Md.: University Press of America, 1986.

———. *Sadat's Stategy*. Montreal: Dawn Publishing Co., 1979.

Einstein, Albert. *Out of My Later Years*. New York: Philosophical Library, 1950.

Fisch, Harold. *The Zionist Revolution*. New York: St. Martin's Press, 1978.

Galileo. *Dialogues Concerning Two Sciences*.

Gottlieb, Eli J. *The Inescapable Truth*. New York: Feldheim, 1971.

Graves, John C. *The Conceptual Foundations of General Relativity Theory*. Cambridge: MIT Press, 1971.

Green, D. F. *Arab Theologians on Jews and Israel*. Geneva: Academy of Islamic Research, 1976.

Grunebaum, G. E. von. *Islam*. London: Routledge & Kegan Paul, 1961.

Harkabi, Y. *Arab Attitudes to Israel*. Jerusalem: Keter Publishing House, 1972.

Hegel, Georg W. H. *The Philosophy of History*. New York: Dover Publications, 1956.

Hess, Moses. *Rome and Jerusalem*. New York: Bloch Publishing Co., 1943.

Hobbes, Thomas. *Leviathan*. Oxford: Basil Blackwell, 1955.

Hoenig, Sidney R. *The Great Sanhedrin*. New York: Bloch Publishing Co., 1953.

Hume, David. *A Treatise of Human Nature*. Oxford: Clarendon Press, 1955.

Jacobs, Louis. *The Talmudic Argument: A Study in Talmudic Reasoning and Methodology*. Cambridge: Cambridge University Press, 1986.

Jammer, Max. *The Philosophy of Quantum Mechanics*. New York: John Wiley & Sons, 1974.

Josephus, Flavius. *Complete Works*. Trans. Haverman. 4 vols. New York: Bigelow, Brown & Co., n.d.

Jung, Leo, ed. *Israel and the World of Tomorrow*. 2nd ed. New York: Herald Square Press, 1949.

———, ed. *The Jewish Library*. Second series. New York: Bloch Publishing Co., 1930.

———, ed. *Judaism in a Changing World*. New York: Oxford University Press, 1939.

Kant, Immanuel. *Critique of Pure Reason*. Trans. N. K. Smith. London: Macmillan, 1956.

Katsh, Abraham I. *The Biblical Heritage of American Democracy*. New York: KTAV Publishing House, 1977.

Kierkegaard, Soren. *Fear and Trembling*. Trans. W. Lowrie. New York: Doubleday Anchor Books, 1954.

The Koran, Trans. Dawood. New York: Penguin Books, 1974.

Leitch, Vincent B. *Deconstructive Criticism*. New York: Columbia University Press, 1983.

Lichtenstein, Aaron. *The Seven Laws of Noah*. New York: Z. Berman Books, 1981.

Locke, John. *Two Treatises of Government*. New York: Hafner Publishing Co., 1947.

Machiavelli, Niccolo. *The Discourses*.

—— *The Prince*. Trans. Leo Paul de Alvarez. Irving, Tex.: University of Dallas Press, 1980.

Mansfield, Harvey, Jr. *Machiavelli's New Modes and Orders*. Ithaca, N.Y.: Cornell University Press, 1979.

Mantel, Hugo. *Studies in the History of the Sanhedrin*. Cambridge: Harvard University Press, 1965.

More, Thomas. *Utopia*. New York: Crofts Classics, 1949.

Nasr, Seyyed H. *Islam and the Plight of Modern Man*. London: Longman, 1975.

——. *Knowledge and the Sacred*. New York: Crossroad, 1981.

Nietzsche, Friedrich. Trans. W. Kaufmann. *Basic Writings of Nietzsche*. New York: Modern Library, 1968.

——. *The Joyful Wisdom*. Trans. T. Common. New York: Frederick Ungar Publishing Co., 1960.

—— *The Will to Power*. Trans. W. Kaufmann. New York: Random House, 1967.

Oppenheimer, J. Robert. *Science and the Common Understanding*. London: Oxford University Press, 1954.

Plato. *Apology*.

——. *Protagoras*.

——. *The Republic*.

——. *Symposium*.

——. *Timaeus*.

Reichenbach, Hans. *The Rise of Scientific Philosophy*. Berkeley: University of California Press, 1959.

Rousseau, Jean-Jacques. *The First and Second Discourses*. Ed. R. D. Masters; Trans. J. R. Masters. New York: St. Martin's Press, 1964.

—— *The Social Contract*. New York: Hafner Publishing Co., 1957.

Ryn, Claes G. *Democracy and the Ethical Life*. Baton Rouge: Louisiana State University Press, 1978.

Sadat, Anwar. *In Search of Identity*. New York: Harper & Row, 1978.

Schatz, Eliyahu A. *Proof of the Accuracy of the Bible*. New York: Jonathan David Publishers, 1973.

Schuon, Frithjof. *Understanding Islam*. London: George Allen & Unwin, Ltd., 1963.

Silberg, Moshe. *Talmudic Law and the Modern State*. Trans. B. Bokser. New York: Burning Bush Press, 1973.

Simon, Yves. *The Philosophy of Democratic Government*. Chicago: University of Chicago Press, 1951.

Skinner, B. F. *Science and Human Behavior*. New York: Free Press, 1953.

Spinoza, Benedict de. 2 vols. Trans. R. H. M. Elwes. *Works*. New York: Dover Publications, 1951.

————. *Ethics*. Trans. R. H. M. Elwes. New York: Tudor Publishing Co., n.d.

Strauss, Leo. *Natural Right and History*. Chicago: University of Chicago Press, 1953.

————. *Thoughts on Machiavelli*. Glencoe, Ill.: Free Press, 1958.

Strauss, Leo and Cropsey, Joseph, eds. 2d ed. *History of Political Philosophy*. Chicago: Rand McNally and Co., 1972.

Tocqueville, Alexis de. *Democracy in America*. 2 vols. New York: Vintage Books, 1945.

Whitehead, Alfred North. *Religion in the Making*. New York: Meridian Books, 1961.

————. *Science and Philosophy*. New York: Philosophical Library, 1948.

Wiesel, Elie. *A Jew Today*. New York: Random House, 1978.

Wigner, Eugene. *Symmetries and Reflections*. Bloomington: Indiana University Press, 1967.

Index

About the Author

PAUL EIDELBERG is a Professor of Political Science at Bar Ilan University. He is the author of *Jerusalem vs. Athens, A Discourse on Statesmanship, The Philosophy of the American Constitution,* and other books and articles.